OLD MOORE'S
EASY GUIDE TO
ASTROLOGY

OLD MOORE'S EASY GUIDE TO ASTROLOGY

W. Foulsham & Co. Ltd.

London • New York • Toronto • Cape Town • Sydney

W. Foulsham & Company Limited
Yeovil Road, Slough, Berkshire, SL1 4JH

ISBN 0-572-01391-4

Printed in Great Britain
at St. Edmundsbury Press
Bury St. Edmunds

CONTENTS

CONTENTS

LIST OF ILLUSTRATIONS

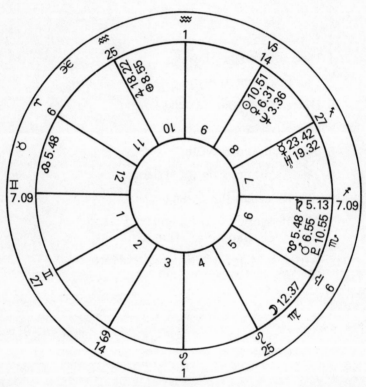

Fig. 1   Horoscope map of an imaginary child born on 1st January
1986 at 1.40 pm Liverpool

OLD MOORE'S EASY GUIDE TO ASTROLOGY

An A B C of Astrology

This guide to astrology is intended for those who do not find the other books, at present in use, sufficiently clear enough in detail and explanation. In fact, I have been asked to write it by my pupils and others, who have told me of their difficulties as well as their mistakes, when they first began this fascinating study.

So I propose to teach on my own lines, which I have found most successful for some time past. I begin, therefore, by supposing that those who intend to try my system know nothing whatever about the way a true astrologer casts a horoscope.

The Way to Begin

Do not buy any other books on astrology! This may seem a strange piece of advice to some, but, as I know from personal experience, it is necessary. Many beginners do buy books, which are not intended for those who have no teachers, to help them 'over their first stiles'!

When you have learned how to cast a horoscope and calculate the aspects without making any mistakes; when you see how to set to work to write out the results of your calculations and observations, the judgment of the influence of the signs, planets, houses and aspects—then it will be time enough to get your books.

But you need not begin with a manual on astronomy. Of course, every astrologer ought to know elementary astronomy at least, but you do not need to begin with it. That can come later on. As long as you know that the Signs of the Zodiac do not change their places, and that the planets are not stars or all the same distance from the Sun; that Venus, for instance, cannot ever be in 'opposition' to the Sun, as it is so close to the Sun that it cannot make the sextile aspect of 60°, and other facts about our solar system which are usually taught to children at school—as long as you know these things, that is all you want to start with. But later on you should read one of the elementary manuals on astronomy which have been recently published.

But it may, perhaps, be as well to state that when an astrologer talks of the Sun 'moving through' the Signs of the Zodiac at the rate of one sign a month or one degree a day, he means that the Sun appears to us to move. The Earth, as you know, makes one complete revolution round the Sun in a year, and it moves round in the Zodiac that is known as the Earth's orbit, or path in the heavens, for the revolution. So the Sun naturally appears to be going in the other direction, just as the landscape seen from a train in motion appears to be moving past the other way. Therefore, when the Sun appears to 'move' into the Sign Aries, on the 21st of March, known as the Vernal Equinox, and then into Taurus on the 21st of April, and so on through all the twelve signs, it simply means, in other words, that the Earth has moved into the opposite signs.

In case any of my readers have studied astronomy, and used Philips' Planisphere to find the constellations and stars, it would be as well to point out here that the Zodiac of the constellations is not the Zodiac used by the astrologer.

You have only to look at the Planisphere or any other sky map to see that the Signs of the Zodiac are of most irregular extent. Compare, for instance, Libra and Aries with Pisces. At the same time you must remember that the signs used in your horoscopes are of equal extent—of 30° each. It is said that these Zodiacs did coincide about A.D. 480. The two Zodiacs are in sympathy with each other and of the same nature; and of course the names and symbols are identical.

So the first lesson you have to learn is how to write out the names and symbols of the signs in their proper order. When you have done this, write them out on a sheet of paper in large, clear characters. Put the sheet where you can constantly look at it. A good plan is to fix it up in your bedroom or private sitting-room, so that you can look at it until you have visualised the names, symbols, and their order so well that you can write them down without a mistake.

Do not make the common error of trying to learn them by heart like a column of spelling in a school book. If you try to learn the different arrangements of the signs by heart, you will muddle up Water Signs on the Fire and Air Triangles, or Mutable Signs on the Cardinal Cross, and so on!

Now, I have a good reason for using this word 'visualise'. I was taught to spell, not by learning long columns of words by heart, but by looking at all the strange and difficult words until I could see their spelling! How is it that you cannot read a book upside down? The letters are just the same; but your eye has got so accustomed to them in a different position that you do not recognise them. Help your memory with your eyes.

Write down the twelve signs with their symbols in their proper order, thus:

The Twelve Signs

♈	♉	♊	♋	♌	♍	♎
ARIES	TAURUS	GEMINI	CANCER	LEO	VIRGO	LIBRA

♏	♐	♑	♒	♓
SCORPIO	SAGITTARIUS	CAPRICORN	AQUARIUS	PISCES

The English names are:

The Ram. The Bull. The Twins. The Crab. The Lion. The Virgin. The Scales. The Scorpion. The Archer. The Goat. The Waterman. The Fishes.

You want to know these English names, of course, but astrologers never use them in writing or in conversation.

When you can write down these names and their symbols at a moment's notice, without any hesitation or a single error, take another sheet of paper and write the names and symbols like this:

The Triplicities

	FIRE			EARTH	
♈	♌	♐	♉	♍	♑
ARIES	LEO	SAGITTARIUS	TAURUS	VIRGO	CAPRICORN

	AIR			WATER	
♊	♎	♒	♋	♏	♓
GEMINI	LIBRA	AQUARIUS	CANCER	SCORPIO	PISCES

Here you have the important triplicities of Fire, Earth, Air, and Water. This order must be most carefully studied, as it is of such importance in making a correct judgment of a horoscope. It is useful in another way, as it enables you to visualise the trine aspect of 120° at a glance.

Beginners are apt to put Aquarius down as a Water Sign at first, because it is named the Waterman. Taurus and Scorpio are sometimes confused with the Fire Signs, as their names sound more in keeping with Fire than Earth and Water. And Virgo is also mistaken for an Airy Sign.

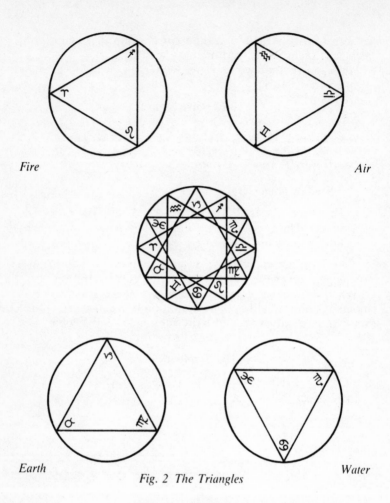

Fire

Air

Earth

Water

Fig. 2 The Triangles

The Quadruplicities

You can now pass on to the other important groups known as the Qualities, or the Quadruplicities. You write them down like this:

CARDINAL

♈	♋	♎	♑
ARIES	CANCER	LIBRA	CAPRICORN

FIXED

♉	♌	♏	♒
TAURUS	LEO	SCORPIO	AQUARIUS

MUTABLE

♊   ♍   ♐   ♓
GEMINI   VIRGO   SAGITTARIUS   PISCES

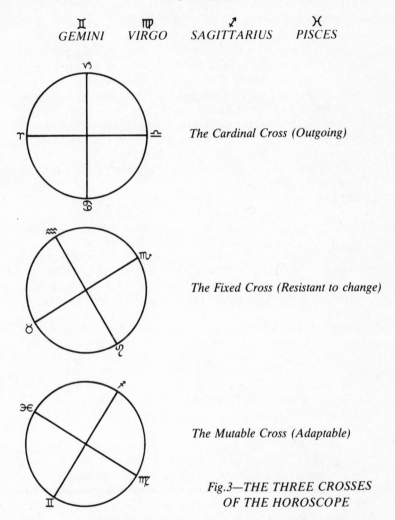

The Cardinal Cross (Outgoing)

The Fixed Cross (Resistant to change)

The Mutable Cross (Adaptable)

*Fig.3—THE THREE CROSSES
OF THE HOROSCOPE*

The Difference Between the Two Groups

The triplicities are made up of four equal triangles. On the points of each of these triangles you find the same kind of signs. All the Fire Signs are on the first, all the Earth Signs are on the second, all the Air Signs are on the third, and all the Water Signs on the fourth.

But on the crosses you find an entirely different arrangement. Look at the first cross. There you find Aries, a Fire Sign, opposite Libra, an Air Sign, and Capricorn, an Earth Sign, opposite Cancer, a Water Sign.

The arrangement is the same on the other crosses: Fire Signs opposite to Air Signs, and Earth Signs opposite to Water Signs.

Now you have arranged the signs in three ways:

(i) In their natural order, as they must always be placed round the rim of the horoscope.

(ii) In the order of the elements, the triplicities of Fire, Earth, Air, and Water. If you draw four lines from the points of the crosses to similar signs, you get the triangles.

(iii) In the order of the qualities, or quadruplicities Cardinal, Fixed, Mutable.

So you must always remember that each sign has its own place, which never alters, in the circle round the heavens, and that each sign has its place at the angles of the four triangles, and also its place at the point of one of the crosses.

You will find it a help to draw these triangles and crosses without the words Fire, Earth, Air, and Water; or Cardinal, Fixed, and Mutable. Have the signs only. Then visualise them until you can put the signs on the points and angles without any mistakes.

Later on you will have to learn your aspects by the aid of these very important diagrams.

The Houses

As well as being divided up into 12 signs, each of 30°, a horoscope chart is divided into 12 'houses'. Each house is referred to by its number, and the points of division between the houses are called the cusps.

As the earth rotates once in every 24 hours, the 12 signs pass through the 12 houses in that period. At the moment of birth, a particular sign and degree is rising on the eastern horizon. This is what is known as the Ascendant, which is also the cusp of the 1st House. Opposite the Ascendant is the Descendant, which is the cusp of the 7th House. The cusp of the 10th House is known as the Upper Meridian, Mid-Heaven or Medium Coeli—or M.C. for short. Opposite the M.C. is the I.C. (Imum Coeli), on the cusp of the 4th House. These four points are known as the Angles.

The houses after the angles are called the Angular Houses. The Houses following the angular ones are known as Succedent, and after these come the Cadent Houses. (Fig. 4.)

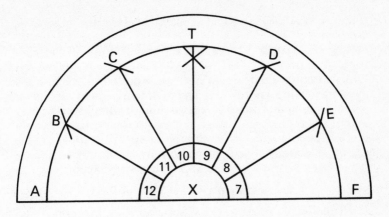

Fig. 4—How to draw a map.

The Sun, Moon and the Planets

You must now study a new set of names and symbols. As before, they should be written out on a sheet of paper until you have visualised them like the others. This is the order in which they are placed for making a list of aspects:

☉	☽	☿	♀	♂
SUN	MOON	MERCURY	VENUS	MARS
♃	♄	♅	♆	♇
JUPITER	SATURN	URANUS	NEPTUNE	PLUTO

So before we go any farther, we should have these expressions properly understood. The Moon, as you know, goes round the Earth, and therefore it moves at a very much quicker rate than Mercury, which is the nearest planet to the Sun. So the Moon is said to 'apply' to all the other planets.

A much better word to use would be 'overtakes'. The Moon goes through the signs in a month, so it overtakes the other planets and passes them.

Therefore, when an astrologer talks about the applications and separations of a planet, he simply means the overtaking and passing in the sky, as we see it.

When the Moon or some other planet comes quite close to another planet, so that they appear to be side by side, the position is called a conjunction; or when it has passed on exactly

15

60° away, that position is called an exact sextile, the name of an aspect.

Now you may ask, 'What does it matter if one planet goes faster than another?' Well, you will find out, later on, that it does matter a good deal. For instance, when you come to study the 7th House in a horoscope, and want to find out what kind of man a woman may marry, or what kind of woman a man may marry, it will be all-important to know to which planet the Sun is applying in the one case, and the Moon in the other! There are other reasons also. A planet is considered to have a more powerful influence when separating than when applying.

The Importance of the Time of Birth

When you are going to cast a horoscope, as it is termed, the first question you ask is this: 'Do you know the exact time that you were born?'

You will very soon discover that most people do not know the time, and, further, that they do not know anyone who does! Even mothers do not remember when their children were born.

You will get vague answers, such as, 'Between 2 and 4 in the morning'; or, 'Somewhere about midnight'; or, 'Just before lunch'; or, 'Soon after dinner-time.'

In the case of a baby these answers are useless. Babies are very much alike. They give no indication by their appearance of any particular sign. They are not old enough to show any signs of character. There is nothing to guide you. What is termed 'rectification by events' is impossible for infants.

But with grown-up people the case is different. Personal appearance, as you can imagine, is a most useful guide. Numbers of astrologers have made special study of personal appearance, in order to be able to tell at a glance the right sign that fits a face and figure, as well as tricks of movement and special mannerisms.

A great deal can be done by asking people to read something about the signs so as to say which gives a description of their character. You can also ask questions about likes and dislikes, favourite occupations, and other details likely to suggest the sign. Photographs are useful when you are asked to do the horoscope for some man or woman you have not seen.

Rectification by important events in the life can be made by expert astrologers, but you need not begin to study this yet. Nor do I advise you to study the method of the Prenatal Epoch until you are advanced enough to undertake it.

But there is one problem that you are certain to have sooner or later, when you are given 'an exact time', as they say. That is when the given time shows you 29° of a sign had risen, or just the 1st degree of a sign. Perhaps you may think that this does not much matter. But it does matter.

A person born, say, under the last degree of Pisces is not the same as one born under the 1st degree of Aries. There is also another very important point to consider. If you place Pisces on the cusp of the Ascendant, you have Virgo on the cusp of the important Marriage House. But if you put Aries on the Ascendant, you have Libra. You would also have Capricorn on the 10th House instead of Sagittarius, and other differences that would alter the house position of the planets.

In a case like this a few questions may decide the question, for you must point out that an error of a few minutes in the clock time would give the wrong sign for the Ascendant. But it is very difficult to make some people understand that astrology is an exact science, and that we attach great importance to minutes!

I very soon discovered that the majority of people who profess to know the exact birth time always gave what I call the Cardinal Cross divisions of their clocks or watches. Children cannot always come into the world exactly at either the hour or the half-hour, or the quarter past or the quarter to!

Now, there is another important point to which I want to draw your attention. You ask for particulars about the birth. You get a letter with a reply something like this: 'I was born on the 10th of May, in 1953, late at night, on Sunday. I am sure it was Sunday.'

So you have to write and explain that 'late at night' is too vague; that it is possible that the birth took place between 11 p.m. and midnight, or about 1 a.m. on Monday morning, as some people would call that late on Sunday night; and that the day of the week does not help longitude or latitude. And you ask if the name of the place where the birth took place could be given, as that is important. Now you may ask, 'Why do we want to know the place of birth? What does it matter? You know the birthday and the time. What has the place got to do with it?'

Well, it matters so much that you find yourself in a fix, if you are asked to do a horoscope for someone born at Cape Town, or Malta, or any other place outside of the latitude of London, Liverpool, and New York. You want two little booklets, one called Raphael's Table of Houses for Northern Latitudes and the other called Raphael's Tables of Houses for Great Britain for different latitudes. Also you must know how far the longitude is east or west of the meridian of Greenwich.

So now you must buy a little paper-covered publication, known to all astrologers as Raphael's Ephemeris. This, and the Tables of Houses booklets are published by W. Foulsham & Co. Ltd., the publishers of this book.

Raphael's Astronomical Ephemeris of the Planets' Places

Raphael's Astronomical Ephemeris is published annually in spring each year for the year following, and copies of any year back to 1860 can be obtained. You need a copy for the year of birth of any person for whom you wish to erect a horoscope. However, all the worked examples in this book apply to the year 1986, and facsimile pages of the 1986 Ephemeris are to be found at the back of this book (p. 89)

When some new students of astrology take up an Ephemeris for the first time, they remark that it looks a most confusing jumble of figures and strange symbols! I once heard the question: 'What are all these little Chinese lanterns? What do they mean?'

Well the 'little Chinese lanterns' are the symbols of the signs and the planets, with which you ought to be quite familiar already. You will very soon understand what the figures mean and how to use them. In fact, I hope that the time will soon arrive when the Ephemeris will be on your writing-table as your daily companion.

Without this Ephemeris you could not make a chart of the sky for anyone's horoscope. For a horoscope is just a chart of the sky at the birth hour, containing the symbols of the Signs of the Zodiac on the outer ring of the circle, and the Sun, Moon, and the planets inside, in the divisions known as the 'houses' of the horoscope. We do not put in the Great Bear or Orion or the Pleiades.

So you can take up your Ephemeris without any fear of finding a troublesome or impossible task for your brains. Look at the Ephemeris for 1986. Look at page 2, for January. Carefully note the top line, and then the one under it:

D D Sidereal ⊙   ⊙   ☽   ☽   ☽   ☽   Midnight.
M W Time.   Long. Dec. Long. Lat. Dec. Node ☽ Long. ☽Dec.

Below this line there are rows of figures for each day of the month. D.W. stands for Days of the Week.

Sidereal Time is an expression which is probably new to you. It will be explained later on.

Lat., Dec., and Long., stand for Latitude, Declination and Longitude.

The symbols for the planets Mercury, Venus, Mars, Jupiter, Saturn, Uranus, Neptune and Pluto, and a column for the lunar aspects, follow on the next page.

Now look at the second part of page 2. Here you find some different columns with the following headings:

D.   MERCURY   VENUS   MARS   JUPITER
M.   Lat.   Dec.   Lat.   Dec.   Lat.   Dec.   Lat.   Dec.

D.M. means Day of the Month. The rest of the planets, Saturn, Uranus etc. continue on page 3 where there is also a column for mutual aspects.

You will also note that the latitudes and declinations are only given for every second day; except for the quicker-moving planets, where the declinations are given for each day of the month.

Among the figures on these and the following pages you will find the capital letters S, N, D and ℞ with a stroke across the tail. S and N mean South and North. D means Direct, but the ℞ with the stroke across the tail stands for Retrograde.

The words Declination and Retrograde will be explained farther on, and also the meaning of the Moon's Nodes.

Now let us see what a simple thing it is to use this Ephemeris. Let us suppose that you want to cast a horoscope for 12 o'clock at London, on the 1st of January 1986. You begin with the column headed 'Sidereal Time'. Write down on a sheet of paper S.T. 18 43 23. On these all-important figures the correctness of your horoscope entirely depends.

Look at the next column. The symbol of the Sun is above it, the circle with the dot in the middle. Under is the word Long. Then opposite the 1st day of the month you find the figures 10 46 33. But between the 10 and the 46 there is a queer, unfamiliar little symbol. This tells you the name of the Sign of the Zodiac in which the Sun was at that time. Copy this on your paper and pass to the next column, in which you find that the Dec. is 23S0. Write that down and go on. Now you come to the Moon. Here you find the figures 11 40 56. Between the 11 and the 40 there is another symbol. Copy it and pass on. Now you find 4N10. This is the latitude, but as beginners do not require the Moon's latitude, you leave it out and put down the declination, 11N2. You also leave out midnight. In the same way you copy out from page 3 the degrees and minutes of the planets Mercury, Venus, Mars, Jupiter, Saturn, Uranus, Neptune and Pluto. Then under Lunar Aspects you find five little symbols which inform you that the Moon is trine the Sun and Venus, square Saturn and sextile Mars and Pluto.

If you have already learned your symbols, you will know that the Sun is in the Sign Capricorn, the Moon in Virgo, and so on.

Now you have on your paper your time, the position of the Sun, Moon, and the planets all ready for casting a horoscope.

But before we leave these two pages, I want you to note the importance of marking the change of signs. Mistakes have been made like this, for instance:

Suppose you wrote down the Sun 11 18 58 in Capricorn for the 31st of January, and also Venus 14 9 in Capricorn for the same day. I have seen mistakes like this, for beginners sometimes to note a change of sign and only look at the top of the column. On the 20th of January the Sun goes into Aquarius, and also on the 20th Venus goes into Aquarius.

Now turn over to page 26. There you have the Daily Motion of the Planets. This is useful, as it saves trouble when you want to use the logarithms.

Other tables follow, an Aspectarian, then the important Tables of Houses, and the Proportional Logarithms.

I do not want you to use the Aspectarian, as I hope to teach you to use your eyes as an aspectarian. You will use the Table of Houses and the Logarithms, as we shall see later on. Note on these pages °′″, marks indicating degrees, minutes, and seconds.

The 'Time' Question

When you are told that a child was born at 2.20 p.m. G.M.T. on the 22nd of May, 1986, in London, and asked to do the horoscope, you open your Ephemeris at page 10, look at the line marked 22, and find out where the Sun and the Moon and the planets were at 12 noon, Greenwich Time. Under the heading Sidereal Time you find the figures 3 59 17; that is, 3 hours, 59 minutes, and 17 seconds. At first sight you might think that this means just on 4 o'clock. But there is no a.m. or p.m. even mentioned; and if you look at the next day you will see that the noon time was only advanced to 4 3 13. Our clocks and watches do not record time like this!

If you turn the pages back to see what the Greenwich time was on the 1st of January at noon, you will be surprised to find that it was 18 43 23. Then if you wonder why this curious time is more in January than it is in May you will discover, if you turn over the pages, that on the morning of May 23rd this clock recorded the time at noon with the figures 4 3 13. The explanation of the mystery is astronomical.

In the Greenwich Observatory, and in all astronomical observatories, there is a carefully adjusted clock which records twenty-four hours exactly, while the earth makes one complete revolution round the Sun. So this clock marks an advance of about four minutes each day of twenty-four hours. That is all that you want to know at present.

Now comes the question: If 3 59 17 on the 22nd of May, 1986, means exactly noon at Greenwich Observatory, and for all the clocks in London, how are we to find the sidereal time which will correspond with the birth time of 2.20 p.m. given from an ordinary clock?

What you want to get at is the 'Local Sidereal Time', as it is called. There is a simple rule for finding Local Sidereal Time from Greenwich Time which you must note and remember.

This time depends upon the longitude of the place, so an astrologer must have a good atlas, or a book giving the latitudes and longitudes for all parts of the world.

At first beginners find it difficult to deal with this time question. There are many people who do not seem to understand why places to the East of Greenwich are later in time, while places to the West are earlier in time than Greenwich.

The rule is to convert this longitude into time, and then add the time to the Greenwich Time if the place of birth is East of Greenwich.

But this longitude time is subtracted if the place of birth is West of Greenwich.

To convert longitude into time is very simple, if you have not got a table of 'Longitude Equivalents' for doing it, such as is found in some books on astrology.

If you had a table, you would find that 15° of longitude is equal to 1 hour, and that 1° is equal to 4 minutes, and that 1 minute of longitude is equal to 4 seconds of time.

Suppose you have longitude 2° 32′ W., the 2° is 8 minutes. The 32′ is 2 minutes and 8 seconds, which is 10 minutes and 8 seconds. Subtract that from 12 noon, and you have 11h. 49m. 52s. That is the time at the place of birth when it is exactly 12 noon at Greenwich.

But if the longitude is 2° 32′ E., you add the 10 minutes and 8 seconds to the 12 noon of Greenwich, which gives you 0h. 10m. 8s. p.m. at the place of birth.

The introduction of the Summer Time Act does not alter the astrologers' Sidereal Time, so remember this in future. People should record a child's birth by the true Standard Time, but many will not do so. Therefore be careful about this, for your horoscopes will be an hour wrong if you use British Summer Time (B.S.T.), or two hours wrong if you use British Double

Summer Time (B.D.S.T.—used in 1941–45 and in 1947 only).

Correcting for Acceleration

As the Sidereal Time is short of Mean Time by nearly 10 seconds for each hour, the number of hours to or from noon should be multiplied by 10. The results, called the 'acceleration', in minutes and seconds, are added to or subtracted from the Sidereal Time.

For an a.m. birth, *subtract* the acceleration from the Sidereal Time.

For a p.m. birth, *add* the acceleration to the Sidereal Time.

To take an example, 7.00 a.m. is 5 hours before noon, so the acceleration for 5 hours is 50s.

Now take 9.00 p.m. Acceleration for 9 hours is +1m. 30s.

At the back of this book, on page 88, you will find an Acceleration Table to help you calculate the time correction quickly and with precision. It is very simple to use; just look up the number of hours at the top and then the minutes on the left. Sometimes the correction is merely a few seconds, and it is never more than two minutes. In the early stages, to make things easier, you may decide to omit calculating the acceleration correction, though your results will be less accurate.

How to Deal With Your Sidereal Time

When a birth takes place in London you have no longitude calculations to make, as London is on the meridian of Greenwich.

So you write down the Sidereal Time for the date of birth, 22nd May 1986, and underneath the birth time 2.20 p.m. As 2.20 p.m. is 2 hours and 20 minutes more than 12.00 noon, you *add* this to the Sidereal Time. Then you add the acceleration correction which is 23 seconds.

You then have what is known as the Local Sidereal Time, which is 6 19 40.

```
  3 59 17
  2 20 0
  0  0 23
  ───────
  6 19 40

 27 59 17
  9 40 00
  ───────
 18 19 17
     3  1
  ───────
 18 16 16
```

But suppose the time of birth had been 2.20 *a.m.* You must not subtract 2.20 from 3 59 17 as beginners sometimes do. Consider what 2.20 a.m. means in relation to 12.00 noon. It means 9 hours 40 minutes before 12.00 noon. You must always subtract the time between the hour that is given for the birth and 12.00 noon. As you cannot subtract 9 from 3, it is the rule to add the 24 hours to the 3 59 17. So you write down 27

59 17 and subtract 9 40 from it, giving 18 19 17. Then subtract the acceleration correction for 9 hours and 40 minutes, which is 3' 1". This leaves you with 18 16 16.

According to the day of the year, the Sidereal Time at noon can be any figures from 0h. 0m. 0s. to 23h. 56m. 0s. The Sidereal Time does not go beyond 24h. 0m. 0s., so when the addition of your p.m. birth times amounts to more than 24, you must subtract 24, and the result will be the Sidereal Time.

The Tables of Houses

Having found that your Local Sidereal Time for 2.20 p.m., on the 22nd of May, 1986, was 6h. 19m. 40s., you now turn to the end of the Ephemeris and look at the Tables of Houses. You find three sets: for London, Liverpool, and New York. (Raphael's Table of Houses for Great Britain, a most useful book, gives Tables for important towns in the British Isles.)

Look at the Table for London, and note the words 'Latitude 51° 32' N'. Then turn over and look at the latitude for Liverpool and New York. So you see that, if you do not know the place of birth, you do not know what Table of Houses to use, for these tables give you the correct Ascendants for your horoscopes.

Now look at the two pages before you, and you will see twelve little columns with the following headings:

Sidereal Time	10	11	12	Ascen.	2	3
	♈	♉	♊	♋	♌	♍

Then follow rows of figures to which you must pay careful attention, or you will make mistakes when you come to copy down on a slip of paper the Ascendant and the signs for the houses, numbered 10, 11, 12, Asc. 2, 3.

You will not find anything about the other six houses, as the signs on them are always the same as the signs which are found opposite to the others in the natural order of the signs.

Now I want you to notice that the top figures under Sidereal Time are 0 0 0, and the last figures on the second page are 24 0 0. But all the degrees of the signs rise between these two figures.

As your Local Sidereal Time is 6 19 40, you look down these columns until you find the nearest figures to that time. It is 6 21 48. This is near enough for the present, so you look under Ascen., where you find the figures 3° 51'. This means that 3 degrees 51 minutes of Libra are rising. For the symbol of Libra is on the top of this column.

You write down Ascendant Libra 3° 51'. Then you look under the columns marked 10, 11, and 12. Here you find Cancer

5°, Leo 11° and Virgo 10°. So you write these on your paper also. Next you look under 2 and 3. Here you have Libra 28° and Scorpio 29°. When you have done this, compare what you have written with the signs and figures in the Ephemeris. It is so very easy to make mistakes.

You must notice here that you have the Sign Libra twice over. What does this mean? On the Ascendant, the 1st House, you have Libra 3° 51'; and on the 2nd House you have Libra 28°. It means that, as Aries has to be put in the map opposite to Libra, with the same figures, Aries will come twice over.

As a little exercise write down these five signs, Libra, Cancer, Leo, and Virgo and Scorpio. Then write down their opposite signs. You will then discover that two of the signs are missing. The best way to visualise and remember the pairs of opposite signs is to write them down like this, in the order of the houses, as they appear on the map of a horoscope:

12	11	10	9	8	7
PISCES	*AQUARIUS*	*CAPRICORN*	*SAGITTARIUS*	*SCORPIO*	*LIBRA*
ARIES	*TAURUS*	*GEMINI*	*CANCER*	*LEO*	*VIRGO*
1	2	3	4	5	6

This is not the usual way of making a list of the opposite pairs, but it is a simple plan to teach the opposite houses as well as the opposite signs.

I have known beginners think that the opposite house to the first is the sixth, the opposite to the third the tenth, and so on!

Here you have Aries and Libra, Gemini and Sagittarius, Leo and Aquarius, the six odd signs.

Then you have Taurus and Scorpio, Cancer and Capricorn, Virgo and Pisces, the six even signs.

This is the way you have to look at them in a horoscope, only here they are written in two straight lines, instead of two curved lines.

Now you can see that if Libra is on two houses, Aries must be on the two opposite houses. So the question is: 'Where are you to put Gemini and Sagittarius?'

This question will be answered when we come to the map and the way to write in the signs and the planets.

Horoscopes for Places Distant from the Meridian of Greenwich

I do not advise you, at first, to attempt any horoscopes for places which are not in the latitudes given in Raphael's Ephemeris for London, Liverpool and New York. In fact, for preliminary practice you had better deal with places where the Standard Time is Greenwich Time.

But in all places where the Standard Time is Greenwich Time there is an important rule which you must observe before you can place the signs and planets in the map of the horoscope. And the meridian of Greenwich is the Standard Time for England, Scotland, Wales, Isle of Man, Ireland, Shetlands and the Orkneys.

Now the important rule is this:

The signs on the cusps of the houses must be calculated for the Local Sidereal Time. The places of the planets must be calculated for Greenwich Mean Time. The best way to make this calculation is by the use of logarithms. How to use logarithms will be explained later on.

In countries where Greenwich Time is not used, you have to deal with the country's Standard Time. A table showing the Standard Times for many countries of the world is given on pages 83.

Supposing you had to do a horoscope for someone in New York. Eastern Standard Time (E.S.T.) is –5. The birth time and date is 11.00 p.m. on 2nd March. You must *add* 5 hours, giving the time and date as 4.00 a.m. G.M.T. on 3rd March. Note that the conversion to G.M.T. in this instance has altered the date.

If the birth took place in a time zone East of Greenwich (Europe side), you will have to subtract.

The same important rule applies here: houses, Local Sidereal Time, planets, Greenwich.

When you are doing horoscopes for Greenwich Standard Time, I advise you to make a practice from the first of calculating the Local Sidereal Time by any degree of longitude, one or more from the meridian of Greenwich. You will not have to go far East, as Yarmouth and Lowestoft are farthest East, only 1° 43'.

But if you go West, say as far as the longitude which runs down from the Orkney Islands, past Edinburgh, Liverpool, Chester, and down to Lyme Regis in Dorset, you must certainly deal with the Local Sidereal Time.

Suppose you have to do a horoscope for Edinburgh. The longitude is 3° 11'. If you subtract this from 12.00 noon, Greenwich, you get 11° 47' 16" at Edinburgh, a.m. You must use this time to get your Ascendant and the other house cusps of the horoscope.

Now, it is quite possible that you may think that these few minutes do not much matter; so I will give you a case to prove that a few minutes matter a great deal in an exact science like astrology.

Let us say that you are going to do a horoscope for the 6th of August, 1986. The child was born exactly at noon. The time, of course, was Greenwich correct time, not Summer Time. We will suppose that the place of birth was York.

You look at your Ephemeris and find that the Sidereal Time for the 6th is:

8 58 55

You write that down. Then you find out from an atlas that the longitude of York is 1° 5'. You have already learned, on page 21, that 1° is equal to 4 minutes, and 1 minute equal to 4 seconds of time. So you multiply the degrees and minutes by 4. The degrees of longitude become, by this simple multiplication, minutes of time, and the minutes of longitude become seconds of time. Now, as you are dealing with West Longitude, you subtract this fraction of time from 12 noon. This gives you 11h. 55m. 40s. a.m. This is the exact birth time, and as it is a.m., you subtract it from the Sidereal Time. That is, you subtract the very short time between the birth and 12 noon.

1° 5'
4
―――
4' 20''

'Hardly worth calculating,' you may say. Well, let us look at the Table of Houses for York.

12 0 0
4 20
―――
11 55 40

What sign does the Sidereal Time for noon give us? You find it is Scorpio 0° 14'. But the true birth time, 8 54 35, gives Libra 29° 33'!

8 58 55
4 20
―――
8 54 35'

So if you had ignored this trifle of 4 minutes and 20 seconds you would have had the 1st degree of Scorpio on the Ascendant instead of the last degree of Libra, and Taurus on the cusp of the important Marriage House, the 7th, instead of the Sign Aries. The horoscope would not have been correct.

As Yarmouth and Lowestoft are the farthest places East of Greenwich, in England, with the longitude 1° 43' East, your calculations will be for East Longitude, and the farther you go East the more important it becomes to calculate them carefully.

If you have to do a horoscope for a birth which took place at Inveraray, you find that it is 5° 5' West. Multiply that by 4 and you get the time 20 minutes and 20 seconds. You are told that the birth time was registered by an accurate clock as 4h. 23m. a.m. You ask if that was Summer Time or Greenwich Standard Time, and you hear that it was Greenwich Time.

You know now, of course, that you must not subtract the figures 4h. 23m. from the Sidereal Time, but the 7h. 37m. between that time and 12 noon.

To make sure of the date, you look at the letter or paper on which the birth data were written. You find that the date is the 27th of February, 1986. Then you write down the Sidereal Time for the 27th, which is 22 28 6. Now you must take care to make no mistakes. You have three times to deal with here. Write down—

22 28 6	You have nothing to add to this, as the birth time being early in the morning, you
7 37 0	subtract the 7h. 37m. Then, as the longitude
14 51 56	is West you subtract the longitude equivalent also.
14 51 56	
20 20	Now we look for the result in Raphael's Tables of Houses for Great Britain, under
14 31 36	the latitude for Dundee. There we find that

Sagittarius 27° 3′ is rising. But suppose that you had forgotten about the longitude, or not thought 20 minutes worth troubling about—you would have had the wrong Ascendant. For 14 51 6 gives Capricorn 1° 32′.

I want to impress upon you the great importance of getting the birth time as exact as possible, before you sit down to cast a horoscope. You will find that people who know nothing about astrology are under the impression that an error of an hour in giving the birth time is of no consequence.

How to Get the Planets Ready for the Map

For this work provide yourself with some plain sheets of paper, school copy-book size. Never do this work on any untidy scraps of paper, as so many do. Get into the habit, if you were not born with it, of doing these preparations for a horoscope neatly, and as carefully as you can. Write your symbols slowly and distinctly, and do not make them so small that one wants a magnifying glass to read them. These injunctions may seem unnecessary, but I know from experience that they are not.

Now let us suppose that you are going to do a horoscope for the 1st of January, in the year 1986. Take the Ephemeris, and under the line marked the 1st, rule a pencil line, and mark the line with a little star on both pages. To some minds this may seem quite superfluous, but experience teaches that it is a precaution against a very common mistake. If you do not rule this line, you may, in writing down a planet, cast your eye for a moment on the line above or below, as the case may be, and write down, for instance, the Moon as Virgo 25° 4′, instead of Virgo 11° 41′.

This would alter the aspects considerably. Now write on top of your paper, 'The Planets for 1st January, 1986'.

I may note here that, in all cases like this, the word 'planets' includes the Sun and the Moon, to avoid repetition.

On the top left-hand side make the symbol of the Sun, and then look at the column under Sun Long. You will find it written down like this, 10°♑46′ 33″.

As it is not usual to write it like this in the maps, put it down, ♑ 10° 47′. The seconds may be left out at first.

Now I must give a word of caution. Suppose that your date was the 25th of January, instead of the 1st. You might put down Capricorn 5° 13′, instead of Aquarius 5° 13′. I have seen this mistake made, and it is not as stupid as some may think. On the 25th the figures 5° 13′ 19″ have no symbol between them, so you might look up to the top of the column, see the Sign Capricorn, and put it down without noticing that the Sun had gone into Aquarius on the 20th. Always look down the columns to see if any planet has changed its sign.

Next, under the Sun, write the symbol of the Moon. But do not copy down the Sign Virgo 11° 41′ just yet. You could only do this if the birth time were given for 12.00 noon, Greenwich Time, exactly. You leave it to be calculated by logarithms.

Next under the Moon put the symbol for Mercury, but do not write down Sagittarius 23° 36′, as it must also be calculated by the logarithms.

Next under Mercury put the symbol for Venus. It is in Capricorn, but as it is not too near the beginning of the sign, it is not so important to calculate its exact position as in the case of the Sun, Moon and Mercury. So write down the Sign Capricorn with the figures 6° 26′.

Next under Venus put the symbol for Mars. Then add the Sign Scorpio with the figures 10° 53′.

Next under Mars put the symbol for Jupiter. Write the Sign Aries after this and the figures 18° 22′.

Next under Jupiter put the symbol for Saturn, with the Sign Sagittarius and the figures 5° 13′.

Next under Saturn put the symbol for Uranus, with the Sign Sagittarius and the figures 19° 32′.

Next under Uranus put the symbol for Neptune, with the Sign Capricorn and the figures 3° 36′.

Finally, put down the symbol for Pluto, with the Sign Scorpio and the figures 6° 55′.

The Meaning of Retrograde

Before passing on to the logarithms, I had better give some explanation of the word Retrograde. Owing to the fact that our Earth and the planets are going round the Sun at different rates of speed, a planet sometimes appears to be moving, not in its proper direction through the sign, but backwards. Then, if you look at the Ephemeris for March, 1986, you will see that Saturn was retrograde on the 19th. Note the letter ℞ with a little stroke across the tail. That is the symbol for the word retrograde. On the 7th August, you will find the symbol D. This indicates when the change takes place from retrograde to direct. There is some difference of opinion among astrologers as to the effect of this retrograde movement. The old astrologers said that a retrograde planet brought bad luck or misfortune. Others think now that there is no evil influence at all. When Mercury or Venus forms a conjunction with the Sun by retrograde movement, the result is considered to be of no importance by some astrologers.

How to Use Your Table of Logarithms

Now the word Logarithm is quite a bogey to some beginners! I once heard a would-be astrologer explain her failure to take up the study with the remark: 'The first pages of your Ephemeris looked very confusing; but when I came to the one with those logarithms, that settled me!'

The word Logarithm, like so many of our scientific English words, is taken from the Greek. If you get a dictionary and look up the word, you will find that it only means *logos*, a ratio; and *arithmos*, a number. The clever invention of these numbers is simply a system of calculating by easy addition and subtraction, instead of by multiplication and division. There is no need for you to get a school book and study the different kinds of logarithms. All you want to know is the way to use one particular table of them, called the Proportional Logarithms for finding the Planets' Places.

Let us begin with the Moon, as that is the most important for you to start with now. There is a very good reason in the fact, which is not well known, that the Moon moves round the Earth at the rate of about 12° to 15° in the twenty-four hours.

So a few hours before noon or after noon would make a difference in the aspects, or in the sign for the Moon.

In cases where accuracy, as complete as possible, is required it is the rule to calculate the Sun, Moon, and all the planets by logarithms.

Now turn to the page of logarithms in your Ephemeris, and carefully read the rule, in very small print at the bottom of the page. In case you find that your eyesight is not strong enough, I propose to copy out the rule here.

RULE.—Add proportional log. of planet's daily motion to log. of time from noon, and the sum will be the log. of the motion required.

Add this to the planet's place at noon, if time be p.m.; but subtract if a.m., and the sum will be planet's true place.

If retrograde, subtract for p.m., but add for a.m. On pages 26-28 of the Ephemeris, you will find a useful set of tables which give the daily motion of the planets. However, it is very easy to calculate the planetary positions. But it must be done carefully, and on one sheet of paper. Always begin a calculation by writing down the date with which it is connected. It saves confusion.

Now consult your birth data. You find that the birth took place on the 1st of January at 1.40 p.m., at Liverpool, in the year 1986.

You want to find the rate at which the Moon was moving. It is in the tables—13 22 49. Put down the longitude at noon on the 1st.

Now open the Ephemeris at the last page, and prepare to make your next calculation by logarithms!

Look at the top of the page, where you see a row of figures, 0 to 15, under the words Degrees or Hours. Then down each side of the page you see another row of figures, from 0 to 59.

Moon's long. at noon:

11° 40′ 56″
1° 40′ 0″
―――――
10° 0′ 56″

Moon's place in the map:

Virgo 10° 1′.

Now look at the Moon's daily rate, 13° 23′. [The 49″ is not far off a minute, and as a rule we omit the seconds.] Does not common sense suggest that you look at the column with 13 at the top, and then at the line under it marked 23 at the side? There you get the figures 2536. Then take the time 1.40 p.m., and look in the column headed by the figure 1 at the 40th line, where you find 1.1584. That is all. Add these together, and the result is the log. 1.4120. That is the nearest you can get.

Now what are you to do with this log. 1.4120? Most people see at once. Some do not see that you must look for the log., and see what degree and minutes it corresponds to. It is in column 0 at the minutes line 56. So you add 0° 56′ to the Moon's longitude at noon, as you find it in the Ephemeris for the 1st of January, 1986. Then you put it on your paper as Virgo 12° 37'.

Whenever you use this Table of Logarithms, with its figures packed so closely together, have a small flat rule to guide your eye in looking down the long columns or across the minute lines. But you need not use these tables at all if you always have this book and its Logarithm pages at hand (see pages 74–82).

The Atlas

It is always advisable to obtain an atlas and one that gives maps in good detail with place names clearly shown. In addition the atlas should contain a list of the more important towns and places in the world with the latitude and longitude, as well as the map reference, against each place.

How to Make a Horoscope Map

Do not buy any printed maps at first. Draw your own for your trial attempts. But, remember, there is a right and a wrong way. Do not use saucers or anything of that kind to get the circle, and then draw the lines by guess-work with a book for a ruler. This is the wrong way, and the results are deplorable. An untidy, badly drawn horoscope on a cheap sheet of ruled paper indicates the sloven and a badly afflicted Venus at birth.

Buy a plain writing-pad, and at the same time get a pair of school compasses, with a lead-pencil holder and an ink bow. You should also have a ruler and a ballpoint pen. If you have a school pocket-case of instruments, all the better; but you need not buy one.

Now, you will save much time and trouble if you make what I call a horoscope stencil card, such as I always use for my own work.

On a rather stiff sheet of paper, draw a line across it, 5 inches (12.5 cm.) long, as in the diagram (Fig. 4), the line AXF. Find the centre X with your compasses. Then from this centre draw the half-circle ATF. Now find the point T in the half-circle. To do this, open your compasses about $3\frac{1}{2}$ inches (9 cm.), and from the centre A draw a short line under T. Then from F draw another to cross it. Draw a straight line from X through the point where the lines cross to T. You have now divided the half-circle into two equal parts.

If you have a protractor or set-square it is easier to get the point T. Next you want to get exactly the points in the half-circle marked $BCDE$. Open your compasses so that the point shall rest on A, and the pencil or ink-point on X. Now, when

31

you turn the drawing-point round to the left, you will make a little line across the half-circle at *C*. Do the same thing from *F* to the right, and you will mark *D*. Now put the point of your compasses on *T*. Turn the pencil point right round so as to pass through *X*, and you will mark *B* and *E*. With a strong needle or long pin prick holes in the half-circle exactly where the lines cross. Before you rule in your straight lines make the two little half-circles at *X*. Now you can put your compasses aside. Get an ordinary lead pencil or your ballpoint pen and with your rule carefully draw the lines from *BCDE* in a line with the point *X*. Fill in the figures and carefully push your needle or pin through the points marked by the eight letters.

Your horoscope stencil is now ready for use. But a paper stencil would not last very long, so you should draw it on a stiff piece of cardboard, when you have got a paper stencil drawn out quite correctly. You may not find your first attempt as satisfactory as you would like. These things are best done in colour.

When you have got a good stencil card, all you have to do is to lay it on your paper, or in your horoscope book and prick through the holes with a needle. But you must hold the card quite steady while you do it, and do not forget a hole.

Then with your compasses and drawing-pen you can make a complete horoscope map in a few minutes. You had better leave the little circle in the middle blank.

Now for people who are born without any manual dexterity and who cannot even make a simple stencil like this, the best thing to do is to buy Raphael's Book of Blank Maps.

Writing in the Signs and Planets

Now take your paper on which you have written out the Ascendant and the signs for the other five houses. Begin at the top, the 10th House, and write the sign with its figures under it.

But I want to give a word of warning to you about writing these symbols. Make a rule of writing your signs and planets slowly and with care. Do not get into that slovenly habit of writing then anyhow, as some astrologers do. I have seen Libra and Aquarius written so that you could not tell them apart. It is very easy to mistake Virgo for Scorpio, if they are not properly formed. I have seen Capricorn made like a contorted Saturn, and Uranus like the letter H tumbling to pieces. Again, Leo should not be written like the Dragon's Head. Get into the habit of forming your symbols carefully, even when making rough notes (see Fig. 1).

At the top of the map and at the lower part of the circle write the sign as in the map. But the Ascendant with its opposite sign is written as in the map. For the other houses you can write the signs like the figures on a clock face, in line with the centre or vertically with the figures under them. Remember that it is usual to put the minutes as well as the degrees to the ascending sign, and to the sign on the 7th.

The Intercepted Signs

You were doing a horoscope for the 1st of January, 1986, the birth time was 1.40 p.m. and the birth place was Liverpool. You find that the house cusps are as follows:

10	11	12	Ascen.	2	3
1° ♒	25° ♒	6° ♈	7° 9′ ♊	27° ♊	14° ♋

When you have written in the signs you will see that the same sign comes on two adjacent houses (but, note, with different degrees). You will also find that some other signs are missing. These are known as the Intercepted Signs. Now what are you to do in this case? Look at Fig. 5 and you will see where two signs are not on the cusps of any house. But they must go somewhere, so they go between their proper signs, as you see in the drawing, but without figures.

You would put Gemini 7° 9′ on the Ascendant, and Aquarius on the cusp of the 10th House. Then you would find that Aquarius 25° was on the cusp of the 11th House, and Aries 6° on the cusp of the 12th. But after you had placed the opposite signs on their houses, you would see no fewer than four signs were missing. For Aquarius cannot come next to Aries, nor can Aries be next to Gemini. And you must not leave out Pisces, Taurus, Virgo and Scorpio. Pisces is put in the 11th House and Taurus in the 12th. Then, of course, the opposite signs, in the same way, go into the opposite houses.

You need not trouble about the explanation of these intercepted signs. They are caused by the latitude of the country. All signs rise in regular rotation at the Equator, but an inequality in their rising happens as one proceeds North or to the South. Some astrologers consider that planets in these signs are considered to have much influence upon the houses in which they happen to be placed, others think that their influence is weakened.

33

What do the Figures Attached to the Signs Mean?

Why have you got 7° 9′ with Gemini, or 1° with Aquarius? These figures are often a difficulty with beginners, especially if they attempt to write the planets in the map before they have clearly understood how they are used (see Fig. 1).

When we say that a planet is in a sign, we mean that it is in one of the 30 degrees of that sign. Now, it is a very important matter to know which degree, for two reasons. One is that you may put it in the right house of the map; the other is that you may know in which decanate it is, as we shall see later on.

Look at the diagram for the intercepted signs (Fig. 5). Then look at the Ephemeris for the 1st of January, 1986. When you make a list of the planets with their signs, you will note at once that Saturn is in Sagittarius; that Mars is in Scorpio, and Pluto also; and that the Moon is in Virgo. So here you have four planets to be put in this quarter of the map. Where do you put them?

Start with Saturn. It is 5° 13′ in Sagittarius. Now Sagittarius is on the cusp of both the 7th and 8th Houses, and Saturn must be placed in the house that is *before* the degree on the cusp. So Saturn should be placed just under the cusp of the 7th House, and therefore in the 6th House of the chart. It's as easy as that.

You must always remember that the Signs of the Zodiac come up, as we say, from the East point, like Gemini in Fig. 1. There 7° 9′ had only just appeared at the birth time—supposing that the birth time had been given exactly.

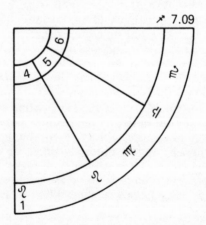

Fig. 5. A Diagram to Illustrate the Intercepted Signs

They go through the 12th and 11th Houses to the 10th, and then go down the West side to the 4th House, when they start to come up again. They go round like the hands of a clock. But the Sun, the Moon, and the planets are, at the same time, moving in the other direction in the order of the houses. You will see in your Ephemeris that the Sun, Moon, and the planets move through Aries, from the first degree to the last, and then go into Taurus, and through that into Gemini, and so on through all the signs.

It is important to remember this, and that the 1st degree of a sign is going up on the Eastern side, head first, and coming down on the Western side with the 1st degree head downwards.

These cautions may seem superfluous to some readers, but I know from experience that they are needed. I will give an instance to prove it. Look at the complete map Fig. 1. There you will find Gemini 7° 9′ on the 1st House, and Gemini 27° on the 2nd. You will also see Aquarius 1° on the 10th, and Capricorn 14° on the 9th.

Now, you might say that no one would be foolish enough to put the 7° 9′ on the 2nd House or the 1° of Aquarius on the 8th House! Well, it can be done. I have seen a horoscope with the figures wrong in this way! I have also had to correct such a mistake as a planet being moved into the 8th House, under the impression that the degrees were going up on the Western side, instead of being placed in the 6th. Beginners make very curious mistakes sometimes.

Next look at Mars and Pluto. You will see that they are both in Scorpio. It is one of the intercepted signs, so there are no figures to consult. You simply put in Mars and Pluto by writing them along the rim of the 6th House. Similarly, the Moon is in the intercepted sign of Virgo and is written along the rim of the 5th House.

How to Place the Planets Properly

There is a recognised way of writing the planets in the map. When you have decided the question of the house, the planet must be written close up to the line of the house on which its sign is. If the degree the planet is in is less than the degree on the cusp, the planet is placed before the cusp, but after the cusp if it is in a greater degree.

For instance, take Jupiter in the map (Fig. 1). It is, we may say, under the line in the 2nd House. But if Saturn had been 16° 27′ in Cancer, it would have been close to the same line, but just above it in the 1st House.

Jupiter is in Aquarius, 18° 24'. Jupiter is close up to the cusp of the 11th, but is kept close to the line to show it belongs to the 10th House. If Jupiter had been at 26° Aquarius, it would have been in the 11th House.

Now, you very often have two or more planets in the same sign, and all of them, sometimes, have to go in the same house. What are you to do then?

It depends whether the planets have to go on the East or West side of the map. If you are dealing with the Eastern side, just remember that the signs are going up—as I have said 'head first'. Then the planet which is highest up in the sign goes close to the cusp, and the others follow according to their figures.

It is very troublesome when you have a lot of planets in one sign, called a satellitium of planets, as it is not easy to write them without making a muddle of them. Always arrange a satellitium on a slip of paper before you attempt to write them in. Also note how many have to be carried over into the next house, where there may be some other planets.

When you are going to arrange the planets for the Western side of the map, remember that the signs are coming down 'head first'. So you put the planets, in the beginning of the sign, nearest to the cusp of the house, and the others farther on in the sign behind them.

Then if you have two or more planets in an intercepted sign, you place the one highest in the sign close to the rim (as the Moon is in the map in Fig. 11, page 61), if it is on the Eastern side of the map. If on the Western, you place the planet with the greater figures nearest to the rim, as Mars in the map in Fig. 1. These may seem trivial details to some people, but they are important to those who like to do their work neatly and well.

The Aspects Between the Sun, Moon and the Planets

When you have written the planets in your map, you are ready to calculate what are called the aspects. This word is misleading to those who know nothing about astrology, as an aspect is known by finding the distance of one planet from another or from the Sun.

These distances are measured by degrees, minutes, and seconds; the seconds are generally left out, except in cases where great accuracy is required.

There is an old mystical meaning for these aspects. Most people know that an interesting amount of lore exists in reference to numbers. In all religions they have played an important part. There is a very ancient reverence for the number 3. So it is very interesting to note that the harmonious astrological aspects are based on the threefold division of the circle. The best aspect of all, the trine, is 120°, the third part of the circle. As we have seen, the four equilateral triangles in the horoscope have the triplicities of Fire, Earth, Air, and Water on their angles. All the signs on each of these triangles are in perfect harmony with each other—that is, they are in trine.

The sextile, 60°, is half a trine, and the semi-sextile half a sextile. But when we turn to the square, we find the discord; for the unharmonious aspects are based upon the 2 and the 4. The circle is divided into two equal parts by the diameter. This is 180°, which is known as the opposition. Then when the circle is quartered, we get the square, a distance of 90°. A semi-square and a sesquiquadrate are parts of the square, naturally, and discordant also.

We must remember, however, that there is no such thing as evil in the heavens. All the evil in the world is caused by our own misuse of our free-will. There is an old astrological saying that 'the wise man rules his Stars; but the fool obeys them'.

A List of the Aspects Generally Used

☌	Conjunction	0°	Variable
⚺	Semi-sextile	30	Weak harmony
∠	Semi-square	45	Weak discord
✳	Sextile	60	Harmony
⧠	Square	90	Discord
△	Trine	120	Harmony
⧠	Sesquiquadrate	135	Weak discord
⚻	Quincunx	150	Weak discord
☍	Opposition	180	Discord
P	Parallel		Variable

The Parallel of Declination must be found from the Ephemeris. It is given in the columns at the top of each page under the heading Dec. It is the distance in degrees and minutes, North or South of the Equator, between any two planets. If there is no other aspect between two planets in the same degree of declination, this is considered to act as a conjunction, or an opposition.

How to Find the Aspects Without Figures

If you learn the above figures by heart, like a column of spelling, you are almost certain to mix them up at first, and you would not find it easy to calculate the distances on the map, especially in the case of the 45 and 135 aspects.

So I propose that you should learn your aspects without any figures at all at first. You can learn the figures afterwards without any difficulty. But I know by experience that you can learn to see any aspect at sight. You must use your eyes and memory together. I have never known this plan to fail yet.

But I do not take the aspects in the order given above. That is the order of the formation of the aspects. Look in your Ephemeris at the monthly progress of the Moon, as it overtakes and passes the Sun and the planets, from the conjunction, when we say there is a New Moon, round to the opposition, when we have the Full Moon. After the Full Moon these aspects are formed again, but in reverse order, until the next New Moon is reached.

Now I am going to take the aspects in a different order altogether. We will begin with the triangles of the horoscope and then take the crosses. After that I will use some simple diagrams to complete my system.

The Triangles and the Trines

Take your four triangles and study them well, until you can visualise them perfectly. Always write them down in the following order, as order helps the eye:

FIRE　　　　EARTH　　　AIR　　　WATER

Take care that you do not put an Air Sign on the Fire Triangle by mistake; or get the symbol for Scorpio on the Earth Triangle instead of the symbol for Virgo.

When you can visualise these triangles at a moment's notice, you can tell the trine aspect at sight. There is no need to count the 120°.

Say that you find the Sun 20° in Leo. All you have to do is to look at your row of signs and planets to see if you have any planets in Aries or Sagittarius. You need not look at any other signs for this trine. Then if you find one or more planets in either of these signs, you examine their figures.

I say 'examine their figures', because you have now to deal with something that is quite new to you. This is the unsettled question of the 'orbs' of the Sun and Moon and the different planets. You want to know when you have got an aspect.

A planet might be in Aries and another in Leo, but it does not follow that they would be in trine or sesquiquadrate to each other. It is not necessary for the aspect to be exact. When the Moon is approaching the Sun to form the conjunction or leaving the Sun to break the conjunction, the influence may be working for 10° on one side and 10° on the other. This 10° influence may be termed its orb for the aspect.

But it will be time enough to deal with the proper orbs later on, when we are done with the best way to find the aspects themselves first.

Your first lesson in aspects is to visualise the trine from the study of the four triangles. The Fire Signs are trine with one another, so are the Earth Signs, so are the Air Signs, and so are the Water Signs. You must never mix them up. So the planets in these signs are trine also, if they are in orbs. But you must never make a Water Sign planet in trine with a planet in a Fire Sign.

Therefore, when you find the Sun, for instance, in a Fire Sign, look first of all for a trine of any other planet in another Fire Sign. Or if it is in an Air Sign, do the same.

Of course, you may look for the squares first, if you like, or the sextile. I only want you to work methodically. If you learn your aspects from this book, it would be as well to look for your aspects in the same order as you learn them.

So now we will pass on to consider—

The Crosses and the Squares

Dismiss the triangles from your mind for the present, and study the crosses. Always write them down and study them in the same order:

CARDINAL   FIXED   MUTABLE

It will not be easy at first, as you are dealing with the same signs as those on the triangles, but with quite a different arrangement. Instead of having four sets of three signs each, you now have three sets of four signs each.

This is rather confusing at first, but with patience and perseverance you will find it quite easy. Suppose that you are dealing with a planet in Leo. First you look for the trine in Aries and Sagittarius. Now you must look for the square in Taurus and Scorpio.

Think of the triangles with their one aspect of harmony; and then, as a strong contrast, think of the three crosses with their two aspects of discord.

Each sign on the points of the crosses is 90° from the next sign. That is the distance which forms the square aspect. For the second discord we come to—

The Crosses and the Opposition

The twelve Signs of the Zodiac are so arranged that each sign has another sign on the other side of the heavens exactly opposite to it. Remember that these positions never change. Aries is always opposite to Libra, Taurus to Scorpio, and so on all round. The distance is 180°, half the circle.

The oppositions have already been noticed above on page 00, but I may as well repeat them here in a different way, in separate crosses:

CAPRICORN   AQUARIUS   PISCES

ARIES   LIBRA   TAURUS   SCORPIO   GEMINI   SAGIT-
TARIUS
    CANCER   LEO   VIRGO

Now, this diagram should help you to visualise the two discords of the three crosses, the square, and the opposition.

You see now how to visualise the trine, the square, and the opposition. You will very soon be able to sit down with a pencil and sheet of paper, and show anyone the four triangles and the three crosses, with the sign accurately placed upon each.

The Qualities and the Sextiles

For the sextiles you have nothing like the triangles and crosses to guide you. So we must adopt another plan.

You will notice, if you look round the circle of the signs, that a Fire Sign is followed by an Earth Sign, and that an Air Sign is followed by a Water Sign. So that all round the circle Fire and Air, Earth and Water, are two signs apart. That is, they are 60° apart. Now, 60° is the distance of the sextile.

The sextile is a very harmonious aspect, so you can visualise it as formed between the excellent blends of Fire and Air, and Earth and Water.

So, after you have looked to see if your Sun in Leo has any trines, squares, or planets in opposition, you next look to see if there are any planets in Gemini or Libra, to form a sextile.

So remember that each Sign of the Zodiac can make two sextiles, as well as an opposition, with those signs with which it makes a good blend. (See Fig. 6.)

Now, someone may ask the very natural question: 'How is it that you can have a harmonious aspect and a discordant aspect between two signs that blend well together, like Fire and Air?'

It is not easy to answer this question. But there are many astrologers who do not consider that the opposition is such a discord as some think. It is founded on the number 2, the circle halved, and so, like the square, is a discord.

But the opposition may be complementary as well as separative. Aries and Libra are complementary. Aries represents the Man; Libra represents the Woman. Man and Woman are complementary: one cannot do without the other, just as Fire cannot exist in flame without Air. So in the same way Earth and Water: they are complementary also; without Water the Earth would be a desert.

The Semi-sextile

As this is half the sextile it is very simple. Planets in orbs in any two signs side by side are in semi-sextile aspect. A planet in Aries may be semi-sextile to another in Pisces and another in Taurus.

Here again comes the question: 'How can Fire and Water, and Fire and Earth, make harmonious aspects?' The best way to answer the question is to point out that an aspect like this brings two things together so as to cause a useful result, although they are antagonistic by nature, like Fire and Water. Throw water on fire and you put the fire out. But fill your kettle with water and place it on the fire, and you can have your tea. This is most harmonious! But even here there is danger of discord. A kettle of boiling water may be upset and cause dangerous injuries. A boiler may explode and kill a number of people.

Again, when fire and earth are brought together, as in the case of a kiln and china clay, you get most beautiful as well as useful results.

The Quincunx, or Inconjunct

The Quincunx, or Inconjunct, as it is sometimes called, is similar in character to the semi-sextile. It is an aspect of 150°. So it is formed by a planet with another planet in either of the signs on each side of its opposite sign.

For instance, a planet in Aries can only form the quincunx with a planet in the Sign of Virgo or Scorpio. And a planet in Libra can only form it with a planet in Taurus and Pisces.

Now, there is a difference of opinion about this aspect, as to whether it should be considered a weak harmony or a weak discord. Many astrologers think now that it acts like the semi-sextile, and there does not seem to be any reason why there should be any difference, except from the difference of their degrees apart.

A planet placed in Libra is in opposition to a planet in Aries. It is also in quincunx to a planet placed in Pisces or Taurus.

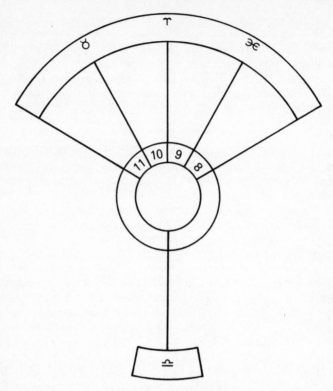

Fig. 6—Diagram Showing Four Aspects: The Opposition, the Sextile, the Semi-sextile and the Quincunx

A planet in Pisces is in sextile with a planet placed in Taurus. This is the Earth and Water sextile. The Fire and Air sextiles are formed on either side of this fan, between Aries and Aquarius on one side, and Aries and Gemini on the other.

Then a planet in Aries is semi-sextile to a planet in Pisces or Taurus. Now it is very easy to visualise this fan, and see these four aspects at a glance.

The Semi-Square and the Sesquiquadrate

I find from my experience that these two aspects cause a great deal of trouble to beginners. They are not calculated like the other aspects, for a semi-square is half a square, and a sesqui-quadrate is a square and a half.

So you cannot take them like trines, squares, and sextiles, either way round the horoscope. The rule for finding these aspects is given as follows:

Add or subtract 15 to the planet's position, as it is nearest the beginning or end of a sign; and see if any other planet is in or near that degree of another sign.

Now let us suppose that a beginner finds Venus is 5° in Aries, and adds 15 to it, making 20. Then it is found that Jupiter is 22° in Gemini, and that Saturn is 21° in Sagittarius. It is quite possible that Venus will be put down as semi-square to Jupiter and sesquiquadrate to Saturn!

Mistakes like this have been made, as I know. Then, again, I have known a beginner to add 15 to 16 or 17, and then put down a semi-square with another planet.

The fact that 15° plus 17° makes 32°, and that there are only 30° in a sign, is quite forgotten!

The first thing for you to remember is that if you add 15 you must stop at 15°, and subtract from 16 or more.

The next thing to do is to look at a Table of Houses, which shows the twelve signs ascending one after the other, and see why these aspects are different distances from a planet, according to the way you count the 45° or the 135°.

Let us suppose that the Sun is 5° in Aries, Mars 20° in Taurus, and Saturn 21° in Aquarius. The Sun is semi-square to them both.

But Taurus is the next sign to Aries and Aquarius is not, but beyond Pisces. At the same time let us suppose that Jupiter is 19° in Scorpio, and that the planet Neptune is 22° in Leo. The Sun is sesquiquadrate to them both.

But Scorpio is farther from Aries than Leo. Look at the Table of Houses for London, and note Aries 5° 19′. Then count downwards into Taurus, till you have counted 45° from Aries 5°19′. You stop at Taurus 20°. For 20° of Taurus added to 25° of Aries make 45°.

Now count from Aries 5° 19′, up through Pisces for the same number 45°. Here you have only got 5° of Aries towards the 45°. So you add the 30° of Pisces, which makes 35°, and go up farther to the 20th degree of Aquarius.

In the same way you will find that the sesquiquadrate will come in the Trine Sign of Leo, if you count in the direction of the signs; but that it must be one sign beyond the other Trine Sign, Sagittarius, if you count through Pisces.

So I think that this will make it clear to you that a semi-square is either one sign forwards or two back. Also that a sesquiquadrate is the Trine Sign, if you count forwards; but if you have to count the other way, it is the sign just beyond the Trine Sign.

Two Tables to see these Aspects at Sight

I have found these tables very much appreciated by those who have used them. As I have been asked if the first table would not do for the subtraction, I must point out that it would not. You only add when a planet is in the first 15°. You subtract from anything over 15.

If you look at the second table carefully, you will see that the arrangement is quite different.

Look at the Cardinal Signs in the two small columns. You will see at a glance that they only make the semi-square and the sesquiquadrate with the Fixed Signs.

Take Aries at the top of the first little column. In front of it you have these four signs: Aquarius and Taurus in the top line, for the semi-square; and Leo and Scorpio in the second line, for the sesquiquadrate.

Then look down to Cancer. There again you have the same four, but in a different order.

Next look at Libra. The same four again, and in another order. And farther down you see a different order in front of Capricorn.

♈	♒ ♌	♉ ♏	♎	♌ ♒	♏ ♉
♉	♓ ♍	♊ ♐	♏	♍ ♓	♐ ♊
♊	♈ ♎	♋ ♑	♐	♎ ♈	♑ ♋
♋	♉ ♏	♌ ♒	♑	♏ ♉	♒ ♌
♌	♊ ♐	♍ ♓	♒	♐ ♊	♓ ♍
♍	♋ ♑	♎ ♈	♓	♑ ♋	♈ ♎

Table for the Addition of 15

44

Now look at Taurus and the other Fixed Signs—Leo, Scorpio, and Aquarius. In front of them you have the Mutable Signs. They also are arranged differently in each case.

In the same way you will see that the Mutable Signs form these two aspects with the Cardinal Signs.

So here you have a most simple method of visualising these aspects without any counting of 45° and 135°. You can see either aspect at a glance.

If you have a planet in Aries to which you can add 15°, all you have to do is to look at the planets in the Fixed Signs, and see if there is one or more within 3° of the number made by the addition; for the orb for these two aspects is 3°.

If there is one in Aquarius or Taurus, you know it is the semi-square, as Taurus and Aquarius are close to Aries.

If it is in Leo or Scorpio, you know that it is the sesquiquadrate, as one is the Trine Sign and the other the sign beyond.

In the same way you deal with planets in the Fixed Signs. You only examine the Mutable Signs for aspects.

Then if your addition planet is in the Mutable Signs, you look for the aspect in the Cardinal Signs.

♈	♓ ♍	♊ ♐	♎	♍ ♓	♐ ♊
♉	♈ ♎	♋ ♑	♏	♎ ♈	♑ ♋
♊	♉ ♏	♌ ♒	♐	♏ ♉	♒ ♌
♋	♊ ♐	♍ ♓	♑	♐ ♊	♓ ♍
♌	♋ ♑	♎ ♈	♒	♑ ♋	♈ ♎
♍	♌ ♒	♏ ♉	♓	♒ ♌	♉ ♏

Table for the Subtraction of 15

After a little experience you need not even look at your tables at all. You can do without them, as you will know these two aspects at sight.

Here you will see why the first table will not do for the subtraction as well as the addition. The order is reversed, for the Mutable Signs make the aspects with the Fixed. The Fixed make theirs with the Cardinal; and the Cardinal make theirs with the Mutable.

I should like you to notice how these tables arrange themselves. You have four rows in each table of the planets which are in opposition to each other.

So you see that the semi-square and the sesquiquadrate aspects are made with two pairs of opposites. And you will also notice that these aspects are made between the Cardinal, Fixed, and Mutable Crosses; for they are discords.

Therefore, the complaints made by so many beginners that the aspects, and these two especially, are difficult to master, turn out to be due only to the ignorance of their simplicity and beautiful symmetry.

The Parallel of Declination

The Parallel of Declination is concerned with the Celestial Equator and the Ecliptic. You can study this in any little manual of astronomy.

For instance, the Sun is said to 'decline' away from the Celestial Equator after the 21st of March, until it arrives at its farthest North Declination about the 21st of June. Then it gets back to the Equator about the 21st of September. Afterwards it goes South till it reaches the maximum South Declination about the 21st of December. The maximum degrees of declination are 23° 27′.

Look at your Ephemeris for 1986, and note the Declination of the Sun on those days. You will find that the figures vary very much in different years.

To get your declinations correctly you must have an Ephemeris for the year. It is a good plan to write out the declinations and then examine them to see if any of them are within orbs. The orb is one degree.

Whenever you find two planets in parallel, and at the same time in square, or any other aspect, you consider the parallel to be the same as the square. But if there is no other aspect, you take the parallel as a conjunction, unless Neptune, Uranus, Saturn, and Mars are concerned. Then you regard it is an opposition.

The Conjunction

This is the union of two planets in the same sign. It means the blending of two in one. Everything depends upon the nature of the planets in conjunction, so you must study the conjunctions carefully later on when you get your astrological books. It is a mistake to suppose, as some beginners do, that Jupiter in conjunction with Mars is harmonious. It is partly good and partly discordant. In judging a conjunction of Jupiter with Saturn, for instance, you must consider the sign in which it takes place. The conjunction in Capricorn would not be harmonious, but a conjunction in Libra would.

The 'Heads and Tails' Aspects

For want of a better name, I call the aspects which I am now going to mention the 'heads and tails' aspects. This name is easily remembered, and there can be no mistake about its meaning. Some astrologers ignore this aspect. They say it is not made in the proper aspecting signs. But the planets concerned are within orbs, and I consider that sufficient. Besides, the aspect is used in Raphael's Ephemeris. Look at the Moon on the 19th of February, 1986. It is 29° 40′ in Gemini, and is put down as opposite to Neptune. Now Neptune is in Capricorn 5° 13′.

This is an example of a 'head and tail' aspect. Count from Gemini 29° 40′ to Capricorn 5° 13′. The Moon has only to go on 20′ to come out of Gemini. To this add the degrees of Cancer, Leo, Virgo, Libra, Scorpio and Sagittarius—180°—making 180° 20′. Then add the 5° 13′ of Neptune. That makes 185° 33′, which is within the orb for the opposite aspect.

There is another example on the 19th of July, 1986. There you find the Moon in the 29th degree of Sagittarius, and Neptune is at Capricorn 3° 50′ and as Capricorn follows Sagittarius, the Moon and Neptune form a conjunction, which has been marked under the lunar aspects.

So make this rule: If you find one or more of your planets in the last two or three degrees of a sign, look if any other planet is in the first two or three degrees of any other sign. Then don't count the degrees apart, as I did above, as there is a much quicker and more simple plan. Take our first example above.

Say: 'The Moon is at 29° 40′ of Gemini, which is practically the same as the 1st degree of Cancer, for aspect purposes. The 1st degree of Cancer is, I know at sight, opposite the 6th degree of Capricorn.' Therefore it is a case of the Moon opposite

Neptune. So don't count.

But do not fail to note whether the quicker planet is in the 'head' or the 'tail'. If the Moon is in the 'tail', it will catch up the other planet and make the exact aspect. But if the Moon is in the 'head', it is going away; that is, is separating from the aspect.

The Orbs of the Aspects

We have not done with the aspects yet, for it is not enough to know in which of the signs they are made. There is something else very important to take into consideration.

You must know what is meant by the orbs. So I may as well take this opportunity to say that an orb is not the same thing as an orbit, although both words are derived from the same Latin word, *orbis*, which means a circle.

'Orbit', in astronomy and astrology, means the path or course described by a celestial body in the heavens. Thus, the Zodiac is the earth's orbit for its revolution round the Sun. The celestial Ecliptic is the orbit in which the Sun appears to move.

But the word 'orb' means a 'sphere of action'. Now, if you happen to be a reader of theosophical literature you will know all about the Aura, which surrounds all living creatures, as well as everything in the vegetable and mineral kingdom.

So we may call the radiating influence of the Sun, Moon, and the planets, their Aura, or orb for aspects.

Now, if this orb of influence extended everywhere into space, there would be no separate aspects. So the orb is limited, according to the aspect. There are certain considerations and rules to be observed, but all astrologers are not agreed about these rules. When I first began to study astrology, I was told to calculate the aspects in three different ways! You see, there are no hard and fast rules.

So the orbs which I propose to recommend to you are those which seem to commend themselves to my ideas of the fitness of things.

Moon in conjunction with, or opposition to, the Sun					12°
Sun and Moon in same aspects with any planet					10°
Planets in conjunction or opposition					8°
For all squares and trines					8°
For sextiles					7°
For semi-square and sesquiquadrate					3°
For semi-sextile and quincunx					2°
For the parallel					1°

However, I may as well give an instance of another method of calculating these orbs, to show how authorities can disagree.

The rule is this: Add the orbs of the two planets together, and take one-half of the sum. That gives the orb.

The list of the orbs is as follows:

Sun and Moon				15°
Jupiter and Saturn				9°
Mercury, Venus, Mars, and Uranus			7°
Neptune				5°
Some writers give the Sun				17°
" " Jupiter				12°

How to Write Out the Aspects

Write them neatly in fair-sized symbols and figures. Do not scribble them in a careless way, or in tiny, badly shaped symbols and indistinct figures.

Write them under the two headings Harmony and Discord. It is not a good plan to jumble them up anyhow, squares and trines together, and so on. If your paper has the harmonies on one side, and the discords on the other, you can see at a glance what you have to deal with. If you jumble them up you cannot.

I also advise my pupils strongly not to write the aspects on the same sheet of paper on which the map is. I know perfectly well that some astrologers do not agree with me about this matter. They love to have a map surrounded with all the aspects, birth data, the triplicities, and the qualities of the planets, etc! But I was born with Venus in exact conjunction with the Moon, Mercury in Libra, and my Sun in the middle of Virgo, so that accounts for my ideas about neatness, order, and the proper way to arrange a horoscope map and the aspects, etc.

The Moon's Nodes

A node is that part of the Ecliptic where a planet passes from North to South Latitude, or from South to North. The Moon's ascending node, when it goes North, is called the Dragon's Head. Its descending node, when it goes South, is called the Dragon's Tail.

The symbol is something like the symbol for Leo, but it is not the same. If you think of the 'hook and eye' used by dressmakers, the 'eye' is the symbol. When the loops are turned down, it stands for the Dragon's Head: ☊ . When the loops are turned up it stands for the Dragon's Tail like this: ☋ .

The old astrologers considered these nodes important, and so do the Hindu astrologers of the present day. They say that the head means 'manas', the thinking power, and that it is harmonious and exalted in the 3rd degree of Gemini. But the tail, which means 'kama', or desire and lust, is regarded as discordant. It is exalted in the 3rd degree of Sagittarius.

Modern astrologers also consider these nodes to exercise considerable power and on no account should they be omitted from the map.

The Part of Fortune

Some astrologers do not think that the Part of Fortune has any value, while others consider that it is very useful. It is certainly used in horary astrology. I will explain how it is found, but I will tell you one thing first.

You may save yourself the trouble of calculating it, unless you happen to know almost the exact time of the birth. For you have to make the calculation with the position of the Ascendant, the Sun, and, what is most important, the position of the Moon.

The rule is to add the longitude of the Ascendant to that of the Moon, and then subtract that of the Sun, adding the circle of 360° if wanted. The result gives you the longitude of the Part of Fortune.

Now, the Part of Fortune is the same distance from the Ascendant as the Sun is from the Moon, counting in the direction of the signs. So if you look at the horoscope in Fig. 1, you will see the Part of Fortune entered in the 10th House in Aquarius 8° 55'. Then if you count the distance from Gemini 7° 9' to Aquarius 8° 55', you will find that it is 118° 14'. Then count from the Sun, which is 10° 51' in Capricorn, to the Moon in Virgo 12° 37', and that is also 118° 14'. But you can find the

50

proper position without this counting, and that is your best and easiest way to do it. You write your little sum like this;

		Sign	Degrees	Minutes
Longitude of Ascendant	..	2	7	9
Longitude of Moon	.. ..	5	12	37
		7	19	46
Longitude of Sun	.. ..	9	10	51
Part of Fortune, ⊕	.. ..	10	8	55

That is, Capricorn 8° 55′

Now let us see how we arrive at this answer. What do the figures under the word 'Sign' mean? How do we get Longitude of Ascendant 2, and Longitude of Moon 5?

It simply means that you take the number of the signs of the Ascendant, Sun and Moon, and use them as you see above.

In this calculation Aries is Zero, 0, and Taurus counts as 1, Gemini as 2, and so on all round. So 2 means Gemini, 5 Virgo, 9 Capricorn, and 10 Aquarius. Quite simple!

Next, 9 from 7 leaving 10 requires explanation for most beginners. Whenever you have to take a higher figure from a lower figure in the sign column, add 12 to the lower figure (because there are 12 signs in 360°, the complete circle).

The symbol used for the Part of Fortune is the symbol that represents our earth, which was called Rhea. It is the circle with a cross in it. It is said to indicate inherited property or worldly prosperity.

After the Map is Finished

We may now consider that your map is correctly finished, and the aspects written out on the page opposite to the map. What next?

You have in front of you a human document. A character is written there. If it is the horoscope of a child, you can see how that child ought to be trained by parents and school teachers. You can tell how the child is likely to behave in youth and as life goes on. You can indicate what occupations and professions would be the best to prepare for. You can give advice on the important subjects of friendship and marriage. You can give valuable information about diet and the care of health; and you can give warnings about possible dangers.

But to read correctly all that is written in that little chart of the sky requires what we term judgment. We could teach any intelligent boy or girl to cast a horoscope, and prepare the map with its aspects, for judgment, but no one can teach judgment.

It is possible, however, to point out to students how they may cultivate such a knowledge of astrology as may develop the intuition required. So I propose now to suggest some guiding notes on the way to begin.

I came to the study of astrology through theosophy. As a theosophist I had very thoroughly grasped the truth about reincarnation. So it struck me that astrology ought to furnish further proof of the truth of evolution by birth after birth.

I was not disappointed, for I saw at once that a horoscope must be a 'human document' from the past, the horoscope of the last life on earth; and that each life in the present is making the horoscope for the next reincarnation.

So I want you to consider each horoscope in this light. When you have studied the different influences of the signs, and the extraordinary variety of the combinations of the planets in those signs, and the houses of the horoscope, you will be in a better position to understand that no human being could possibly become 'fit for the Kingdom of Heaven' in a single life on earth!

The vulgar idea that all children are born 'like peas in a pod', all of them indeed brand-new, and of the same age and growth, is absolutely idiotic!

Astrology will teach you that you are never likely to find two horoscopes alike or even approximately alike. It explains difficulties and questions about all the problems of life in the most remarkable way, if you clearly understand that your horoscope is not an accidental arrangement of the planets, just because you happened to be born, as people say, in that particular year. Horoscopes are not accidental documents. Not only the parents, but the year, the month, the day, and the exact minute of time for the birth, depend upon the kind of lives we led when we were on this earth for our last experience in the 'school' of evolution.

If you know nothing about reincarnation, or think there is no truth in it, as no highly evolved men and women do now, you will look upon one horoscope as only 'an unlucky one' and another as only 'a lucky one.'

But you will never be able to explain to anyone but a child or an adult bigot why the Almighty gives out lucky and unlucky horoscopes to children whose souls He is supposed to have just created!

First Impressions from the Map

Leave books alone for the present. Take a sheet of paper and a pen, and sit down with your map and the aspects. You have some work to do before you lay aside this document, and start reading and study.

Look at the horoscope, with expectant eyes and intelligent desire, in search of something which can tell you a story.

In Fig. 1, you have before you a map divided into twelve houses, as we call them, and six of these houses are above the horizon, and six are below. Six of them are also on the Oriental side of the map, and six on the Occidental side.

Then four of these divisions are known as very important angles: The Ascendant and Descendant, the M.C. and the I.C. Four more are called Succedent Houses, and the other four as Cadent Houses (See Fig. 7.)

You know that you have Fire, Earth, Air, and Water Signs round the circle; also that the divisions are made by the Cardinal, Fixed and Mutable Crosses.

Now, how are the planets arranged in relation to these signs and houses? The eye looks to see where the majority of the planets are: what houses are tenanted, and how many are empty.

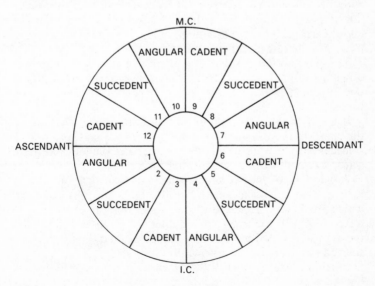

Fig. 7   The Houses

You begin to make notes. For instance, you see that the majority of the planets are above the horizon, but at the same time the majority are on the Oriental side setting.

You note that Saturn is in the 6th, and that it is close to the Descendant. Then you make your list of the positions of the planets as follows:

3 CARDINAL	3 FIRE	2 ANGULAR
3 FIXED	4 EARTH	4 SUCCEDENT
4 MUTABLE	1 AIR	3 CADENT
0 EXALTED	2 WATER	1 ORIENTAL
0 DETRIMENT		9 OCCIDENTAL

You will find this table most useful when you come to write out the judgment of a horoscope, as we shall see later on. But there is another little table which I also advise you to make for reference, for the same purpose, relating to the important decanates of the signs. These decanates will be explained later.

If a planet is in one of the first 10° of a sign, it is in the 1st decanate; if in the second 10°, in the second; and if in the third 10°, in the third.

The Exaltation of the Planets

Now take your little list of the planets in the signs. You begin with the Sun, and ask yourself: 'Is this a good sign for the Sun or not?' And so you go down the list, asking the same question about each planet. And as you go along, if there is anything to note, and there generally is, you record it.

You want to see if any of the planets in your list can be put down as 'exalted' or not. Now what does this mean? It means one of the important things which help you to judge a horoscope.

It is only natural to suppose, if you think of the divisions of the signs, in the triangles and on the crosses, that there will be some affinity or want of affinity between the planets and these signs. You will learn now that there is.

A planet is, of course, very strong in its own sign, or 'house', as it is termed. But a planet can also be powerful in the sign which has been considered that of its exaltation. Some astrologers think that the nature of a planet is entirely transmuted in the sign of its exaltation. So a planet exalted would be considered stronger than in its own house.

When a planet happens to be in the sign opposite to its own house, it is said to be in its 'detriment'. And when it is in the sign opposite to that of its exaltation, it is said to be in its 'fall'.

A List of the Exaltations

The Sun is exalted in Aries; the Moon in Taurus; Mercury in Virgo; Venus in Pisces; Mars in Capricorn; Jupiter in Cancer; and Saturn in Libra.

The planets Uranus, Neptune, Pluto do not rule signs, but Uranus has an affinity with Aquarius, Neptune has an affinity with Pisces and Pluto has an affinity with Scorpio.

I do not suggest that you should learn these exaltations by heart, although it does not seem to be difficult in any way. But I know by experience that many beginners are apt to forget them or muddle them up.

So you must know something about these exaltations, and then learn to visualise them. But just look at that little list again, and see if you can find anything in it to note as a guide to memory.

Let us go back to our Cardinal, Fixed, and Mutable Crosses. Here they are again with the planets added on the signs of their exaltations (see Fig. 8).

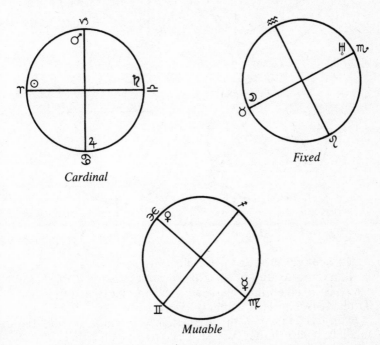

Cardinal

Fixed

Mutable

Fig. 8—The Exaltation of the Planets Shown on the Crosses

Here is something better than a list, something you can look at and visualise. Now you notice at once that the Cardinal Cross exalts the Sun, the great Jupiter, and Saturn and Mars also.

The Fixed Cross has the Moon and Uranus exalted on it. Uranus is given in some books as exalted in Scorpio.

The Mutable Cross has Venus and Mercury exalted on it. But you may wonder why Mercury is in Virgo! The reason is that tradition has always made Virgo not only the house but the sign of Mercury's exaltation. Some astrologers consider that Aquarius ought to be the sign of Mercury's exaltation.

There is another way of looking at these exaltations, which some readers might prefer, and that is to see them in the triangles, like this:

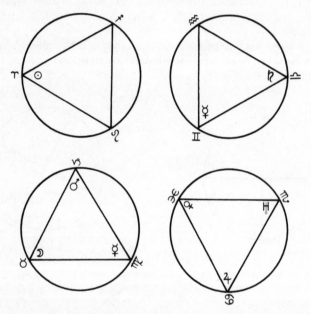

Fig. 9—The Exaltation of the Planets Shown in the Triangles

The Sun is exalted on the Cardinal Cross, in Aries, because it is the symbol of the head. The Sun rules Leo and the heart influence is taken into the head. And the Fiery and Spiritual Triplicity is naturally in affinity with the Sun.

Saturn is exalted in the Air Triplicity because it rules the intellect; and in Libra, the Sign of Love, so that its cold and unemotional influence may be softened.

Mars, the planet of desire and passion, is exalted in the Earthly Triplicity, as might be expected; and in Capricorn, because the hot and impulsive Mars is purified by coming into contact with Saturn as mind.

Jupiter and Venus together, compassion and love, are exalted in Cancer and Pisces, of the emotional Water Triplicity. For Cancer is the sign of the home, where the compassion and the religious spirit of Jupiter is exercised. And Pisces is 'the mystic sign of love and self-sacrifice'.

Then the Moon is exalted in Taurus, so that its changeable emotions may be given the benefit of the influence of the practical, calm, and steady Fixed Sign.

The Rulers of the Signs

You have now to learn how the twelve signs are ruled. I think that the best way to show this is to have our triangle diagrams again. It is easier to visualise them in the triangles than on the crosses. So I have put the rulers in each triangle next to the signs which they rule.

Now look at these triangles carefully, and think if there is anything to note in the way the rulers are arranged. What would you note first?

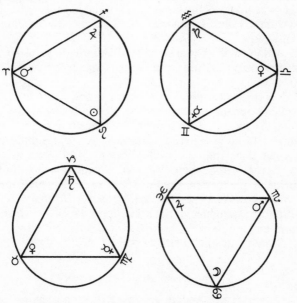

Fig.10—The Rulers of the Signs in the Triangles

Look at the Fire and Water Triangles. The Sun is in the Fiery, Regal Sign, Leo, and the moist and changeable, unstable Moon in the Water Sign of Cancer, which rules the sea.

Then take Mars, the planet which clearly fits the fiery, impetuous Aries, and also the sign of the extremes of good and evil, Scorpio.

When you come to study the nature of the signs and planets, you will understand how Jupiter, the planet of expansion, freedom, and compassion, is in sympathy with the signs Sagittarius and Pisces, which represent justice and benevolence, and universal love.

Now look at the Earth and Air Triangles. Here we have Venus ruling Taurus. This sign produces people capable of very lasting affection. Taurean women make some of the best and most affectionate mothers. Taurus is said to rule Ireland, and is responsible for the pretty colleens! So Venus seems a most suitable ruler.

Then Saturn rules Capricorn. This is the sign of the climbing goat, and Saturn in Capricorn gives ambition and helps people to rise in life through diplomacy. And they always follow the upward path.

In the Air Triangle we have Venus ruling Libra. Here this planet, which affects the higher part of the nature, separates the mind from the senses, making it tend more towards comparison and justice.

Then Saturn in Aquarius, Fixed Air Sign, gains by quiet, persistent determination, and refines the mind by study and observation.

Mercury rules Gemini and Virgo, Air and Earth Signs. Now, this planet means intelligence of all kinds, from the lowest cunning to the greatest genius. So it well suits the dualistic Gemini, which, in esoteric symbology, is represented by two apes—the chattering ape, and imitator; and the divine ape.

As regards Virgo, there are some astrologers who think that the invisible planet near the Sun, Vulcan, is the true Ruler, and that Mercury is exalted in Virgo. However, Mercury is said to represent the influence of the mind upon the body in health and disease; and Virgo in the horoscope rules the 6th House, which is connected with the health of the physical body.

The Decanates of the Signs

The Signs of the Zodiac are divided, as we have seen, into three parts of 10° each. These divisions are called the Decanates. You may ask, 'What is the use of these divisions, and how do they help the astrologer?'

To answer this question, we must have another look at our triangles. Take the Fire Triangle as an example. Here you have three signs: Aries ruled by Mars, Leo ruled by the Sun, and Sagittarius ruled by Jupiter.

These signs together form a triplicity of Fire. But they are more than companions in the triangles. They are blended together. So we have this result. The first decanate is pure Aries, ruled by Mars; the second decanate is of the Leo nature, ruled by the Sun; and the third is of the Sagittarius nature, and so brings in the rule of Jupiter.

This is very simple and easily understood; but you must clearly see how the three signs are blended. When we say that the first decanate is of the nature of the sign itself, and that the second is of the nature of the next sign of the same triplicity, we mean the next sign in the proper order of the signs. So when you have to deal with Leo, the next sign is Sagittarius; and when you have Sagittarius to deal with, the next sign is Aries.

You deal with the other triplicities in just the same way. So the second sign to Taurus is Virgo; the second to Gemini, Libra; and the second to Cancer is Scorpio; and so on all round. Therefore, if you find, for instance, a planet in the last decanate of Sagittarius, you will note it and say, 'This brings in Leo, and will not only influence the personal appearance, but the character.'

Elevation

It is very important to note planets in 'elevation'. This word may apply to any planet higher in the horoscope than another, but it chiefly applies to planets which are above the horizon. The highest point of elevation is, of course, the cusp of the 10th House.

The elevated planet has more power than the one below with which it is in some aspect. Suppose, for instance, that Saturn was in the 10th House, and that the Moon was in opposition to it from the 4th. Such an aspect would show a much harder and more sorrowful struggle in life than would be the case if the Moon were in elevation and Saturn below the horizon. When you see the horoscope of Napoleon I, you will see this aspect. He had Saturn in Cancer near the cusp of the 10th, and the Moon in Capricorn in the 4th.

To take another instance, say you find Venus in opposition to Mars in elevation well above the horizon. You could plainly predict that there would be difficulty in controlling the passions. But if the positions were reversed, the struggle to overcome passion would be much easier.

Reception

Mutual Reception is the term given to any case where two planets are in one another's houses. For instance, in Napoleon I's horoscope the Moon is in Capricorn, the House of Saturn, and Saturn is in Cancer, the House of the Moon.

Reception adds strength to a harmonious aspect, and reduces the evil of a discordant one. Some astrologers consider receptions in exaltations, or even in the decanates. A case of this may be found in Ruskin's horoscope. He had the Moon in the 28th degree of Cancer, and Saturn in the 18th degree of Pisces.

The two planets were in the same triplicity, and Saturn was in the Cancer Decanate of Pisces. But the Moon was in Saturn's detriment. This could not be called an important reception. Several receptions are used in horary astrology.

Notes for the Temperament

To judge the temperament, you look at your list of planets as arranged in the triplicities and quadruplicities. You want to see if a majority of planets can be found on one of the triangles and on one of the crosses.

Look at the horoscope in Fig. 11. There you find no less than seven planets on the Cardinal Cross, and four on the Fire Triangle. There is no question here as to the nature of the temperament. We should call it Cardinal-Fire.

Then when you come to examine this majority, you find that it is very strong. For you have the Sun and the Moon and all the planets together with the exception of Uranus. When you come to study a combination like this, with the Sun and Moon in Capricorn and Aries; Saturn in his detriment; and then Jupiter and Venus in the two Fiery Signs; and all of them in square or opposition with one another, with the exception of Venus, which was sesquiquadrate with the Moon—then you will understand why the judgment of a horoscope requires careful consideration, knowledge of the conflicting influences, and the intuition to blend them correctly and give an answer to the question: 'What does it all mean?'

But in our map (Fig. 1), you do not find the majority question settled so easily. We have four planets in Mutable Signs, three planets in Cardinal signs, three in Fire and four in Earth signs. In such a situation, how are you to decide between Mutable

Fire and Earth and Cardinal Fire and Earth?

You examine the lists and see what planets are in the Fire Triangle, and how they differ from the three in the Earth Triangle. If you find the Sun or the Moon in one of the triangles, give the preference to that one. If the Sun and the Moon are not there, or if the Sun is in one triangle and the Moon in the other, give the casting vote to the Ascendant. In the map in Fig. 1, the temperament is a decidedly earthy ore.

Sometimes you will get a balanced temperament—three in Cardinal, three in Fixed, and three in Mutable Signs; and only a majority of one in the triangles. This at first sight might seem to be quite good, but it is not always considered so, except in the case of advanced souls.

In the case of the degenerate and undeveloped men and women this balance only seems to produce inertia and want of incentive.

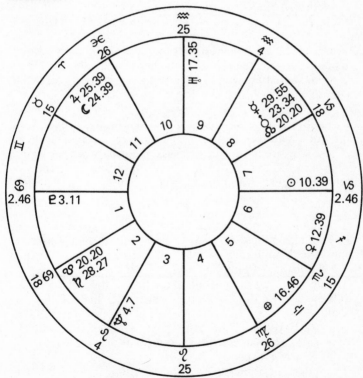

Fig. 11—A Horoscope of an Imaginary Person with a 'Cardinal-Fire' Temperament

What the Houses of the Horoscope Mean

The 'houses' or 'mansions' of the horoscope are the twelve divisions of the map that you must now get well acquainted with, as it is most important to know what they have to do with our daily lives, literally from the cradle to the grave.

But do not forget that the signs are of the first importance, as these houses are called after them. So the natural rulers never alter. The temporary rulers, as you must see, depend upon the sign rising at birth.

House I

This is the house of birth. It rules the personality, chiefly the head and face, as Aries, the Sign of the Ram, is the sign of the 1st House. So Mars, the ruler of Aries, is the natural ruler of this house. Therefore, you should always take a special note of the position of Mars in every horoscope, to see whether it is in a favourable sign and in good aspect with the other planets or not.

For instance, take the Mars in Fig. 11. Although it is exalted, it is not in a fortunate position in the house of death at any time; and to make matters worse, it has not a single good aspect, but is square with the Moon and Jupiter as well as in opposition to Saturn.

Women are generally interested to know the proper Birth Stones or Mystical Gems to get, and the proper colours to wear.

Those who are born with Aries rising, or between the 21st of March and the 21st of April, should have amethyst and diamond ornaments. The proper colour is scarlet or red carmine.

House II

This house is concerned with money, finance, commerce, the way to make money or lose it. The position and aspects of Venus, the natural ruler, and the ruler of the sign on the cusp of the 2nd must be carefully noted.

Taurus, the Sign of the Bull, is the first of the Earthly Signs, and is the sign for the 2nd House, which rules the neck and the throat.

The old Egyptian glyph for property was the circle with the cross inside. The same glyph is used for Rhea, the Earth, and for the Part of Fortune.

The judgment of financial prospects requires careful study of the horoscope in general, and especially the position and aspects of Venus, Jupiter, and Saturn.

Those born under the Sign of the Bull should have emeralds and mossagates for wear. Their colours are pale blue, lemon yellow, and art tints.

Also those born with the Sun in Taurus, between the 21st of April and the 21st of May, can wear the same stones and colours.

House III

This house rules near relatives and neighbours. It is concerned with letters, short journeys, means of communication, and changes generally. It also rules the mind, mental qualifications generally, and therefore the sign on the cusp and the ruler, as well as the natural ruler, must be studied.

Gemini is the ruling sign, and Mercury the natural ruler. It governs the lungs, arms and shoulders, and the nerves. It is also said to rule the tongue and organs of speech.

Those born under the Sign of the Twins, or between the 21st of May and the 21st of June, should have aquamarines and beryls. Their colours are orange, yellow, any spotted mixtures, and slate colours.

House IV

Cancer is the sign on this house, so the Moon is the natural ruler. This house relates to the environment, the home or residence, the father or the mother, as the Hindus say, and the end of life. Planets in this house have, naturally, much importance with regard to the domestic conditions and the last years of a life.

The parts of the body ruled are the breasts, the chest, the liver, and also the stomach. The Moon has rule over the eyes and the etheric double of the body.

Those born under Cancer, and between the 21st of June and the 21st of July, should get emeralds, moonstones, and black onyx; some say also opals. The colours are violet, silvery white, pearl, opal, green, and iridescent silvery hues.

House V

This house is ruled by Leo and the Sun. It governs children, social pleasures, love affairs, and courtships. It also relates to speculations, investments, and to any enterprises connected with our natural desires.

Leo rules the heart and the back, and the Sun rules the heart also, with the eyes, the spinal cord, the arteries, the circulation, and the vital force.

Those born under the Sun, and between the 21st of July and the 21st of August, should wear diamonds, rubies, and carbuncles. Their colours are orange, gold, the deeper shades of yellow, and yellow-brown.

House VI

This house has much to do with the health, the physical body, food and clothes, hygiene and sanitation. Its ruler Virgo is also concerned with service and servants of all kinds, and especially uniformed and liveried servants, as the house is related to all forms and ceremonies.

If there are no planets in this house it is a good thing, as any planet there means some kind of sickness connected with that planet.

Those who are born under Virgo, or between the 21st of August and the 21st of September, should wear some pink jasper and hyacinths. The colours have been mentioned above under Gemini.

House VII

This is the Marriage House. It is ruled by Libra and Venus. At the same time, it has a good deal to do with partners in other ways, legal matters, contracts, lawsuits, and public adversaries. In the body it is related to the loins, kidneys, and the vital fluids.

If there are no planets in the 7th House, it is easier to write about marriage prospects. This is very often the case, but you may sometimes get several planets in this house, and then it is not so easy to judge what may happen.

Here you find that astrology has to make a difference between the men and the women about the matter of the marriage partner. So you could not take a baby's horoscope and write a judgment on it unless you knew the sex. When you are dealing with a woman's horoscope, you take the Sun to act as significator of her marriage partner. But in a man's horoscope you take the Moon. Then the planets to which the Sun and Moon apply describe the type of the partner.

In the horoscope in Fig. 11, you can see that the boys and girls who were born on that day would have had, in adulthood, quite different types for their marriage partners.

The woman's Sun applies to the planet Uranus, but the man's Moon applies to the planet Jupiter. If you look at the aspects, you will see that the women will come off best, as Uranus has no discordant aspects. If you study this unlucky horoscope, you will find that you could write above it the old Eastern saying: 'Yet man is born unto trouble, as the sparks fly upward.'

This horoscope is an example of the numerous horoscopes which astrologers have to deal with, that prove what a blessing it will be when all children have their horoscopes cast, in order that they may be trained and educated so as to do all they can to overcome their faults, and fight against the restrictions of so many squares and oppositions. It is very unfortunate to be born when the Moon is square with Saturn from Fire and Water Signs, but it makes matters much worse when Mars at the same time is square with the Moon and in opposition to Saturn.

Those who are born under Libra, and between the 21st of September and the 21st of October, may wear opals as well as diamonds. The colours were given under the Venus Sign of Taurus.

House VIII

The sign of this house is Scorpio, and it is ruled by Mars. Here Scorpio rules the generative system.

This is known as the house of death, and all matters connected with death, such as executor's duties, the property of the dead, wills, legacies, and funerals.

Planets in this house have a most important influence, as you will find when you come to study their relation to the way in which death comes.

I do not advise you to make any predictions about death, except for your own study and information. Very few people like to read the story which the 8th House of the horoscope can tell.

Those who are born under Scorpio, or between the 21st of October and the 21st of November, should have malachite and topaz ornaments, and the colours to wear are the dark reds and deep crimsons.

House IX

This house is ruled by Sagittarius and Jupiter. It is connected with all our religious beliefs, philosophy, science and books on these subjects. It is also concerned with long voyages and distant travels. It also governs dreams, visions, and prophecy. The religious views are naturally very much influenced by the particular planet or planets which may be there at birth. This house not only makes the theosophist and the occultist, but the bigot, the fanatic, and the sceptic.

In the body it rules the thighs, the liver, the blood, the

digestion to some extent, and the growth of the body.

Those born under Sagittarius, and between the 21st of November and the 21st of December, should have their ornaments made with the turquoise and carbuncle. The proper colour is indigo, but purple, violet, and mixed red may be worn also.

House X

Capricorn is on this house and Saturn is the ruler. It is the house of the profession or occupation. It is also concerned with the honour and reputation.

This is a very important house when you are asked to give an opinion as to the best profession or occupation for a boy or a girl to prepare for. You must study the sign on the 10th, its ruler, any planet or planets in the house, and also the position and aspects of Saturn, the natural ruler, as Saturn rules Capricorn. In the body this house rules the knees, the skin, the bones, the teeth, and the spleen.

Those who are born under Capricorn, and between the 21st of December and the 21st of January, should wear moonstones and white onyx. The colours are dark brown, indigo, and black.

House XI

The sign of this house is Aquarius. The ruler is Saturn. But many modern astrologers consider that Uranus exercises a sub-influence, and this is my own opinion.

I have no space here to give the arguments, but they are in accordance with modern investigations regarding the action of Uranus upon character and modern conditions of life.

This sign is said to rule the eyes, the ankles, and the blood. The house is the house of friends, social relations, societies and companies. It is also concerned with our hopes and wishes.

As might be expected, this house must be connected with the Marriage House, for, as a rule, people marry those who have been their friends before marriage.

Planets in this house indicate the kind of friends who will influence your life as long as it lasts. So the aspects, as you may suppose, are most important. Good aspects will bring fortunate results in the family life, and the social relations of all kinds. The best aspects are those from the Marriage House and the 3rd, the house which rules your kindred. For these three houses are the trine houses on the Air Triangle. Discordant aspects are sure to bring some discord all round.

When there are no planets in this house the sign on the cusp and the position of the ruler must be considered. Note if it is in the 3rd or 7th, or, in cases of intercepted planets, if it is in the same triplicity. Of course, the influence of this house is very much weaker if there are no planets in it.

In a general way our friends and enemies, open and secret, private and public, are indicated by the rest of the horoscope, especially the 12th House, that of secret enemies, as well as the houses of the Air Triplicity. The aspects of the Sun and Moon have an important part to play in this matter.

You can make an interesting experiment to see how astrology may help people to cultivate friendships and avoid enemies as far as possible.

Write down the houses and longitudes of the planets Mars, Saturn, Uranus, and Neptune. Then look in an Ephemeris for the dates when the Sun is in the same longitude as those planets, in your own horoscope or that of a friend.

For instance, take Mars. Say you find Mars in the 7th House in Taurus 18° 30′. Now you will find the Sun is in Taurus 18° 30′ on the 9th of May. So to marry anyone born on that date would mean discord and trouble afterwards. Nor would it be wise to go into partnership with anyone born on that date.

Then take the positions and longitude of Venus, Jupiter, and the Moon. Find the Sun dates in the same way, and you will know that people who were born on those dates would be the best friends you could get!

As an example of this, if you look at the horoscope in Fig. 11, you will see that Venus is in Sagittarius 12° 39′. Now the Sun is in that degree of the Zodiac on approximately 5th of December of each year and consequently anyone born on 5th of December could become a very good friend.

Those born under Aquarius, or between the 21st of January and the 21st of February, may wear opals and sapphires. The colour to wear is light green; but if Uranus is taken as the ruler, you should wear the tartan or any mixed colours.

House XII

Pisces, the Sign of the Fishes, is on this house, and the traditional ruler has always been Jupiter. But many modern astrologers think now that Neptune is really the proper ruler. This sign rules the feet, so you see now that every part of the body from the head to the feet is ruled by the signs in their proper order. This is no accident, as the doctors will some day find out to their great advantage!

The 12th House has been called the House of Self-undoing. It relates to prisons and other places of confinement, such as asylums and hospitals. Almshouses and infirmaries, with similar institutions, come under this house. It is also the house of secret enemies, moral and mental bondage, suffering, misery and suicide.

But it is also said to be the house of the voluntary recluse, such as monks and nuns. And a well-aspected Jupiter in this house favours the officials of public institutions, such as hospitals, philanthropic establishments, and schools of various kinds.

Those who are born under Pisces, or between the 21st of February and the 21st of March, should wear moonstones and chrysolite. The colours are pale heliotrope, mauve, and lavender.

Please note that the Sun does not always go into a sign exactly on the 21st of a month. This should be put right when a birthday comes about the 21st of any month by a reference to the Ephemeris for the year of birth.

The Progressed Horoscope

I find that beginners when they know their birth times, are generally eager to do their own progressed horoscopes. This is very natural, as a progressed horoscope is not only most interesting, but most useful.

To some people the idea of a progressed horoscope may come as a surprise. They do not realise that the influences of the planets at their birth are not the only influences which will affect their lives. The horoscope changes.

The birth Ascendant moves up. The Sun, and the Moon especially, move round and change their places. The planets sometimes move out of the signs that they occupied at birth. and go into other signs, and naturally the aspects change.

There are people who do not realise that the Earth rotates through the 360° of the diurnal circle in the day, as we call it, of twenty-four hours; and that at the same time it is revolving through the 360° of the annual circle of our Spring, Summer, Autumn, and Winter, in twelve months. So you have a different progressed horoscope for each birthday of your life.

The Two Methods of Calculation

The first method is by axial rotation, and this is called the Primary System. Those who wish to adopt this method must understand that a knowledge of trigonometry is required. Also for the Primary Directions, as they are called, you must have the correct birth time, or find it by rectification. So I do not advise you to attempt this method at first, unless you have considerable ability for calculation.

The second method is by orbital revolution. You will probably be surprised to know how this calculation for each year of life is made. You would naturally be inclined to think that, if you were going to do a progressed horoscope for your twenty-first birthday, you would do it with an Ephemeris for the year in which that birthday occurred.

But that is not the way which has been handed down to us from the past. You use your birth year Ephemeris for the whole of your life, unless you happen to have been born at the end of a year (then you will require an additional Ephemeris for the next year as well).

In this system the measure of time is one day. The planetary changes in the heavens during the first day of life symbolise the events which may occur during the first year of life. The second day symbolises the second year, and so on all through life.

Now, the time between one day and another by the sidereal clock, already mentioned, is only four minutes. So there is only four minutes between one birthday and the next.

You can understand, therefore, from this fact how important it is to know the exact time of birth, if you can get it, for the progressed horoscope as well as for the birth one.

It is a good plan, when you are going to do a progressed horoscope, to mark the particular day required with a pencil mark, so that you will not make any mistake and use the wrong line of figures. Then take the Sidereal Time for the day and cast the new horoscope just as you did the birth one, and calculate the Moon also in the same way, as well as Mercury and Venus, if required. Then when you have finished the map you will find that there are some changes to note.

We have already calculated the horoscope for an imaginary person born in Liverpool at 1.40 p.m. on 1st January 1986. Let us see what kind of progressed horoscope he or she would have on his or her 21st birthday. Taking a day for a year, you must add 21 days to 1st January, which is 22nd January 1986. Now you must calculate the birth chart for this date also. This is quickly done for all you have to do

22.1.86	20 6 10	S.T.
1.1.86	18 43 23	L.S.T.
	1 22 47	
	20 11 59	
	21 34 46	

is to deduct the sidereal time at noon GMT for 22nd January from that for 1st January. Add the result to the Local Sidereal Time that you calculated when doing the natal chart (20 11 59). This gives the

Local Sidereal Time of the progressed horoscope which you now look up in the table of houses for Liverpool to obtain the house cusps. The positions of the planets for 1.40 p.m. on 22nd January 1986 are now calculated just as you did for the natal chart.

You have now done the progressed horoscope which shows the end of Gemini on the progressed Ascendant. You will note that the Sun, Venus and Jupiter have gone into Aquarius, Mercury is in Capricorn and the Moon is in Gemini.

The Lunar Aspects for Each Month

Now you must calculate the lunar aspects for each month of the coming year. You start by finding the daily motion of the Moon. You find that the Moon is entered in the Ephemeris as Gemini 21° 46′ 39″. In these calculations always use the seconds as they mount up into minutes. So put down:

$$30° \ 0′ \ 0″$$
$$21° \ 46′ \ 39″$$
_____
$$8° \ 13′ \ 21″$$
$$3° \ 57′ \ 47″$$
_____

12° 11′ 8″ = the Moon's motion from noon 22.1.86 to noon 23.1.86.

1° 0′ 56″ You now divide the figures 12° 11′ 8″ by 12. This gives you within a few seconds 1° 0′ 56″. These figures have to be added to the Moon for a year. After that you must see again what the rate is, as it changes so much.

January	22° ♊ 37′ 39″	(progressed Moon)
	+ 1° 0′ 56″	
February	23° ♊ 38′ 35″	Trine Jupiter, p
		Quincunx Mars, p
	+ 1° 0′ 56″	Opposite Mercury, r
March	24° ♊ 39′ 31″	
	+ 1° 0′ 56″	
April	25° ♊ 40′ 27″	
	+ 1° 0′ 56″	
May	26° ♊ 41′ 23″	

Simply go through the months in this way. There is nothing difficult about these lunar aspects, but they must be done very carefully. It is so easy to make mistakes when dealing with figures.

Remember that aspects between the progressed planets and between the progressed planets and those of the natal chart are only noted when they are within one degree of exactitude. The former are denoted by a little 'p' (progressed) and the latter by a little 'r' (radical).

The Changes in the Map

For several years after birth there are not likely to be many changes, unless some of the planets were in the end of their signs at birth. But when you find that any planet has gone into another sign, you naturally make a note of it, for a new influence affects the planet. Do not, however, suppose that the influence of the sign in which the planet was at birth disappears from your life. The change only modifies it.

Of course, when you do the aspects you will write the symbols. I have used the words 'Trine Jupiter' etc., for clearness, as I am now writing for those who are not familiar with the symbols.

The Transits Over the Sun, Moon and the Planets

A transit is the passage of a planet over the exact place of the Sun, the Moon, the Ascendant and the Mid-heaven. Or a transit may be the passage of a planet in opposition to any of these places. Or, again, it may be a passage through any house of the horoscope.

A transit is really a conjunction. But an opposition is not to be ignored, as it always has some effect. Trines and squares sometimes may be strong and are worth noting. The other aspects are sometimes used too.

There are transits over our horoscopes every day. We never can evade them, but the progressed birthday transits are considered to be of the most consequence, as they probably influence the whole year.

The transits of the most importance are those of Mars, Jupiter, Saturn, Uranus, Neptune and Pluto. Always note when they are retrograde—that is, marked with the ℞, as already explained. And note when they are 'stationary', also. You can tell this when the change comes from D to ℞ or ℞ to D. For examples, see Ephemeris for 1986, February 10th (Pluto) and March 30th (Mercury). Their influence is more marked then.

New Moon and Eclipses as Transits

Always get the new Ephemeris as soon as it is published, and then make a list of the New Moons and Eclipses. It saves a lot of trouble afterwards, as you will often want to use it. Look at page 30 in the 1986 Ephemeris. There at the top of the page you see how the Eclipses are marked. Then, on page 32, on the 9th of April, is Moon conjunction Sun, with the little black disc marking an eclipse. A New Moon is the conjunction and a Full Moon is the opposition. So you write down as follows: January 10th, Capricorn 19° 45′; February 9th, Aquarius 26° 18′, and so on.

You must not, however, attach too much importance to these transits, unless it happens that they come in months when there are no progressed aspects, as often is the case. As the New Moons during the year form both harmonious and discordant aspects, you will find that some months are fortunate and others unfortunate. As you may suppose, a great deal depends upon the nature of the birth horoscope.

By way of an exercise, you might make a list of the New Moons, Full Moons and Eclipses for 1986, and then see how they affect our New Year's Day horoscope.

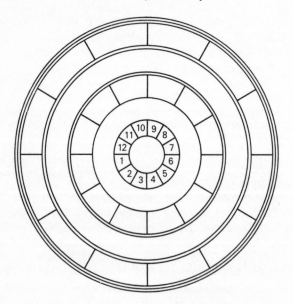

Fig. 12—A Blank Map for a Progressed Horoscope

The Blank Map

I prefer to do my progressed horoscopes with this map. The radical horoscope is copied into the centre circle. Then the progressed horoscope comes into the large circle round it. The transits are arranged round the outer circle.

Of course, a map like this cannot be properly drawn without some knowledge of geometrical drawing and practice with mathematical instruments.

The Horoscope for 1st January 1986, 1.40 p.m., Liverpool

The General Aspects

Planet	Sign	Harmony	Discord
SUN	CAPRICORN	△ ☽ ♂ ♀ ✶ ♂ ⊻ ♄ ✶ ♇	♂ Ψ
MOON	VIRGO	△ ♀ ✶ ♂ ✶ ♇	□ ♄ □ ♅
MERCURY	SAGITTARIUS	✶ ♃	♂ ♅ ∠ ♇
VENUS	CAPRICORN	✶ ♂ ✶ ♇	♂ Ψ
MARS	SCORPIO		□ ♃ ♂ ♇
JUPITER	AQUARIUS	✶ ♅	∠ Ψ
SATURN	SAGITTARIUS	⊻ Ψ ⊻ ♇	
URANUS	SAGITTARIUS		
NEPTUNE	CAPRICORN	✶ ♇	

The Logarithms

NOTE.—Instead of having all these logarithms packed together on one page, I have arranged them in sections on nine pages. This arrangement will enable them to be used with perfect ease. You will notice that the larger numbers come on the first page, and that they gradually get smaller, until you come to the smallest number, 1765.

Then you will note that the first three pages are headed with the numbers 0 to 3; the next three pages are headed with the numbers 4 to 9; and the last three pages are headed with the numbers 10 to 15; so you will very soon get familiar with this new but very clear arrangement.

These logarithms will be useful to old as well as new students of astrology.

I.

	0	1	2	3	
0	3.1584	1.3802	1.0792	9031	0
1	3.1584	1.3730	1.0856	9007	1
2	2.8573	1.3660	1.0720	8983	2
3	2.6812	1.3590	1.0685	8959	3
4	2.5563	1.3522	1.0649	8935	4
5	2.4594	1.3454	1.0614	8912	5
6	2.3802	1.3388	1.0580	8888	6
7	2.3133	1.3323	1.0546	8865	7
8	2.2553	1.3258	1.0511	8842	8
9	2.2041	1.3195	1.0478	8819	9
10	2.1584	1.3133	1.0444	8796	10
11	2.1170	1.3071	1.0411	8773	11
12	2.0792	1.3010	1.0378	8751	12
13	2.0444	1.2950	1.0345	8728	13
14	2.0122	1.2891	1.0313	8706	14
15	1.9823	1.2833	1.0280	8683	15
16	1.9542	1.2775	1.0248	8661	16
17	1.9279	1.2719	1.0216	8639	17
18	1.9031	1.2663	0.0185	8617	18
19	1.8796	1.2607	1.0153	8595	19

II.

	0	1	2	3	
20	1.8573	1.2553	1.0122	8573	20
21	1.8361	1.2499	1.0091	8552	21
22	1.8159	1.2445	1.0061	8530	22
23	1.7966	1.2393	1.0030	8509	23
24	1.7781	1.2341	1.0000	8487	24
25	1.7604	1.2289	0.9970	8466	25
26	1.7434	1.2239	0.9940	8445	26
27	1.7270	1.2188	0.9910	8424	27
28	1.7112	1.2139	0.9881	8403	28
29	1.6960	1.2090	0.9852	8382	29
30	1.6812	1.2041	0.9823	8361	30
31	1.6670	1.1993	0.9794	8341	31
32	1.6532	1.1946	0.9765	8327	32
33	1.6398	1.1899	0.9737	8300	33
34	1.6269	1.1852	0.9708	8279	34
35	1.6143	1.1806	0.9680	8259	35
36	1.6021	1.1761	0.9652	8239	36
37	1.5902	1.1716	0.9625	8219	37
38	1.5786	1.1671	0.9557	8199	38
39	1.5673	1.1627	0.9570	8179	39

III.

	0	1	2	3	
40	1.5563	1.1584	0.9542	8159	40
41	1.5456	1.1540	0.9515	8140	41
42	1.5351	1.1498	0.9488	8120	42
43	1.5249	1.1455	0.9462	8101	43
44	1.5149	1.1413	0.9435	8081	44
45	1.5051	1.1372	0.9409	8062	45
46	1.4956	1.1331	0.9383	8043	46
47	1.4863	1.1290	0.9356	8023	47
48	1.4771	1.1249	0.9330	8004	48
49	1.4682	1.1209	0.9305	7985	49
50	1.4594	1.1170	0.9279	7966	50
51	1.4508	1.1130	0.9254	7947	51
52	1.4424	1.1091	0.9228	7929	52
53	1.4341	1.1053	0.9203	7910	53
54	1.4260	1.1015	0.9178	7891	54
55	1.4180	1.0977	0.9153	7873	55
56	1.4102	1.0939	0.9128	7854	56
57	1.4025	1.0902	0.9104	7836	57
58	1.3949	1.0865	0.9079	7818	58
59	1.3875	1.0828	0.9055	7800	59

IV

	4	5	6	7	8	9	
0	7781	6812	6021	5351	4771	4260	0
1	7763	6798	6009	5341	4762	4252	1
2	7745	6784	5997	5330	4753	4244	2
3	7728	6769	5985	5320	4744	4236	3
4	7710	6755	5973	5310	4735	4228	4
5	7692	6741	5961	5300	4726	4220	5
6	7674	6726	5949	5289	4717	4212	6
7	7657	6712	5937	5279	4708	4204	7
8	7639	6698	5925	5269	4699	4196	8
9	7622	6684	5913	5259	4690	4188	9
10	7604	6670	5902	5249	4682	4180	10
11	7587	6656	5890	5239	4673	4172	11
12	7570	6642	5878	5229	4664	4164	12
13	7552	6628	5866	5219	4655	4156	13
14	7535	6614	5855	5209	4646	4148	14
15	7518	6600	5843	5199	4638	4141	15
16	7501	6587	5832	5189	4629	4133	16
17	7484	6573	5820	5179	4620	4125	17
18	7467	6559	5809	5169	4611	4117	18
19	7451	6546	5797	5159	4603	4109	19

V.

	4	5	6	7	8	9	
20	7434	6532	5786	5149	4594	4102	**20**
21	7417	6519	5774	5139	4585	4094	**21**
22	7401	6505	5763	5129	4577	4086	**22**
23	7384	6492	5752	5120	4568	4079	**23**
24	7368	6478	5740	5110	4559	4071	**24**
25	7351	6465	5729	5100	4551	4063	**25**
26	7335	6451	5718	5090	4542	4055	**26**
27	7318	6438	5706	5081	4534	4048	**27**
28	7302	6425	5695	5071	4525	4040	**28**
29	7286	6412	5684	5061	4516	4032	**29**
30	7270	6398	5673	5051	4508	4025	**30**
31	7254	6385	5662	5042	4499	4017	**31**
32	7238	6372	5651	5032	4491	4010	**32**
33	7222	6359	5640	5023	4482	4002	**33**
34	7206	6346	5629	5013	4474	3994	**34**
35	7190	6333	5618	5003	4466	3987	**35**
36	7174	6320	5607	4994	4457	3979	**36**
37	7159	6307	5596	4984	4449	3972	**37**
38	7143	6294	5585	4975	4440	3964	**38**
39	7128	6282	5574	4965	4432	3957	**39**

VI.

	4	5	6	7	8	9	
40	7112	6269	5563	4956	4424	3949	40
41	7097	6256	5552	4947	4415	3942	41
42	7081	6243	5541	4937	4407	3934	42
43	7066	6231	5531	4928	4399	3927	43
44	7050	6218	5520	4918	4390	3919	44
45	7035	6205	5509	4909	4382	3912	45
46	7020	6193	5498	4900	4374	3905	46
47	7005	6180	5488	4890	4365	3897	47
48	6990	6168	5477	4881	4357	3890	48
49	6975	6155	5466	4872	4349	3882	49
50	6960	6143	5456	4863	4341	3875	50
51	6945	6131	5445	4853	4333	3868	51
52	6930	6118	5435	4844	4324	3860	52
53	6915	6106	5424	4835	4316	3853	53
54	6900	6094	5414	4826	4308	3846	54
55	6885	6081	5403	4817	4300	3838	55
56	6871	6069	5393	4808	4292	3831	56
57	6856	6057	5382	4798	4284	3824	57
58	6841	6045	5372	4789	4276	3817	58
59	6827	6033	5361	4780	4268	3809	59

VII

	10	11	12	13	14	15	
0	3802	3388	3010	2663	2341	2041	0
1	3795	3382	3004	2757	2336	2036	1
2	3788	3375	2998	2652	2330	2032	2
3	3780	3368	2992	2646	2325	2027	3
4	3773	3362	2986	2640	2320	2022	4
5	3766	3355	2980	2635	2315	2017	5
6	3759	3349	2974	2629	2310	2012	6
7	3752	3342	2968	2624	2305	2008	7
8	3745	3336	2962	2618	2300	2003	8
9	3737	3329	2056	2613	2295	1998	9
10	3730	3323	2950	2607	2289	1993	10
11	3723	3316	2944	2602	2284	1988	11
12	3716	3310	2938	2596	2279	1984	12
13	3709	3303	2933	2591	2274	1979	13
14	3702	3297	2927	2585	2269	1974	14
15	3695	3291	2921	2580	2264	1969	15
16	3688	3284	2915	2574	2259	1965	16
17	3681	3278	2909	2569	2254	1960	17
18	3674	3271	2903	2564	2249	1955	18
19	3667	3265	2897	2558	2244	1950	19

VIII.

	10	11	12	13	14	15	
20	3660	3258	2891	2553	2239	1946	20
21	3653	3252	2885	2547	2234	1941	21
22	3646	3246	2880	2542	2229	1936	22
23	3639	3239	2874	2536	2223	1932	23
24	3632	3233	2868	2531	2218	1927	24
25	3625	3227	2862	2526	2213	1922	25
26	3618	3220	2856	2520	2208	1917	26
27	3611	3214	2850	2515	2203	1913	27
28	3604	3208	2845	2509	2198	1908	28
29	3597	3201	2839	2504	2193	1903	29
30	3590	3195	2833	2499	2188	1899	30
31	3583	3189	2827	2493	2183	1894	31
32	3576	3183	2821	2488	2178	1889	32
33	3570	3176	2816	2483	2173	1885	33
34	3563	3170	2810	2477	2168	1880	34
35	3556	3164	2804	2472	2164	1875	35
36	3549	3157	2798	2467	2159	1871	36
37	3542	3151	2793	2461	2154	1866	37
38	3535	3145	2787	2456	2149	1862	38
39	3529	3139	2781	2451	2144	1857	39

IX.

	10	11	12	13	14	15	
40	3522	3133	2775	2445	2139	1852	40
41	3515	3126	2770	2440	2134	1848	41
42	3508	3120	2764	2435	2129	1843	42
43	3501	3114	2758	2430	2124	1838	43
44	3495	3108	2753	2424	2119	1834	44
45	3488	3102	2747	2419	2114	1829	45
46	3481	3096	2741	2414	2109	1825	46
47	3475	3089	2736	2409	2104	1820	47
48	3468	3083	2730	2403	2099	1816	48
49	3461	3077	2724	2398	2095	1811	49
50	3454	3071	2719	2393	2090	1806	50
51	3448	3065	2713	2388	2085	1802	51
52	3441	3059	2707	2382	2080	1797	52
53	3434	3053	2702	2377	2075	1793	53
54	3428	3047	2696	2372	2070	1788	54
55	3421	3041	2691	2367	2065	1784	55
56	3415	3034	2685	2362	2061	1779	56
57	3408	3028	2679	2356	2056	1774	57
58	3401	3022	2674	2351	2051	1770	58
59	3395	3016	2668	2346	2046	1765	59

Zone and Standard Times for Different Parts of the World

All countries now have Standard or Zone Time but some have adopted it comparatively recently. When in doubt as to whether a birth date was before or after the date of adoption of Standard Time, inquiries can be made to the embassy of that particular country.

Some countries keep Summer Time, and these are marked with an asterisk in the list below.

	hours		hours
Algeria	00	Romania	+2
Angola	+1	Russia, W. of 40°E.	+2
Argentina	−3	40°–52°30′E.	+3
Australia		E. of 52°30′E.	+4
Broken Hill, N.S.W.	+9½	Sardinia	+1
Capital Territory	+10	Seychelles	+4
N.S.W. (excl. Broken		Sicily	+1
Hill area)	+10	Sierra Leone	00
Northern Territory	+9½	Singapore	+7
Queensland	+10	South Africa	+2
South Australia	+9½	Spain (time in	
Victoria	+10	normal use)	+1
Western Australia	+8	Sri Lanka	+5½
Austria	+1	Sudan	+2
Bahamas	−5	Swaziland	+2
Bangladesh	+6	Sweden	+1
Barbados	−4	Switzerland	+1
Belgium	+1	Syria	+2
Bermuda*	−4	Tanzania	+3
Bolivia	−4	Tangier*	00
Botswana	+2	Tasmania	+10
Brazil (Eastern)*	−3	Thailand	+7
Bulgaria	+2	Tobago	−4
Canada		Trinidad	−4
Alberta*	−7	Tunisia	+1
British Columbia*	−8	Turkey*	+2
Labrador*	−3½	Uganda	+3
Manitoba*	−6	Uruguay	−3
New Brunswick*	−4	U.S.A.	
Newfoundland*	−3½	Alabama*	−6
Nova Scotia*	−4	Arizona*(time in	
Ontario*, E. of 90°W	−5	normal use)	−7
W. of 90°W	−6	Arkansas*	−7

Place	Offset
Quebec*, E. of 68°W	−4
W. of 68°W	−5
Saskatchewan* (except S.E.)	−7
Yukon	−9
Chile	−4
Costa Rica	−6
Crete	+2
Cuba	−5
Cypress	+2
Czechoslovakia*	+1
Denmark	+1
Ecuador	−5
Finland	+2
France (time in normal use)	+1
Gambia	00
Germany	+1
Ghana (Winter Time is kept in this country)	00
Great Britain*	00
Greece	+2
Guatemala	−6
Holland	+1
Hong Kong*	+8
Hungary*	+1
Iceland	−1
India	$+5\frac{1}{2}$
Iran	$+3\frac{1}{2}$
Iraq	+3
Irish Republic	00
Israel*	+2
Italy	+1
Ivory Coast	00
Jamaica	−5
Japan	+9
Java	$+7\frac{1}{2}$
Jordan	+2
Kenya	+3
Korea	+9
Kuwait	+3
Lebanon	+2
Madagascar	+3
Malawi	+2
California*	−8
Colorado*	−7
Connecticut*	−5
Delaware*	−5
Florida*(most of state)	−5
Georgia*	−5
Idaho*(most of state)	−7
Illinois*	−6
Indiana*	−6
Iowa*	−6
Kansas*(most of state)	−6
Kentucky*(most of state)	−6
Louisiana*	−6
Maine*	−5
Maryland*	−5
Massachusetts*	−5
Michigan*(most of state)	−5
Minnesota*	−6
Mississippi*	−6
Missouri*	−6
Montana*	−7
Nebraska*, eastern part	−6
western part	−7
Nevada*	−8
New Hampshire*	−5
New Jersey*	−5
New Mexico*	−7
New York*	−5
North Carolina*	−5
North Dakota*(most of state)	−6
Ohio*	−5
Oklahoma*	−6
Oregon*	−8
Pennsylvania*	−5
Rhode Island*	−5
South Carolina*	−5
South Dakota* eastern part	−6
western part	−7
Tennessee*(most of	

Malaya	$+7\frac{1}{2}$	state)	−6
Malta	+1	Texas*(most of state)	−6
Mauritius	+4	Utah*(most of state)	−7
Mozambique	+2	(Salt Late City,	
New Zealand	+12	Garfield)	−8
Nicaragua*	−6	Vermont*	−5
Nigeria	+1	Virginia*	−5
Norway	+1	Washington state*	−8
Pakistan	$+4\frac{1}{2}$	West Virginia*	−5
Papua New Guinea	+10	Wisconsin*	−6
Paraguay	−4	Wyoming*	−7
Peru	−5	Venezuela	$-4\frac{1}{2}$
Philippine Repub.	+8	Vietnam	+8
Poland*	+1	Yugoslavia	+1
Portugal*	00	Zimbabwe	+2
Puerto Rico	−4		

Summary of Stages in Calculating a Horoscope

Example For a person born 1.40 p.m., 1st January 1986, Liverpool (longitude 2° 55′W).
NB. There is no Summer Time or Zone Standard to be taken into account in this example.

Sidereal time at noon, Greenwich for 1.1.86		18	43	23
Hours and minutes from noon GMT		1	40	00
Acceleration, from table (*add* for p.m. birth)				16
Greenwich Sidereal Time at birth	=	20	23	39
Longitude equivalent of Liverpool (*subtract* for W)			11	40
(*Multiply longitude by 4 and call the result minutes and seconds of time.*)		20	11	59

Rounding off, Local Sidereal Time is therefore 20 hr. 12 min.

From Table of Houses for Liverpool, nearest Sidereal Time is 20 12 54, which gives the Ascendant as 7°9′♊, 10th House cusp (M.C.) 1° ≈, 11th 25°≈, and so on.

(*NB.* For the Southern Hemisphere, you would have to add 12 hours to the Local Sidereal Time of birth, and reverse signs, e.g. for Aries, read Libra.)

The planetary positions for the time, 1.40 p.m. GMT, are now found, using the table of proportional logarithms for faster moving planets.

How to Calculate the Ascendant More Accurately (By Interpolation)

Simple proportional arithmetic will enable you to calculate the Ascendant to a greater degree of accuracy.

From the Table of Houses –

					M.C.
Nearest sidereal times to 20	11	59 are:	20	08 45	0°≈
			20	12 54	1°≈
		Difference		04 09	= 1°≈
			20	11 59	
			20	8 45	
		Difference		3 14	

(Convert to seconds) $\dfrac{194s\ (3m\ 14s) \times 60 \times 60\ (1°)}{249s\ (4m\ 09s)} = 2804.8s = 46.7$

(or 47)m.

Add 47m to the M.C. position: 0°47'≈

From the motion of the Ascendant, you can then calculate the position of the Ascendant –

$$\frac{47}{60} \times 84m\ (1°24) = 65.8\ (or\ 66)m$$

(Ascendant for Sidereal Time of 20 08 45 is 5°45' ♊. Add 66m to this.)
Ascendant is therefore 6°51' ♊.

How to Determine the Ascendant when the Given Latitude Lies between the Latitudes in the Table of Houses

Proportional arithmetic must again be used in solving this problem. However, unless you know the exact birthtime there is no point in working to within seconds of accuracy as has been done in the following example – round them off to the nearest minute.

Let us assume that someone was born at 3.20 p.m. on 1st January 1986 at Milford Haven, Wales. The latitude of Milford Haven is 51°44' N and the longitude is 5°02'W.

The Local Sidereal Time (found as shown above) is 21 43 48. In *Raphael's Table of Houses for Great Britain*, this is between 21 41 23 and 21 45 16 and the latitude falls between 51° 32'N and 51° 59'N (London and Buckingham are on these latitudes. The difference between the two sidereal times is 3m 53s and the difference between the lower sidereal time and the Local Sidereal Time for Milford Haven is 2m 25s. The difference between latitudes 51° 32'N and 51° 59'N is 27', and the difference between 51° 32'N and 51°44'N is 12'.

From the Table of Houses, we must now find the M.C. at both sidereal times and the Ascendant at both sidereal times and latitudes. Then the necessary adjustments are calculated to find the Ascendant and MC. for 51°44'N.

S.T.	*Ascendants* *lat. 51°32'*	*lat. 51°59'*	*Diff. for* *27'*	*12'*	*Asc, for* *51°44'N*	*M.C.*
21 41 23	28°34' ♊	29°09' ♊	+35'	+15'	28°49' ♊	23°≈
21 45 16	29°29' ♊	0°02' ♋	+33'	+15'	29°44' ♊	24°≈
Diff. for 3m 53s					0°55'	1°
Diff. for 2m 25s (add to Asc. and M.C. for 21 41 23)					34'	37'
					28°49' ♊	23°≈
					29°23' ♊	23°37≈

The required Ascendant is therefore 29°23'♊ and the M.C. 23°37'≈.
Note You will need to note in the Table of Houses whether the Ascendant is increasing or decreasing as the latitude increases. In this instance, the Ascendant is increasing so the differences in latitude for 27' and 12' are *added* to the Ascendants at latitude 51°32'N for the respective sidereal times (if the Ascendant had been decreasing, you would *subtract*).

Acceleration Table

MEAN TIME Mins. — WHOLE HOURS OF MEAN TIME

MEAN TIME Mins.	0 m.	0 s.	1 m.	1 s.	2 m.	2 s.	3 m.	3 s.	4 m.	4 s.	5 m.	5 s.	6 m.	6 s.	7 m.	7 s.	8 m.	8 s.	9 m.	9 s.	10 m.	10 s.	11 m.	11 s.
0	0	0	0	10	0	20	0	30	0	39	0	49	0	59	1	9	1	19	1	29	1	39	1	48
4	0	1	0	11	0	20	0	30	0	40	0	50	1	0	1	10	1	20	1	29	1	39	1	49
8	0	1	0	11	0	21	0	31	0	41	0	51	1	1	1	10	1	20	1	30	1	40	1	50
12	0	2	0	12	0	22	0	32	0	41	0	51	1	1	1	11	1	21	1	31	1	41	1	50
16	0	3	0	13	0	22	0	32	0	42	0	52	1	2	1	12	1	22	1	31	1	41	1	51
20	0	3	0	13	0	23	0	33	0	43	0	53	1	2	1	12	1	22	1	32	1	42	1	52
24	0	4	0	14	0	24	0	34	0	43	0	53	1	3	1	13	1	23	1	33	1	43	1	52
28	0	5	0	15	0	24	0	34	0	44	0	54	1	4	1	14	1	24	1	33	1	43	1	53
32	0	5	0	15	0	25	0	35	0	45	0	55	1	4	1	14	1	24	1	34	1	44	1	54
36	0	6	0	16	0	26	0	36	0	45	0	55	1	5	1	15	1	25	1	35	1	45	1	54
40	0	7	0	16	0	26	0	36	0	46	0	56	1	6	1	16	1	25	1	35	1	45	1	55
44	0	7	0	17	0	27	0	37	0	47	0	57	1	6	1	16	1	26	1	36	1	46	1	56
48	0	8	0	18	0	28	0	38	0	47	0	57	1	7	1	17	1	27	1	37	1	46	1	56
52	0	9	0	18	0	28	0	38	0	48	0	58	1	8	1	18	1	27	1	37	1	47	1	57
56	0	9	0	19	0	29	0	39	0	49	0	59	1	8	1	18	1	28	1	38	1	48	1	58

Ephemeris of the Planets' Places

for 1986

A Complete Aspectarian

Mean Obliquity of the Ecliptic, 1986, 23° 26′ 28″.

INTRODUCTION

Greenwich Mean Time (G.M.T.) has been used as the basis for all tabulations and times. The tabular data are for Green-wich Mean Noon (12h. G.M.T.), except for the Moon tabulations headed "MIDNIGHT". All phenomena and aspect times are now in G.M.T.

This edition follows the layout of the new form which was introduced in 1980.

BRITISH SUMMER TIME

British Summer Time begins on March 30 and ends on October 26. When *British Summer Time* (one hour in advance of G.M.T.) is used, subtract one hour from B.S.T. before entering this Ephemeris.

These dates are correct according to the acts in force as at the time of printing.

[Some of the information in this Ephemeris is reproduced, with permission,]
   from data supplied by the Science Research Council.

Published by

LONDON: W. FOULSHAM & CO., LTD.

YEOVIL ROAD, SLOUGH, BERKS. ENGLAND

NEW YORK   TORONTO   CAPE TOWN   SYDNEY

RAPHAEL'S EPHEMERIS.
An annual publication giving the longitudes of the planets, and
Sidereal time for noon on each day of the year. Declinations
of Sun, Moon, Mercury, Venus and Mars for each day of the
year, and of the other planets for every alternate day. It con-
tains all the necessary information for casting horoscopes for
all places in the world, both North and South of the Equator.
The more recent issues contain a complete Aspectarian, and
much other useful information. *Cr. 8vo. This Ephemeris has
been published annually since 1821 and copies are available for
any year from 1860 to date.*

Obtainable from all booksellers or direct from:
W. FOULSHAM & CO. LTD
YEOVIL ROAD, SLOUGH, SL1 4JH, ENGLAND

NEW MOON—January 10, 0h. 22m. p.m. (19° ♑ 58')

| 2 | | | JANUARY, 1986 | | | | | | [RAPHAEL'S |

D M	D W	Sidereal Time	☉ Long.	☉ Dec.	☽ Long.	☽ Lat.	☽ Dec.	☽ Node	MIDNIGHT ☽ Long.	☽ Dec.
		H. M. S.	° ′ ″	° ′	° ′ ″	° ′	° ′	° ′	° ′ ″	° ′
1	W	18 43 23	10♑46 33	23 S 0	11♏40 56	4 N 10	11 N 2	5 ♉ 48	18♏20 40	8 N 6
2	TH	18 47 19	11 47 41	22 55	25 3 44	3 23	5 N 4	5 45	1≏50 18	1 N56
3	F	18 51 16	12 48 50	22 50	8≏40 30	2 23	1 S 15	5 41	15 34 28	4 S 26
4	S	18 55 12	13 50 0	22 43	22 32 18	1 N15	7 37	5 38	29 34 4	10 44
5	☉	18 59 9	14 51 10	22 37	6♏39 45	0 13	13 44	5 35	13♏49 13	16 35
6	M	19 3 5	15 52 20	22 30	21 2 15	1 S 16	19 14	5 32	28 18 30	21 37
7	T	19 7 2	16 53 30	22 23	5 ♐37 28	2 27	23 40	5 29	12 ♐58 31	25 20
8	W	19 10 58	17 54 41	22 15	20 20 53	3 30	26 35	5 26	27 43 41	27 21
9	TH	19 14 55	18 55 51	22 6	5♑3 56	4 18	27 39	5 22	12♑26 39	27 26
10	F	19 18 52	19 57 1	21 58	19 44 48	4 49	26 45	5 19	26 59 25	25 38
11	S	19 22 48	20 58 11	21 48	4≈≈ 9 35	5 1	24 5	5 16	11≈≈14 32	22 12
12	☉	19 26 45	21 59 21	21 39	18 13 41	4 54	20 2	5 13	25 6 32	17 37
13	M	19 30 41	23 0 30	21 29	1 ✕52 49	4 31	15 1	5 10	8 ✕32 28	12 17
14	T	19 34 38	24 1 38	21 18	15 5 31	3 53	9 27	5 6	21 32 11	6 34
15	W	19 38 34	25 2 46	21 8	27 52 49	3 5	3 S 40	5 3	4 ♈ 7 53	0 S 46
16	TH	19 42 31	26 3 53	20 56	10 ♈17 54	2 9	2 N 6	5 0	16 23 29	4 N56
17	F	19 46 27	27 4 59	20 45	22 25 17	1 8	7 41	4 57	28 24 1	10 20
18	S	19 50 24	28 6 5	20 33	4 ♉20 22	0 S 5	12 53	4 54	10 ♉15 3	15 18
19	☉	19 54 21	29♑ 7 9	20 20	16 8 46	0 N57	17 35	4 51	22 2 13	19 41
20	M	19 58 17	0≈≈ 8 13	20 7	27 52 1	1 57	21 36	4 47	3 Ⅱ50 50	23 17
21	T	20 2 14	1 9 16	19 54	9 Ⅱ47 12	2 51	24 45	4 44	15 45 39	25 56
22	W	20 6 10	2 10 18	19 41	21 46 39	3 39	26 50	4 41	27 50 35	27 25
23	TH	20 10 7	3 11 20	19 27	3♋57 47	4 18	27 41	4 38	10♋ 8 28	27 35
24	F	20 14 3	4 12 20	19 13	16 22 49	4 45	27 9	4 35	22 40 56	26 21
25	S	20 18 0	5 13 19	18 58	29 2 49	4 58	25 13	4 32	5 ♌28 25	23 45
26	☉	20 21 56	6 14 18	18 43	11 ♌57 37	4 57	21 57	4 28	18 30 15	19 53
27	M	20 25 53	7 15 16	18 28	25 6 7	4 40	17 33	4 25	1 ♏45 0	14 59
28	T	20 29 50	8 16 13	18 12	8 ♏26 38	4 8	12 14	4 22	15 10 50	9 19
29	W	20 33 46	9 17 9	17 56	21 57 22	3 21	6 N16	4 19	28 46 3	3 N 8
30	TH	20 37 43	10 18 4	17 40	5≏36 46	2 22	0 S 3	4 16	12≏29 23	3 S 15
31	F	20 41 39	11≈≈18 58	17 S 23	19≏23 51	1 N15	6 S 27	4 ♉12	26≏20 7	9 S 34

D M	Mercury Lat.	Dec.	Venus Lat.	Dec.	Mars Lat.	Dec.	Jupiter Lat.	Dec.
	° ′	° ′	° ′	° ′	° ′	° ′	° ′	° ′
1	0 N13	23 S 4	0 S 21	23 S 38	1 N 2	14 S 7	0 S 48	16 S 5
3	0 S 2	23 26	0 26	23 34	1 1	14 30	0 48	15 57
5	0 17	23 43	0 30	23 27	1 0	14 53	0 48	15 49
7	0 31	23 56	0 35	23 17	1 0	15 15	0 48	15 41
9	0 44	24 4	0 39	23 4	0 59	15 37	0 48	15 33
11	0 56	24 7	0 43	22 48	0 58	15 59	0 48	15 24
13	1 8	24 4	0 47	22 30	0 57	16 20	0 48	15 16
15	1 19	23 56	0 51	22 9	0 57	16 40	0 48	15 7
17	1 29	23 51	0 55	21 45	0 56	17 0	0 48	14 58
19	1 38	23 25	0 59	21 18	0 55	17 20	0 48	14 49
21	1 46	23 0	1 2	20 49	0 54	17 39	0 48	14 40
23	1 52	22 30	1 5	20 17	0 53	17 58	0 48	14 31
25	1 58	21 54	1 8	19 43	0 52	18 16	0 48	14 22
27	2 2	21 12	1 11	19 7	0 51	18 34	0 48	14 12
29	2 4	20 24	1 14	18 29	0 50	18 51	0 49	14 3
31	2 S 5	19 S 30	1 S 16	17 S 48	0 N49	19 S 8	0 S 49	13 S 54

FIRST QUARTER—January 17, 10h. 13m. p.m. (27° ♈ 31')

92

FULL MOON—January 26, 0*h*. 31*m*. *a.m*. (5° ♌ 45′)

D M	☿ Long. ° ′	♀ Long. ° ′	♂ Long. ° ′	♃ Long. ° ′	♄ Long. ° ′	♅ Long. ° ′	♆ Long. ° ′	♇ Long. ° ′	Lunar Aspects ☉	☿	♀	♂	♃	♄	♅	♆	♇
1	23 ♐ 36	6 ♑ 26	10 ♏ 53	18 ♒ 22	5 ♐ 13	19 ♐ 32	3 ♑ 36	6 ♏ 55	△		△	✶		□			✶
2	25 3	7 42	11 29	18 35	5 19	19 35	3 39	6 57		□		∠			□		∠
3	26 31	8 57	12 6	18 47	5 25	19 39	3 41	6 58	□		□	⊻	⚼	✶		□	⊻
4	27 59	10 13	12 42	19 0	5 31	19 42	3 43	6 59		✶			△	∠	✶		
S	29 ♐ 28	11 28	13 19	19 14	5 37	19 46	3 45	7 0			✶	☌		⊻	∠	✶	☌
6	0 ♑ 57	12 44	13 55	19 27	5 43	19 49	3 48	7 2	✶	∠			□		⊻	∠	
7	2 27	13 59	14 32	19 40	5 49	19 52	3 50	7 3	∠	⊻	∠			☌		⊻	⊻
8	3 57	15 15	15 9	19 53	5 55	19 56	3 52	7 4	⊻		⊻	⊻	✶		☌		∠
9	5 28	16 30	15 45	20 6	6 1	19 59	3 54	7 5		☌		∠	∠	⊻		☌	✶
10	6 59	17 46	16 21	20 20	6 7	20 2	3 56	7 6	☌		☌	✶	⊻	∠	⊻		
11	8 31	19 1	16 58	20 33	6 13	20 6	3 59	7 7		⊻				✶	∠	⊻	□
S	10 3	20 17	17 34	20 47	6 19	20 9	4 1	7 8	⊻		⊻	□	☌		✶	∠	
13	11 36	21 32	18 10	21 0	6 24	20 12	4 3	7 9	∠	∠	∠			□		✶	△
14	13 9	22 47	18 47	21 14	6 30	20 15	4 5	7 10		✶		△	⊻		□		
15	14 42	24 3	19 23	21 27	6 35	20 19	4 7	7 11	✶		✶						⚼
16	16 16	25 18	19 59	21 41	6 41	20 22	4 9	7 12				⚼	∠	△		□	
17	17 51	26 34	20 35	21 55	6 46	20 25	4 12	7 13	□	□	□		✶	⚼	△		
18	19 26	27 49	21 11	22 8	6 52	20 28	4 14	7 13							⚼	△	☍
S	21 2	29 ♑ 5	21 47	22 22	6 57	20 31	4 16	7 14		△						⚼	
20	22 38	0 ♒ 20	22 23	22 36	7 2	20 34	4 18	7 15	△		△	☍	□				
21	24 15	1 36	22 59	22 50	7 7	20 37	4 20	7 16		⚼				☍			
22	25 52	2 51	23 35	23 4	7 12	20 40	4 22	7 16	⚼		⚼		△		☍		⚼
23	27 30	4 6	24 11	23 18	7 17	20 43	4 24	7 17				⚼	⚼			☍	△
24	29 ♑ 8	5 22	24 47	23 32	7 22	20 46	4 26	7 17						⚼			
25	0 ♒ 47	6 37	25 23	23 46	7 27	20 49	4 28	7 18		☍		△					
S	2 27	7 53	25 59	24 0	7 32	20 52	4 30	7 19	☍		☍			△	⚼		□
27	4 7	9 8	26 35	24 14	7 37	20 54	4 32	7 19				□	☍		△	⚼	
28	5 48	10 23	27 10	24 28	7 41	20 57	4 34	7 19						□		△	✶
29	7 30	11 39	27 46	24 42	7 46	21 0	4 36	7 20	⚼	⚼	⚼	✶			□		∠
30	9 12	12 54	28 22	24 56	7 50	21 3	4 38	7 20	△	△			⚼	✶		□	⊻
31	10 ♒ 56	14 ♒ 9	28 ♏ 57	25 ♒ 10	7 ♐ 55	21 ♐ 5	4 ♑ 40	7 ♏ 20			△	∠	△	∠	✶		

D M	Saturn Lat. ° ′	Saturn Dec. ° ′	Uranus Lat. ° ′	Uranus Dec. ° ′	Neptune Lat. ° ′	Neptune Dec. ° ′	Pluto Lat. ° ′	Pluto Dec. ° ′
1	1 N48	19 S 24	0 S 3	23 S 5	1 N 4	22 S 20	16 N21	1 N40
3	1 49	19 26	0 3	23 6	1 4	22 20	16 22	1 40
5	1 49	19 28	0 3	23 6	1 4	22 20	16 23	1 40
7	1 49	19 30	0 4	23 7	1 4	22 20	16 24	1 40
9	1 49	19 32	0 4	23 7	1 4	22 19	16 25	1 41
11	1 49	19 33	0 4	23 8	1 4	22 19	16 26	1 41
13	1 49	19 35	0 4	23 8	1 4	22 19	16 27	1 41
15	1 49	19 37	0 4	23 9	1 4	22 19	16 28	1 42
17	1 50	19 39	0 4	23 9	1 4	22 19	16 29	1 42
19	1 50	19 40	0 4	23 10	1 4	22 19	16 31	1 43
21	1 50	19 42	0 4	23 10	1 4	22 19	16 32	1 43
23	1 50	19 43	0 4	23 11	1 4	22 18	16 33	1 44
25	1 50	19 45	0 4	23 11	1 4	22 18	16 34	1 45
27	1 51	19 46	0 4	23 12	1 4	22 18	16 35	1 45
29	1 51	19 47	0 4	23 12	1 4	22 18	16 36	1 46
31	1 N51	19 S 48	0 S 4	23 S 12	1 N 4	22 S 18	16 N37	1 N47

Mutual Aspects

1. ☉ **P** ☿, ✶ ♂, ⊥ ♄. ☿ **P** ♅. ♀ ✶ ♇.
2. ♃ ∠ ♆.
3. ☉ ⊥ ♃.
4. ☿ **P** ♀, ∠ ♂.
5. ♀ ⊥ ♄.
6. ♂ ⊥ ♅.
7. ☉ **P** ♆. ♀ ⊥ ♃.
8. ☿ ☌ ♆. ♀ ✶ ♂. ♃ ✶ ♅.
9. ☉ **Q** ♇. ☿ ∠ ♃, ⊻ ♄. ♀ **P** ♅. ♂ **P** ♃.
10. ☉ ⊻ ♃, ⊻ ♅. ☿ ✶ ♇.
11. ☉ ∠ ♄. ♀ **Q** ♇.
12. ♀ ⊻ ♃, ⊻ ♅.
13. ♀ ∠ ♄.
14. ☿ ⊥ ♄. ♀ **P** ♆.
15. ♂ ∠ ♆.
16. ☉ ⊥ ♅. ☿ ⊥ ♃.
17. ♀ ⊥ ♅. ♂ ⊻ ♅.
18. ☿ **Q** ♇.
19. ☉ ☌ ♀. ☿ ⊻ ♅
20. ☿ ✶ ♂, ⊻ ♃, ∠ ♄, **P** ♅.
21. ♂ □ ♃.
22. ☉ **P** ♄.
23. ☿ ⊥ ♅. ♀ ⊻ ♆. ♄ ⊻ ♇.
24. ☉ ⊻ ♆. ☿ **P** ♆. ♀ ∠ ♅.
25. ♀ **P** ♄.
26. ☉ ∠ ♅. ♀ **Q** ♂, ✶ ♄, □ ♇.
27. ☉ **P** ♂, ✶ ♄, □ ♇. ☿ ⊻ ♆.
28. ☿ ∠ ♅. ♀ **P** ♂, ⊥ ♆.
29. ☿ ✶ ♄, □ ♇.
30. ☉ **Q** ♂, ⊥ ♆. ☿ **P** ♄. ♂ ⊥ ♆.
31. ☿ **Q** ♂, ⊥ ♆.

LAST QUARTER—January 3, 7*h*. 47*m*. *p.m*. (13° ♎ 9′)

NEW MOON—February 9, 0h. 55m. a.m. (19° ≈ 59′)

| 4 | | | | | FEBRUARY, 1986 | | | | | [RAPHAEL'S |

D M	D W	Sidereal Time	⊙ Long.	⊙ Dec.	☽ Long.	☽ Lat.	☽ Dec.	Node	MIDNIGHT ☽ Long.	☽ Dec.
		H. M. S.	° ′ ″	° ′	° ′ ″	° ′	° ′	° ′	° ′ ″	° ′
1	S	20 45 36	12≈19 52	17 S 6	3♏18 10	0 N 2	12 S 35	4 ♉ 9	10♏18 0	15 S 28
2	⊙	20 49 32	13 20 46	16 49	17 19 35	1 S 12	18 9	4 6	24 22 52	20 36
3	M	20 53 29	14 21 38	16 32	1 ♐27 46	2 22	22 46	4 3	8 ♐34 7	24 35
4	T	20 57 25	15 22 30	16 14	15 41 40	3 23	26 2	4 0	22 50 8	27 4
5	W	21 1 22	16 23 21	15 56	29 59 6	4 12	27 38	3 57	7♑ 8 3	27 45
6	Th	21 5 19	17 24 11	15 37	14♑16 25	4 45	27 24	3 53	21 23 36	26 36
7	F	21 9 15	18 25 0	15 19	28 28 53	5 0	25 22	3 50	5≈31 36	23 45
8	S	21 13 12	19 25 47	15 0	12≈31 6	4 57	21 48	3 47	19 26 46	19 33
9	⊙	21 17 8	20 26 34	14 41	26 18 2	4 36	17 5	3 44	3 ✕ 4 29	14 25
10	M	21 21 5	21 27 19	14 21	9 ✕45 46	4 1	11 37	3 41	16 21 42	8 44
11	T	21 25 1	22 28 2	14 2	22 52 10	3 13	5 S 47	3 38	29 17 15	2 S 49
12	W	21 28 58	23 28 44	13 42	5 ♈37 5	2 17	0 N 8	3 34	11♈51 58	3 N 4
13	Th	21 32 54	24 29 25	13 22	18 2 16	1 15	5 55	3 31	24 8 27	8 42
14	F	21 36 51	25 30 4	13 1	0 ♉11 1	0 S 11	11 22	3 28	6 ♉10 35	13 55
15	S	21 40 47	26 30 41	12 41	12 7 45	0 N 52	16 19	3 25	18 3 13	18 33
16	⊙	21 44 44	27 31 16	12 20	23 57 38	1 53	20 36	3 22	29 51 42	22 26
17	M	21 48 41	28 31 50	11 59	5 ♊46 6	2 49	24 3	3 18	11♊41 32	25 24
18	T	21 52 37	29≈32 22	11 38	17 38 38	3 38	26 29	3 15	23 38 2	27 16
19	W	21 56 34	0 ✕32 52	11 17	29 40 20	4 17	27 44	3 12	5♋46 2	27 52
20	Th	22 0 30	1 33 21	10 55	11♋55 36	4 46	27 39	3 9	18 9 26	27 6
21	F	22 4 27	2 33 48	10 34	24 27 51	5 2	26 11	3 6	0♌51 2	24 55
22	S	22 8 23	3 34 12	10 12	7♌19 6	5 3	23 19	3 3	13 52 5	21 25
23	⊙	22 12 20	4 34 35	9 50	20 29 53	4 48	19 13	2 59	27 12 17	16 44
24	M	22 16 16	5 34 57	9 28	3♍59 0	4 17	14 2	2 56	10♍49 42	11 9
25	T	22 20 13	6 35 16	9 6	17 43 55	3 31	8 5	2 53	24 41 13	4 N54
26	W	22 24 10	7 35 34	8 43	1≏41 4	2 31	1 N 38	2 50	8≏43 0	1 S 40
27	Th	22 28 6	8 35 50	8 21	15 46 31	1 21	4 S 57	2 47	22 51 10	8 12
28	F	22 32 3	9 ✕36 5	7 S 58	29≏56 33	0 N 6	11 S 21	2 ♉43	7♏ 2 17	14 S 22

D M	Mercury			Venus			Mars			Jupiter	
	Lat.	Dec.		Lat.	Dec.		Lat.	Dec.		Lat.	Dec.
	° ′	° ′	° ′	° ′	° ′	° ′	° ′	° ′	° ′	° ′	° ′
1	2 S 5	19 S 0		1 S 17	17 S 27		0 N48	19 S 16		0 S 49	13 S 49
3	2 3	17 57	18 S 30	1 19	16 43	17 S 5	0 47	19 32	19 S 24	0 49	13 39
5	2 0	16 48	17 24	1 21	15 58	16 21	0 46	19 48	19 40	0 49	13 30
7	1 54	15 34	16 12	1 23	15 11	15 34	0 45	20 3	19 55	0 49	13 20
9	1 46	14 13	14 54	1 24	14 22	14 46	0 44	20 17	20 10	0 49	13 10
			13 31			13 57			20 24			
11	1 36	12 47	12 2	1 25	13 31	13 5	0 42	20 31	20 38	0 49	13 0
13	1 23	11 17		1 26	12 39	12 13	0 41	20 44	20 51	0 49	12 51
15	1 7	9 42	10 30	1 27	11 46	11 19	0 40	20 57	21 3	0 49	12 41
17	0 49	8 4	8 53	1 27	10 52	10 24	0 38	21 9	21 15	0 49	12 31
19	0 28	6 24	7 14	1 27	9 56	9 28	0 37	21 21	21 27	0 50	12 21
			5 34								
21	0 S 5	4 45	3 56	1 27	8 59	8 30	0 35	21 33	21 38	0 50	12 11
23	0 N21	3 7	2 20	1 27	8 1	7 32	0 34	21 43	21 48	0 50	12 1
25	0 49	1 35	0 S 51	1 26	7 3	6 33	0 32	21 54	21 58	0 50	11 51
27	1 17	0 S 10	0 N29	1 25	6 4	5 34	0 30	22 3	22 8	0 50	11 40
29	1 46	1 N 5	1 N38	1 24	5 4	4 S 34	0 28	22 12	22 S 17	0 50	11 30
31	2 N15	2 N 6		1 S 22	4 S 3		0 N27	22 S 21		0 S 50	11 S 20

FIRST QUARTER—February 16, 7h. 55m. p.m. (27° ♉ 51′)

94

Full Moon—February 24, 3*h.* 2*m.* *p.m.* (5° ♍ 43′)

D	☿	♀	♂	♃	♄	♅	♆	♇	Lunar Aspects								
M	Long.	Long.	Long.	Long.	Long.	Long.	Long.	Long.	☉	☿	♀	♂	♃	♄	♅	♆	♇
	° ′	° ′	° ′	° ′	° ′	° ′	° ′	° ′									
1	12♒39	15♒25	29♏33	25♒25	7♐59	21♐ 8	4♑42	7♏21				⊻		⊻	∠	✱	☌
S	14 24	16 40	0♐ 8	25 39	8 3	21 11	4 44	7 21	□	□	□				⊻	∠	
3	16 9	17 55	0 44	25 53	8 8	21 13	4 46	7 21				☌	□	☌		⊻	⊻
4	17 55	19 10	1 19	26 7	8 12	21 16	4 48	7 21	✱	✱	✱				☌		∠
5	19 41	20 26	1 54	26 22	8 16	21 18	4 49	7 22	∠	∠	∠	⊻	✱			☌	
6	21 28	21 41	2 30	26 36	8 20	21 21	4 51	7 22	⊻			∠	∠	⊻	⊻		✱
7	23 16	22 56	3 5	26 50	8 24	21 23	4 53	7 22		⊻	⊻	✱	⊻	∠		⊻	
8	25 4	24 12	3 40	27 5	8 27	21 25	4 55	7 22						✱	∠		□
S	26 52	25 27	4 15	27 19	8 31	21 28	4 56	7 22	☌	☌	☌		☌		✱	∠	
10	28♒41	26 42	4 50	27 33	8 35	21 30	4 58	7℞22				□		□		✱	△
11	0♓30	27 57	5 25	27 48	8 38	21 32	5 0	7 22	⊻		⊻		⊻		□		⚼
12	2 20	29♒12	6 0	28 2	8 42	21 34	5 2	7 22	∠	⊻		△		△		□	
13	4 9	0♓28	6 35	28 17	8 45	21 36	5 3	7 21		∠	∠	⚼	∠	⚼	△		
14	5 58	1 43	7 10	28 31	8 48	21 39	5 5	7 21	✱		✱		✱			△	
15	7 46	2 58	7 44	28 45	8 51	21 41	5 6	7 21		✱					⚼		☍
S	9 34	4 13	8 19	29 0	8 55	21 43	5 8	7 21	□				□			⚼	
17	11 21	5 28	8 54	29 14	8 57	21 45	5 10	7 20			□	☍		☍			
18	13 7	6 43	9 28	29 29	9 0	21 47	5 11	7 20		□					☍		⚼
19	14 51	7 58	10 3	29 43	9 3	21 48	5 13	7 20	△				△			☍	
20	16 32	9 13	10 37	29♒58	9 6	21 50	5 14	7 19	⚼	△	△		⚼				△
21	18 11	10 28	11 11	0♓12	9 9	21 52	5 15	7 19			⚼	⚼		⚼			
22	19 47	11 43	11 45	0 26	9 11	21 54	5 17	7 18		⚼		△		△	⚼		□
S	21 19	12 58	12 20	0 41	9 14	21 55	5 18	7 18							△	⚼	
24	22 47	14 13	12 54	0 55	9 16	21 57	5 20	7 17	☍				☍	□		△	✱
25	24 9	15 28	13 28	1 10	9 18	21 59	5 21	7 17			☍	□			□		∠
26	25 27	16 43	14 2	1 24	9 20	22 0	5 22	7 16		☍						□	⊻
27	26 37	17 58	14 35	1 38	9 22	22 2	5 23	7 16				✱	⚼	✱	✱		
28	27♓41	19♓13	15♐ 9	1♓53	9♐24	22♐ 3	5♑25	7♏15	⚼	·	⚼	∠	△	∠		✱	

D	Saturn		Uranus		Neptune		Pluto	
M	Lat.	Dec.	Lat.	Dec.	Lat.	Dec.	Lat.	Dec.
	° ′	° ′	° ′	° ′	° ′	° ′	° ′	° ′
1	1 N51	19 S 49	0 S 4	23 S 13	1 N 4	22 S 18	16 N38	1 N47
3	1 51	19 50	0 4	23 13	1 4	22 18	16 39	1 48
5	1 52	19 51	0 4	23 13	1 4	22 17	16 40	1 49
7	1 52	19 52	0 4	23 14	1 4	22 17	16 41	1 50
9	1 52	19 53	0 4	23 14	1 4	22 17	16 42	1 51
11	1 52	19 54	0 4	23 14	1 4	22 17	16 43	1 52
13	1 53	19 55	0 4	23 15	1 4	22 17	16 44	1 53
15	1 53	19 55	0 4	23 15	1 4	22 17	16 45	1 54
17	1 53	19 56	0 4	23 15	1 4	22 16	16 46	1 56
19	1 53	19 57	0 4	23 15	1 4	22 16	16 47	1 57
21	1 54	19 57	0 4	23 16	1 4	22 16	16 48	1 58
23	1 54	19 58	0 4	23 16	1 4	22 16	16 49	1 59
25	1 54	19 58	0 4	23 16	1 4	22 16	16 50	2 0
27	1 54	19 58	0 4	23 16	1 4	22 16	16 51	2 2
29	1 55	19 59	0 4	23 17	1 4	22 16	16 52	2 3
31	1 N55	19 S 59	0 S 4	23 S 17	1 N 4	22 S 15	16 N53	2 N 4

Mutual Aspects

1. ☉ ☌ ☿. ☿ **P** ♂.
5. ☉ **P** ♀. ☿ **Q** ♄, ∠ ♆. ♀ **Q** ♄, ∠ ♆. ♂ **P** ♄.
6. ☿ ☌ ♀, ✱ ♅. ♀ ✱ ♅.
8. ☉ **P** ☿, ∠ ♆. ☿ **P** ♀.
9. ☉ **Q** ♄. ☿ ☌ ♃. ♇ **Stat.**
10. ☉ ✱ ♅. ♂ ⊻ ♆.
11. ☿ **P** ♃. ♀ ☌ ♃.
12. ♀ **P** ♃.
13. ☿ **Q** ♅.
14. ☿ ✱ ♆. ♂ ⊻ ♇.
15. ☉ **P** ♃. ☿ □ ♂, △ ♇.
16. ☿ □ ♄. ♀ **Q** ♅.
17. ♀ ✱ ♆. ♂ ☌ ♄.
18. ☉ ☌ ♃. ♀ △ ♇.
20. ☿ **Q** ♆. ♀ □ ♄.
22. ☉ **Q** ♅. ♀ □ ♂.
23. ☿ □ ♅.
24. ☉ ✱ ♆. ☿ ⚼ ♇, **P** ♇.
25. ♂ ⊥ ♇.
26. ☉ △ ♇.
27. ♀ **Q** ♆.
28. ☉ □ ♄.

Last Quarter—February 2, 4*h.* 41*m.* *a.m.* (13° ♏ 2′)

6				MARCH, 1986					[RAPHAEL'S	

D M	D W	Sidereal Time	☉ Long.	☉ Dec.	☽ Long.	☽ Lat.	☽ Dec.	Node	MIDNIGHT ☽ Long.	☽ Dec.
		H. M. S.	° '	° '	° ' "	° '	° '	° '	° ' "	° '
1	S	22 35 59	10♓36 18	7 S 36	14♏ 8 5	1 S 10	17 S 12	2 ♉40	21♏13 41	19 S 47
2	♋	22 39 56	11 36 30	7 13	28 18 52	2 21	22 5	2 37	5 ♐23 27	24 3
3	M	22 43 52	12 36 41	6 50	12 ♐27 15	3 24	25 40	2 34	19 30 10	26 52
4	T	22 47 49	13 36 50	6 27	26 32 1	4 14	27 38	2 31	3 ♑32 38	27 57
5	W	22 51 45	14 36 57	6 4	10 ♑31 51	4 49	27 49	2 28	17 29 27	27 15
6	Th	22 55 42	15 37 3	5 40	24 25 12	5 6	26 16	2 24	1 ♒18 50	24 53
7	F	22 59 39	16 37 7	5 17	8 ♒10 5	5 5	23 9	2 21	14 58 40	21 6
8	S	23 3 35	17 37 10	4 54	21 44 16	4 48	18 48	2 18	28 26 36	16 17
9	♋	23 7 32	18 37 10	4 30	5 ♓ 5 26	4 15	13 36	2 15	11 ♓40 31	10 47
10	M	23 11 28	19 37 9	4 7	18 11 41	3 29	7 52	2 12	24 38 50	4 S 54
11	T	23 15 25	20 37 6	3 43	1 ♈ 1 54	2 32	1 S 55	2 9	7 ♈20 55	1 N 3
12	W	23 19 21	21 37 1	3 20	13 35 57	1 30	3 N59	2 5	19 47 10	6 51
13	Th	23 23 18	22 36 54	2 56	25 54 50	0 S 24	9 38	2 2	1 ♉59 13	12 18
14	F	23 27 14	23 36 44	2 32	8 ♉ 0 43	0 N42	14 50	1 59	13 59 44	17 13
15	S	23 31 11	24 36 33	2 9	19 56 45	1 45	19 25	1 56	25 52 19	21 25
16	♋	23 35 8	25 36 20	1 45	1 ♊46 57	2 43	23 11	1 53	7 ♊41 17	24 43
17	M	23 39 4	26 36 4	1 21	13 35 55	3 34	25 59	1 49	19 31 28	26 58
18	T	23 43 1	27 35 46	0 57	25 28 35	4 17	27 39	1 46	1 ♋27 54	28 0
19	W	23 46 57	28 35 26	0 34	7 ♋30 3	4 48	28 2	1 43	13 35 37	27 43
20	Th	23 50 54	29♓35 3	0 S 10	19 45 11	5 8	27 4	1 40	25 59 15	26 4
21	F	23 54 50	0 ♈34 39	0 N14	2 ♌18 17	5 13	24 43	1 37	8 ♌42 39	23 4
22	S	23 58 47	1 34 12	0 37	15 12 40	5 3	21 5	1 34	21 48 30	18 50
23	♋	0 2 43	2 33 42	1 1	28 30 13	4 36	16 18	1 30	5 ♍17 48	13 33
24	M	0 6 40	3 33 11	1 25	12 ♍11 3	3 53	10 35	1 27	19 9 40	7 27
25	T	0 10 37	4 32 37	1 48	26 13 13	2 55	4 N11	1 24	3 ♎21 10	0 N50
26	W	0 14 33	5 32 1	2 12	10 ♎32 52	1 45	2 S 34	1 21	17 47 36	5 S 57
27	Th	0 18 30	6 31 23	2 35	25 4 37	0 N27	9 17	1 18	2 ♏23 7	12 30
28	F	0 22 26	7 30 43	2 59	9 ♏42 19	0 S 53	15 34	1 15	17 1 28	18 24
29	S	0 26 23	8 30 2	3 22	24 19 51	2 10	20 57	1 11	1 ♐36 50	23 11
30	♋	0 30 19	9 29 19	3 46	8 ♐51 50	3 18	25 3	1 8	16 4 22	26 29
31	M	0 34 16	10♈28 34	4 N 9	23 ♐14	3 4 S 13	27 S 29	1 ♉ 5	0 ♑20 35	28 S 1

D M	Mercury			Venus			Mars			Jupiter	
	Lat.	Dec.		Lat.	Dec.		Lat.	Dec.		Lat.	Dec.
	° '	° '	° '	° '	° '	° '	° '	° '	° '	° '	° '
1	1 N46	1 N 5	1 N38	1 S 24	5 S 4	4 S 34	0 N28	22 S 12	22 S 17	0 S 50	11 S 30
3	2 15	2 6	2 31	1 22	4 3	3 32	0 27	22 21	22 25	0 50	11 20
5	2 41	2 52	3 8	1 21	3 2	2 32	0 25	22 29	22 33	0 51	11 10
7	3 4	3 20	3 27	1 19	2 1	1 31	0 23	22 37	22 41	0 51	11 0
9	3 21	3 29	3 26	1 17	1 S 0	0 S 29	0 21	22 44	22 47	0 51	10 50
11	3 33	3 19	3 7	1 14	0 N 2	0 N33	0 18	22 51	22 54	0 51	10 40
13	3 37	2 50	2 31	1 11	1 4	1 34	0 16	22 57	23 0	0 51	10 29
15	3 33	2 7	1 41	1 9	2 5	2 36	0 14	23 3	23 5	0 52	10 19
17	3 22	1 13	0 N43	1 5	3 7	3 37	0 12	23 8	23 10	0 52	10 9
19	3 3	0 N11	0 S 20	1 2	4 8	4 38	0 9	23 13	23 15	0 52	9 59
21	2 39	0 S 52	1 22	0 59	5 9	5 39	0 7	23 17	23 19	0 52	9 49
23	2 11	1 52	2 20	0 55	6 9	6 39	0 4	23 21	23 23	0 53	9 39
25	1 41	2 46	3 11	0 51	7 9	7 39	0 N 1	23 25	23 26	0 53	9 29
27	1 10	3 33	3 52	0 47	8 8	8 38	0 S 1	23 28	23 29	0 53	9 19
29	0 39	4 9	4 S 24	0 42	9 7	9 N36	0 4	23 31	23 S 32	0 53	9 9
31	0 N10	4 S 36		0 S 38	10 N 4		0 S 7	23 S 33		0 S 54	8 S 59

FULL MOON—March 26, 3*h.* 2*m.* *a.m.* (5° ♎ 10′)

D M	☿ Long.	♀ Long.	♂ Long.	♃ Long.	♄ Long.	♅ Long.	♆ Long.	♇ Long.	Lunar Aspects ⊙	☿	♀	♂	♃	♄	♅	♆	♇
	° ′	° ′	° ′	° ′	° ′	° ′	° ′	° ′									
1	28 ♓ 38	20 ♓ 28	15 ♐ 43	2 ♓ 7	9 ♐ 26	22 ♐ 4	5 ♑ 26	7 ♏ 14	△	⚼	△	⚺		⚺	∠	∠	☌
𝕾	29 ♓ 27	21 43	16 16	2 21	9 28	22 6	5 27	7 ℞ 14		△			□		⚺		
3	0 ♈ 7	22 58	16 50	2 36	9 29	22 7	5 28	7 13	□			☌		☌		⚺	⚺
4	0 39	24 13	17 23	2 50	9 31	22 8	5 29	7 12		□	□		✱		☌		∠
5	1 1	25 27	17 57	3 4	9 32	22 10	5 31	7 11	✱					⚺		☌	✱
6	1 15	26 42	18 30	3 19	9 34	22 11	5 32	7 10	∠	✱	✱	⚺	∠	∠	⚺		
7	1 ℞ 19	27 57	19 3	3 33	9 35	22 12	5 33	7 9			∠	∠	⚺	✱	∠	⚺	□
8	1 14	29 ♓ 12	19 36	3 47	9 36	22 13	5 34	7 9	⚺	∠		✱			✱	∠	
𝕾	1 0	0 ♈ 26	20 9	4 1	9 37	22 14	5 35	7 8		⚺	⚺		☌	□		✱	△
10	0 38	1 41	20 42	4 15	9 38	22 15	5 36	7 7	☌			□			□		⚼
11	0 ♈ 8	2 56	21 14	4 30	9 39	22 16	5 36	7 6		☌	☌		⚺			□	
12	29 ♓ 31	4 10	21 47	4 44	9 40	22 16	5 37	7 5						△			
13	28 48	5 25	22 19	4 58	9 40	22 17	5 38	7 4	⚺	⚺		△	∠	⚼	△		
14	28 0	6 40	22 52	5 12	9 41	22 18	5 39	7 2	∠	∠	⚺	⚼	✱		⚼	△	☍
15	27 8	7 54	23 24	5 26	9 41	22 19	5 40	7 1	✱		∠					⚼	
𝕾	26 13	9 9	23 56	5 40	9 42	22 19	5 40	7 0		✱			□				
17	25 17	10 23	24 28	5 54	9 42	22 20	5 41	6 59			✱			☍			
18	24 20	11 38	25 0	6 8	9 42	22 20	5 42	6 58	□	□		☍			☍		⚼
19	23 25	12 52	25 31	6 22	9 ℞ 42	22 21	5 43	6 57			□		△			☍	△
20	22 31	14 7	26 3	6 36	9 42	22 21	5 43	6 55		△			⚼	⚼			
21	21 41	15 21	26 34	6 49	9 42	22 21	5 44	6 54	△	⚼					⚼		□
22	20 55	16 35	27 6	7 3	9 42	22 22	5 44	6 53	⚼		△	⚼		△		⚼	
𝕾	20 13	17 50	27 37	7 17	9 41	22 22	5 45	6 52			⚼	△			△		
24	19 36	19 4	28 8	7 31	9 41	22 22	5 45	6 50					☍	□		△	✱
25	19 5	20 18	28 39	7 44	9 40	22 22	5 46	6 49		☍		□			□		∠
26	18 39	21 33	29 9	7 58	9 40	22 22	5 46	6 48	☍					✱		□	⚺
27	18 19	22 47	29 ♐ 40	8 11	9 39	22 22	5 47	6 46			☍	✱	⚼	∠	✱		
28	18 6	24 1	0 ♑ 10	8 25	9 38	22 ℞ 22	5 47	6 45		⚼		∠	△	⚺	∠	✱	☌
29	17 58	25 15	0 41	8 38	9 37	22 22	5 47	6 43	⚼	△		⚺			⚺	∠	
𝕾	17 D 56	26 29	1 11	8 52	9 36	22 22	5 48	6 42	△		⚼		□	☌		⚺	⚺
31	17 ♓ 59	27 ♈ 43	1 ♑ 41	9 ♓ 5	9 ♐ 35	22 ♐ 22	5 ♑ 48	6 ♏ 41		□	△				☌		∠

D M	Saturn Lat.	Saturn Dec.	Uranus Lat.	Uranus Dec.	Neptune Lat.	Neptune Dec.	Pluto Lat.	Pluto Dec.
	° ′	° ′	° ′	° ′	° ′	° ′	° ′	° ′
1	1 N 55	19 S 59	0 S 4	23 S 17	1 N 4	22 S 16	16 N 52	2 N 3
3	1 55	19 59	0 4	23 17	1 4	22 15	16 53	2 4
5	1 55	19 59	0 4	23 17	1 5	22 15	16 54	2 6
7	1 56	19 59	0 4	23 17	1 5	22 15	16 55	2 7
9	1 56	19 59	0 4	23 17	1 5	22 15	16 55	2 8
11	1 56	19 59	0 4	23 17	1 5	22 15	16 56	2 10
13	1 56	19 59	0 4	23 17	1 5	22 15	16 57	2 11
15	1 57	19 59	0 4	23 18	1 5	22 15	16 58	2 13
17	1 57	19 59	0 4	23 18	1 5	22 14	16 59	2 14
19	1 57	19 59	0 4	23 18	1 5	22 14	16 59	2 15
21	1 58	19 58	0 4	23 18	1 5	22 14	17 0	2 17
23	1 58	19 58	0 4	23 18	1 5	22 14	17 1	2 18
25	1 58	19 57	0 4	23 18	1 5	22 14	17 1	2 20
27	1 58	19 57	0 5	23 18	1 5	22 14	17 2	2 21
29	1 59	19 56	0 5	23 18	1 5	22 14	17 2	2 22
31	1 N 59	19 S 56	0 S 5	23 S 18	1 N 5	22 S 14	17 N 3	2 N 24

Mutual Aspects

2. ♀ □ ♅, ⚼ ♇. ♂ **P** ♆.
3. ☿ **P** ♇. 5. ☿ **P** ♀.
6. ☿ ± ♇. ♅ ∠ ♇.
7. ☿ **Stat.** ♀ **P** ♇. 8. ⊙ **Q** ♆.
9. ☿ ☌ ♀, ± ♇.
10. ♀ ± ♇. ♃ **Q** ♅.
12. ⊙ □ ♂, ⚼ ♇.
13. ⊙ □ ♅. ♀ ⚺ ♃, □ ♆. ♂ ☌ ♅, ∠ ♇.
14. ♀ ⚻ ♇.
15. ⊙ **P** ♀, **P** ♇. ☿ **P** ♀, **P** ♇. ♀ **P** ♇. ♂ **Q** ♃.
16. ⊙ ☌ ☿. ♀ △ ♄. ♃ ✱ ♆.
18. ☿ □ ♂. ♀ ⊥ ♃.
19. ♄ **Stat.**
20. ⊙ **P** ☿. ☿ □ ♅.
21. ⊙ ± ♇. ☿ ⚼ ♇. ♂ **P** ♅. ♃ △ ♇.
24. ☿ ⚺ ♀, **P** ♇.
26. ⊙ □ ♆, **P** ♇.
27. ⊙ ⚻ ♇. ♀ ∠ ♃, △ ♅. ♅ **Stat.**
28. ☿ ⊥ ♀. ♀ ⚼ ♄.
29. ⊙ ⚺ ♃. ♀ **P** ♃.
30. ⊙ △ ♄. ☿ **Stat.**

LAST QUARTER—March 3, 0*h.* 17*m.* *p.m.* (12° ♐ 37′)

NEW MOON—April 9, 6h. 8m. a.m. (19° ♈ 6')

APRIL, 1986 [*RAPHAEL'S*

D M	D W	Sidereal Time	☉ Long.	☉ Dec.	☽ Long.	☽ Lat.	☽ Dec.	☽ Node	MIDNIGHT ☽ Long.	☽ Dec.
		H. M. S.	° ′ ″	° ′	° ′ ″	° ′	° ′	° ′	° ′ ″	° ′
1	T	0 38 12	11♈27 47	4 N32	7♈23 42	4 S51	28 S 5	1 ♉ 2	14♑23 15	27 S42
2	W	0 42 9	12 26 59	4 55	21 19 8	5 12	26 53	0 59	28 11 17	25 41
3	Th	0 46 6	13 26 8	5 18	4≈59 41	5 15	24 6	0 55	11≈44 20	22 13
4	F	0 50 2	14 25 16	5 41	18 25 17	5 0	20 3	0 52	25 2 34	17 40
5	S	0 53 59	15 24 22	6 4	1♓36 14	4 29	15 6	0 49	8♓ 6 23	12 23
6	☉	0 57 55	16 23 26	6 27	14 33 3	3 45	9 33	0 46	20 56 21	6 39
7	M	1 1 52	17 22 29	6 49	27 16 20	2 51	3 S42	0 43	3♈33 8	0 S45
8	T	1 5 48	18 21 29	7 12	9♈46 50	1 49	2 N12	0 40	15 57 35	5 N 6
9	W	1 9 45	19 20 27	7 34	22 5 32	0 S43	7 56	0 36	28 10 51	10 41
10	Th	1 13 41	20 19 24	7 57	4♉13 44	0 N24	13 18	0 33	10♉14 26	15 48
11	F	1 17 38	21 18 18	8 19	16 13 13	1 29	18 7	0 30	22 10 21	20 15
12	S	1 21 35	22 17 10	8 41	28 6 13	2 30	22 11	0 27	4♊ 1 9	23 52
13	☉	1 25 31	23 16 0	9 3	9♊55 35	3 24	25 11	0 24	15 49 56	26 28
14	M	1 29 28	24 14 48	9 24	21 44 42	4 10	27 20	0 21	27 40 22	27 54
15	T	1 33 24	25 13 34	9 46	3♋37 28	4 45	28 8	0 17	9♋36 33	28 3
16	W	1 37 21	26 12 18	10 7	15 38 11	5 8	27 37	0 14	21 42 55	26 52
17	Th	1 41 17	27 10 59	10 28	27 51 19	5 17	25 46	0 11	4♌ 3 58	24 22
18	F	1 45 14	28 9 38	10 49	10♌21 22	5 12	22 39	0 8	16 44 1	20 39
19	S	1 49 10	29♈ 8 15	11 10	23 12 21	4 52	18 22	0 5	29 46 45	15 51
20	☉	1 53 7	0♉ 6 50	11 31	6♍27 30	4 16	13 6	0♉ 1	13♍14 46	10 9
21	M	1 57 4	1 5 22	11 51	20 8 35	3 24	7 2	29♈58	27 8 54	3 N46
22	T	2 1 0	2 3 52	12 12	4≈15 27	2 18	0 N25	29 55	11≈27 51	2 S59
23	W	2 4 57	3 2 20	12 32	18 45 32	1 N 2	6 S24	29 52	26 7 49	9 45
24	Th	2 8 53	4 0 47	12 52	3♏33 50	0 S20	13 1	29 49	11♏ 2 39	16 7
25	F	2 12 50	4 59 11	13 11	18 33 12	1 41	18 58	29 46	26 4 26	21 32
26	S	2 16 46	5 57 34	13 31	3♐35 13	2 56	23 45	29 42	11♐ 4 32	25 33
27	☉	2 20 43	6 55 53	13 50	18 31 23	3 58	26 54	29 39	25 54 52	27 46
28	M	2 24 39	7 54 15	14 9	3♑14 16	4 43	28 8	29 36	10♑28 57	28 0
29	T	2 28 36	8 52 33	14 28	17 38 27	5 10	27 24	29 33	24 42 28	26 22
30	W	2 32 33	9♉50 49	14 N46	1≈40 48	5 S17	24 S56	29♈30	8≈33 26	23 S10

D M	Mercury Lat.	Mercury Dec.	Mercury Dec.	Venus Lat.	Venus Dec.	Venus Dec.	Mars Lat.	Mars Dec.	Mars Dec.	Jupiter Lat.	Jupiter Dec.
	° ′	° ′	° ′	° ′	° ′	° ′	° ′	° ′	° ′	° ′	° ′
1	0 S 4	4 S45		0 S36	10 N33		0 S 9	23 S34		0 S54	8 S55
			4 S52			11 N 1			23 S35		
3	0 31	4 57		0 31	11 29		0 12	23 36		0 54	8 45
			4 59			11 57			23 37		
5	0 55	4 59		0 26	12 24		0 15	23 38		0 54	8 35
			4 56			12 51			23 39		
7	1 17	4 51		0 21	13 18		0 19	23 39		0 55	8 26
			4 44			13 45			23 40		
9	1 37	4 35		0 16	14 11		0 22	23 40		0 55	8 16
			4 25			14 37			23 41		
11	1 54	4 12		0 11	15 2		0 26	23 41		0 55	8 7
			3 57			15 27			23 42		
13	2 8	3 41		0 6	15 52		0 29	23 42		0 55	7 57
			3 22			16 16			23 42		
15	2 20	3 3		0 S 1	16 40		0 33	23 43		0 56	7 48
			2 41			17 4			23 43		
17	2 30	2 18		0 N 5	17 27		0 37	23 43		0 56	7 39
			1 54			17 49			23 43		
19	2 37	1 28		0 10	18 11		0 42	23 43		0 56	7 30
			1 1			18 33			23 43		
21	2 42	0 S32		0 15	18 54		0 46	23 43		0 57	7 21
			0 S 2			19 15			23 43		
23	2 45	0 N29		0 21	19 35		0 50	23 43		0 57	7 12
			1 N 1			19 55			23 43		
25	2 45	1 35		0 26	20 14		0 55	23 43		0 58	7 4
			2 10			20 33			23 43		
27	2 44	2 45		0 31	20 51		1 0	23 43		0 58	6 55
			3 22			21 8			23 43		
29	2 40	4 0		0 37	21 25		1 5	23 43		0 58	6 47
			4 N39			21 N41			23 S43		
31	2 S33	5 N18		0 N42	21 N57		1 S10	23 S44		0 S59	6 S38

FIRST QUARTER—April 17, 10h. 35m. a.m. (27° ♋ 8')

FULL MOON—April 24, 0*h.* 46*m.p.*˙*m.* (4° ♏ 3′)

EPHEMERIS]			APRIL, 1986						9
D M	☿ Long.	♀ Long.	♂ Long.	♃ Long.	♄ Long.	♅ Long.	♆ Long.	♇ Long.	
	° ′	° ′	° ′	° ′	° ′	° ′	° ′	° ′	
1	18 ♓ 8	28 ♈ 57	2 ♑ 10	9 ♓ 19	9 ♐ 34	22 ♐ 22	5 ♑ 48	6 ♏ 39	
2	18 23	0 ♉ 11	2 40	9 32	9 ℞ 32	22 ℞ 22	5 48	6 ℞ 38	
3	18 42	1 25	3 9	9 45	9 31	22 21	5 48	6 36	
4	19 6	2 39	3 39	9 58	9 29	22 21	5 49	6 34	
5	19 34	3 53	4 8	10 11	9 28	22 20	5 49	6 33	
𝕾	20 7	5 7	4 36	10 24	9 26	22 20	5 49	6 31	
7	20 44	6 21	5 5	10 37	9 24	22 19	5 ℞ 49	6 30	
8	21 25	7 35	5 33	10 50	9 22	22 19	5 49	6 28	
9	22 10	8 49	6 2	11 3	9 20	22 18	5 49	6 27	
10	22 58	10 3	6 30	11 16	9 18	22 17	5 49	6 25	
11	23 49	11 16	6 57	11 29	9 16	22 17	5 48	6 23	
12	24 44	12 30	7 25	11 41	9 14	22 16	5 48	6 22	
𝕾	25 41	13 44	7 52	11 54	9 11	22 15	5 48	6 20	
14	26 42	14 57	8 19	12 6	9 9	22 14	5 48	6 19	
15	27 45	16 11	8 46	12 19	9 7	22 13	5 48	6 17	
16	28 50	17 25	9 12	12 31	9 4	22 12	5 47	6 15	
17	29 ♓ 58	18 38	9 39	12 43	9 1	22 11	5 47	6 14	
18	1 ♈ 9	19 52	10 5	12 56	8 59	22 10	5 47	6 12	
19	2 22	21 5	10 30	13 8	8 56	22 9	5 46	6 10	
𝕾	3 37	22 18	10 56	13 20	8 53	22 8	5 46	6 9	
21	4 54	23 32	11 21	13 32	8 50	22 7	5 45	6 7	
22	6 14	24 45	11 46	13 44	8 47	22 6	5 45	6 5	
23	7 35	25 58	12 11	13 55	8 44	22 4	5 44	6 3	
24	8 59	27 12	12 35	14 7	8 40	22 3	5 44	6 2	
25	10 24	28 25	12 59	14 19	8 37	22 2	5 43	6 0	
26	11 52	29 ♉ 38	13 23	14 30	8 34	22 0	5 43	5 58	
𝕾	13 21	0 ♊ 51	13 46	14 42	8 30	21 59	5 42	5 57	
28	14 52	2 4	14 9	14 53	8 27	21 57	5 42	5 55	
29	16 25	3 17	14 32	15 4	8 23	21 56	5 41	5 53	
30	18 ♈ 0	4 ♊ 31	14 ♑ 54	15 ♓ 16	8 ♐ 20	21 ♐ 54	5 ♑ 40	5 ♏ 52	

Lunar Aspects

D M	☉	☿	♀	♂	♃	♄	♅	♆	♇
1	□			☌	✱	⚺		☌	✱
2		✱			∠	∠	⚺		
3		∠	□	⚺	⚺	✱	∠	⚺	□
4	✱	⚺		∠			✱	∠	
5	∠		✱	✱				✱	△
𝕾	⚺	☌	∠		☌	□			
7							□		⚼
8			⚺	□	⚺	△		□	
9	●	⚺			∠	⚼	△		
10		∠		△			⚼	△	☍
11	⚺		☌		✱			⚼	
12		✱		⚼					
𝕾	∠		⚺		□	☍			
14	✱	□					☍		⚼
15			∠	☍				☍	△
16			✱		△				
17	□	△			⚼	⚼			
18						△	⚼		□
19	△	⚼	□	⚼			△	⚼	
𝕾				△		□		△	✱
21	⚼		△		☍		□		∠
22		☍	⚼			✱		□	⚺
23				□		∠	✱		
24	●●				⚼	⚺	∠	✱	☌
25				✱	△		⚺	∠	
26		⚼	☍	∠		☌		⚺	⚺
𝕾	⚼	△		⚺	□		☌		∠
28	△					⚺		☌	✱
29		□	⚼	☌	✱	∠	⚺		
30			△		∠	✱	∠	⚺	□

D M	Saturn Lat.	Saturn Dec.	Uranus Lat.	Uranus Dec.	Neptune Lat.	Neptune Dec.	Pluto Lat.	Pluto Dec.
	° ′	° ′	° ′	° ′	° ′	° ′	° ′	° ′
1	1 N59	19 S 56	0 S 5	23 S 18	1 N 5	22 S 14	17 N 3	2 N24
3	1 59	19 55	0 5	23 18	1 5	22 14	17 4	2 26
5	2 0	19 54	0 5	23 18	1 5	22 14	17 4	2 27
7	2 0	19 53	0 5	23 18	1 5	22 14	17 4	2 28
9	2 0	19 53	0 5	23 18	1 5	22 14	17 5	2 30
11	2 0	19 52	0 5	23 18	1 6	22 13	17 5	2 31
13	2 0	19 51	0 5	23 18	1 6	22 13	17 5	2 32
15	2 1	19 50	0 5	23 18	1 6	22 13	17 5	2 33
17	2 1	19 49	0 5	23 18	1 6	22 13	17 6	2 34
19	2 1	19 48	0 5	23 17	1 6	22 13	17 6	2 36
21	2 1	19 47	0 5	23 17	1 6	22 13	17 6	2 37
23	2 1	19 46	0 5	23 17	1 6	22 13	17 6	2 38
25	2 1	19 45	0 5	23 17	1 6	22 13	17 6	2 39
27	2 2	19 43	0 5	23 17	1 6	22 13	17 6	2 40
29	2 2	19 42	0 5	23 17	1 6	22 13	17 6	2 41
31	2 N 2	19 S 41	0 S 5	23 S 17	1 N 6	22 S 13	17 N 6	2 N42

Mutual Aspects

2. ☉ **P** ☿. ♃ □ ♄.
5. ♀ △ ♂, ± ♄.
6. ☉ ⊥ ♃. ☿ ∠ ♀.
7. ♀ △ ♆, ☍ ♇. ♆ **Stat.**
8. ☿ ⚼ ♇. ♀ ⚼ ♅.
9. ☿ □ ♅. ♀ ▿ ♄. ♂ ☌ ♆.
10. ♂ ✱ ♇.
11. ☉ **P** ♃. ♀ ✱ ♃.
12. ☉ △ ♅.
14. ☉ ⚼ ♄.
15. ♀ ± ♅.
16. ☿ **P** ♇. ♂ ⚺ ♄.
17. ☿ ± ♇.
18. ☉ ∠ ♃.
19. ♀ ⚼ ♆.
20. ♀ ▿ ♅.
22. ☿ □ ♆, ▿ ♇.
23. ☉ ± ♄. ♀ **Q** ♃.
24. ☿ △ ♄. ♀ ⚼ ♂, **P** ♄.
26. ☉ △ ♆, ☍ ♇. ♀ ± ♆.
27. ☉ ⚼ ♅. ☿ □ ♂, **P** ♇.
28. ☿ ⚺ ♃.
29. ☉ ▿ ♄. ♂ ⊥ ♄.

LAST QUARTER—April 1, 7*h.* 30*m.* *p.m.* (11° ♑ 46′)

NEW MOON—May 8, 10h. 10m. p.m. (18° ♉ 1′)

10			MAY, 1986						[RAPHAEL'S

D M	D W	Sidereal Time	⊙ Long.	⊙ Dec.	☽ Long.	☽ Lat.	☽ Dec.	Node	MIDNIGHT ☽ Long.	☽ Dec.
		H. M. S.	° ′ ″	° ′	° ′ ″	° ′	° ′	° ′	° ′ ″	° ′
1	Th	2 36 29	10 ♉ 49 4	15 N 4	15 ≈ 20 24	5 S 6	21 S 6	29 ♈ 27	22 ≈ 1 52	18 S 48
2	F	2 40 26	11 47 17	15 22	28 38 4	4 38	16 18	29 23	5 ♓ 9 15	13 38
3	S	2 44 22	12 45 29	15 40	11 ♓ 35 46	3 57	10 52	29 20	17 57 57	8 1
4	⊚	2 48 19	13 43 40	15 58	24 16 8	3 5	5 S 7	29 17	0 ♈ 30 41	2 S 11
5	M	2 52 15	14 41 49	16 15	6 ♈ 41 58	2 6	0 N44	29 14	12 50 18	3 N38
6	T	2 56 12	15 39 56	16 32	18 56 0	1 S 1	6 29	29 11	24 59 23	9 15
7	W	3 0 8	16 38 2	16 49	1 ♉ 0 44	0 N 6	11 55	29 7	7 ♉ 0 20	14 28
8	Th	3 4 5	17 36 6	17 5	12 58 27	1 11	16 52	29 4	18 55 20	19 6
9	F	3 8 2	18 34 9	17 21	24 51 14	2 13	21 8	29 1	0 ♊ 46 25	22 57
10	S	3 11 58	19 32 10	17 37	6 ♊ 41 8	3 9	24 32	28 58	12 35 38	25 50
11	⊚	3 15 55	20 30 9	17 53	18 30 14	3 56	26 52	28 55	24 25 12	27 36
12	M	3 19 51	21 28 7	18 8	0 ⊚ 20 52	4 34	28 0	28 52	6 ⊚ 17 36	28 6
13	T	3 23 48	22 26 3	18 23	12 15 45	5 0	27 51	28 48	18 15 44	27 17
14	W	3 27 44	23 23 58	18 38	24 17 57	5 13	26 23	28 45	0 ♌ 22 53	25 11
15	Th	3 31 41	24 21 51	18 52	6 ♌ 30 59	5 12	23 41	28 42	12 42 45	21 53
16	F	3 35 37	25 19 41	19 6	18 58 40	4 57	19 50	28 39	25 19 14	17 32
17	S	3 39 34	26 17 31	19 20	1 ♍ 44 56	4 26	15 0	28 36	8 ♍ 16 13	12 16
18	⊚	3 43 31	27 15 18	19 33	14 53 30	3 42	9 21	28 32	21 37 7	6 N18
19	M	3 47 27	28 13 3	19 46	28 27 19	2 43	3 N 7	28 29	5 ♎ 24 16	0 S 10
20	T	3 51 24	29 ♉ 10 48	19 59	12 ♎ 27 59	1 33	3 S 30	28 26	19 38 18	6 50
21	W	3 55 20	0 ♊ 8 30	20 11	26 54 57	0 N15	10 8	28 23	5 ♏ 17 25	13 21
22	Th	3 59 17	1 6 11	20 23	11 ♏ 44 59	1 S 5	16 24	28 20	19 16 49	19 14
23	F	4 3 13	2 3 50	20 35	26 51 52	2 23	21 47	28 17	4 ♐ 28 57	23 58
24	S	4 7 10	3 1 29	20 46	12 ♐ 6 47	3 31	25 44	28 13	19 44 4	27 2
25	⊚	4 11 6	3 59 6	20 57	27 19 29	4 24	27 49	28 10	4 ♑ 51 50	28 4
26	M	4 15 3	4 56 42	21 7	12 ♑ 19 57	4 58	27 49	28 7	19 42 56	27 3
27	T	4 19 0	5 54 17	21 18	26 59 58	5 11	25 51	28 4	4 ≈ 10 31	24 14
28	W	4 22 56	6 51 51	21 28	11 ≈ 14 12	5 22	21 51	28 1	18 10 51	20 3
29	Th	4 26 53	7 49 25	21 37	25 0 28	4 41	17 35	27 58	1 ♓ 43 14	14 57
30	F	4 30 49	8 46 57	21 46	8 ♓ 19 24	4 2	12 11	27 54	14 49 21	9 20
31	S	4 34 46	9 ♊ 44 28	21 N55	21 ♓ 13 34	3 S 12	6 S 25	27 ♈ 51	27 ♓ 32 33	3 S 29

D M	Mercury		Venus			Mars			Jupiter	
	Lat.	Dec.	Lat.	Dec.		Lat.	Dec.		Lat.	Dec.
	° ′	° ′	° ′	° ′	° ′	° ′	° ′	° ′	° ′	° ′
1	2 S 33	5 N18	0 N42	21 N57	22 N12	1 S 10	23 S 44	23 S 44	0 S 59	6 S 38
3	2 25	6 40	5 N59	0 47	22 27	22 41	1 15	23 44	23 44	0 59	6 30
5	2 15	8 5	7 22	0 52	22 54	23 7	1 21	23 44	23 44	0 59	6 22
7	2 3	9 33	8 49	0 57	23 19	23 30	1 26	23 45	23 45	1 0	6 14
9	1 48	11 2	10 17	1 2	23 41	23 51	1 32	23 46	23 46	1 0	6 7
11	1 32	12 33	11 48	1 7	24 0	24 9	1 38	23 47	23 47	1 1	5 59
13	1 15	14 5	13 19	1 12	24 17	24 27	1 45	23 48	23 47	1 1	5 52
15	0 55	15 36	14 50	1 16	24 31	24 37	1 51	23 50	23 51	1 2	5 45
17	0 35	17 2	16 20	1 21	24 42	24 46	1 58	23 52	23 51	1 2	5 38
19	0 S 14	18 31	17 48	1 25	24 50	24 53	2 4	23 54	23 53	1 3	5 31
21	0 N 7	19 53	19 13	1 29	24 56	24 57	2 12	23 57	23 56	1 3	5 25
23	0 28	21 8	20 31	1 33	24 58	24 57	2 19	24 1	23 59	1 4	5 18
25	0 48	22 16	21 43	1 36	24 58	24 57	2 26	24 3	24 3	1 4	5 12
27	1 6	23 14	22 46	1 40	24 55	24 52	2 34	24 9	24 9	1 4	5 6
29	1 23	24 3	23 40	1 43	24 49	24 45	2 41	24 14	24 11	1 5	5 1
31	1 N37	24 N40	24 N23	1 N46	24 N40	24 N45	2 S 50	24 S 20	24 S 17	1 S 6	4 S 55

FIRST QUARTER—May 17, 1h. 0m. a.m. (25° ♌ 51′)

FULL MOON—May 23, 8*h.* 45*m.* *p.m.* (2° ♐ 25′)

D M	☿ Long.	♀ Long.	♂ Long.	♃ Long.	♄ Long.	♅ Long.	♆ Long.	♇ Long.
	° ′	° ′	° ′	° ′	° ′	° ′	° ′	° ′
1	19 ♈ 37	5 ♊ 44	15 ♑ 16	15 ♓ 27	8 ♐ 16	21 ♐ 52	5 ♑ 39	5 ♏ 50
2	21 16	6 56	15 38	15 38	8 ℞ 12	21 ℞ 51	5 ℞ 39	5 ℞ 48
3	22 57	8 9	15 59	15 49	8 9	21 49	5 38	5 47
S	24 39	9 22	16 20	15 59	8 5	21 47	5 37	5 45
5	26 23	10 35	16 41	16 10	8 1	21 46	5 36	5 43
6	28 9	11 48	17 1	16 21	7 57	21 44	5 35	5 42
7	29 ♈ 57	13 1	17 20	16 31	7 53	21 42	5 35	5 40
8	1 ♉ 47	14 13	17 40	16 42	7 49	21 40	5 34	5 38
9	3 39	15 26	17 58	16 52	7 45	21 38	5 33	5 37
10	5 33	16 39	18 17	17 2	7 41	21 36	5 32	5 35
S	7 28	17 51	18 34	17 12	7 37	21 34	5 31	5 33
12	9 26	19 4	18 52	17 22	7 33	21 32	5 30	5 32
13	11 25	20 16	19 9	17 32	7 28	21 30	5 29	5 30
14	13 26	21 29	19 25	17 41	7 24	21 28	5 28	5 29
15	15 28	22 41	19 41	17 51	7 20	21 26	5 26	5 27
16	17 32	23 54	19 57	18 0	7 16	21 24	5 25	5 25
17	19 38	25 6	20 12	18 10	7 11	21 22	5 24	5 24
S	21 45	26 18	20 26	18 19	7 7	21 20	5 23	5 22
19	23 54	27 30	20 40	18 28	7 3	21 18	5 22	5 21
20	26 3	28 43	20 53	18 37	6 58	21 15	5 21	5 19
21	28 ♉ 14	29 ♊ 55	21 6	18 46	6 54	21 13	5 19	5 18
22	0 ♊ 25	1 ♋ 7	21 18	18 55	6 49	21 11	5 18	5 16
23	2 37	2 19	21 30	19 3	6 45	21 9	5 17	5 15
24	4 48	3 31	21 41	19 12	6 40	21 6	5 16	5 13
S	7 0	4 43	21 51	19 20	6 36	21 4	5 14	5 12
26	9 11	5 54	22 1	19 28	6 32	21 2	5 13	5 10
27	11 22	7 6	22 10	19 36	6 27	20 59	5 12	5 9
28	13 32	8 18	22 19	19 44	6 23	20 57	5 10	5 8
29	15 40	9 30	22 27	19 52	6 18	20 55	5 9	5 6
30	17 47	10 41	22 34	20 0	6 14	20 52	5 7	5 5
31	19 ♊ 53	11 ♋ 53	22 ♑ 40	20 ♓ 7	6 ♐ 9	20 ♐ 50	5 ♑ 6	5 ♏ 4

Lunar Aspects

D M	☉	☿	♀	♂	♃	♄	♅	♆	♇
1	□	✱		⊻	⊻		✱	∠	
2				∠					
3	✱	∠	□	✱	☌	□		✱	△
S	∠	⊻					□		⚼
5			✱			△		□	
6	⊻			□	⊻	⚼	△		
7		☌	∠		∠		⚼	△	☍
8	☌		⊻	△	✱				
9								⚼	
10		⊻		⚼		☍			
S	⊻	∠	☌		□		☍		⚼
12								☍	△
13	∠	✱			△				
14	✱		⊻	☍		⚼			
15			∠		⚼	△	⚼		□
16		□	✱				△	⚼	
17	□			⚼		□		△	✱
S				△	☍		□		∠
19	△	△	□					□	⊻
20	⚼	⚼				✱			
21			△	□	⚼	∠	✱		
22			⚼		△	⊻	∠	✱	☌
23	☍	☍		✱			⊻	∠	
24				∠	□	☌		⊻	⊻
S				⊻			☌		∠
26			☍		✱	⊻		☌	✱
27	⚼	⚼		☌		∠	⊻		
28	△	△			∠	✱	∠	⊻	□
29			⚼	⊻	⊻		✱	∠	
30	□		△	∠		□		✱	△
31		□		✱	☌		□		⚼

D M	Saturn Lat.	Saturn Dec.	Uranus Lat.	Uranus Dec.	Neptune Lat.	Neptune Dec.	Pluto Lat.	Pluto Dec.
	° ′	° ′	° ′	° ′	° ′	° ′	° ′	° ′
1	2 N 2	19 S 41	0 S 5	23 S 17	1 N 6	22 S 13	17 N 6	2 N 42
3	2 2	19 40	0 5	23 16	1 6	22 13	17 5	2 43
5	2 2	19 39	0 5	23 16	1 6	22 13	17 5	2 43
7	2 2	19 37	0 5	23 16	1 6	22 13	17 5	2 44
9	2 2	19 36	0 5	23 16	1 6	22 13	17 5	2 45
11	2 2	19 35	0 5	23 16	1 6	22 14	17 4	2 46
13	2 2	19 33	0 5	23 15	1 6	22 14	17 4	2 46
15	2 2	19 32	0 5	23 15	1 6	22 14	17 3	2 47
17	2 2	19 30	0 5	23 15	1 6	22 14	17 3	2 47
19	2 2	19 29	0 5	23 15	1 6	22 14	17 3	2 48
21	2 2	19 28	0 5	23 14	1 6	22 14	17 2	2 48
23	2 2	19 26	0 5	23 14	1 6	22 14	17 1	2 49
25	2 2	19 25	0 5	23 14	1 6	22 14	17 1	2 49
27	2 2	19 23	0 5	23 13	1 6	22 14	17 0	2 49
29	2 2	19 22	0 5	23 13	1 7	22 14	16 59	2 50
31	2 N 1	19 S 21	0 S 5	23 S 13	1 N 7	22 S 14	16 N 59	2 N 50

Mutual Aspects

1. ♀ ⊼ ♆, ⊼ ♇.
2. ☿ ⊥ ♃, △ ♅. ♀ **P** ♆. ♂ ✱ ♃.
3. ☿ ∠ ♀, **P** ♃, ⚼ ♄. ♀ ☍ ♄.
5. ♀ ± ♂. 6. ☉ ± ♅. ♀ ± ♇.
7. ♀ **P** ♅, ☉ ✱ ♃.
8. ☉ △ ♂. ☿ ∠ ♃, ± ♄. ♂ **Q** ♇.
9. ♀ **P** ♂.
10. ☿ △ ♆, ☍ ♇. ♀ □ ♃.
11. ☉ ⚼ ♆. ☿ ⊼ ♄, ⚼ ♅.
12. ☉ ⊼ ♅. ♀ ⊼ ♂.
13. ♀ ⚼ ♇. ♃ **Q** ♆. 14. ♀ ☍ ♅.
15. ☿ ± ♅. 16. ☿ ⊥ ♀, ✱ ♃. ♆ ✱ ♇.
17. ☿ △ ♂, ⚼ ♆.
18. ☉ **P** ♄. ☿ ⊼ ♅.
20. ☉ ± ♆. ☿ **P** ♄.
21. ☿ ± ♆. ♂ ⊻ ♅.
22. ☉ **P** ☿, ⊻ ♀, **Q** ♃. ☿ **Q** ♃.
23. ☉ ☌ ☿, ☿ ⊻ ♀.
24. ☿ ⊼ ♆, ⊼ ♇. ♂ ∠ ♄.
25. ☿ ⚼ ♂, ☍ ♄, **P** ♆.
♀ ☍ ♆, △ ♇.
26. ☉ ⊼ ♆, ⊼ ♇. ♀ ⊼ ♄.
27. ☿ **P** ♅, ± ♇. 28. ☉ ☍ ♄.
29. ☉ ⚼ ♂. ☿ ± ♂. 30. ☿ **P** ♂.
31. ☿ **P** ♀, □ ♃, ☍ ♅, ⚼ ♇.
♀ ± ♄. ♃ ⚼ ♇.

LAST QUARTER—May 1, 3*h.* 22*m.* *a.m.* (10° ♒ 28′) and May 30, 0*h.* 55*m.* *p.m.* (8° ♓ 49′)

NEW MOON—June 7, 2h. 0m. p.m. (16° ♊ 32′)

12					JUNE, 1986					[RAPHAEL'S	

D M	D W	Sidereal Time	☉ Long.	☉ Dec.	☽ Long.	☽ Lat.	☽ Dec.	Node	MIDNIGHT ☽ Long.	☽ Dec.
		H. M. S.	° ′ ″	° ′	° ′ ″	° ′	° ′	° ′	° ′ ″	° ′
1	♋	4 38 42	10♊41 59	22 N 3	3♈46 49	2 S 14	0 S 33	27♈48	9♈56 55	2 N21
2	M	4 42 39	11 39 29	22 11	16 3 25	1 12	5 N13	27 45	22 6 49	8 0
3	T	4 46 35	12 36 58	22 19	28 7 39	0 S 7	10 42	27 42	4 ♉ 6 24	13 18
4	W	4 50 32	13 34 26	22 26	10 ♉ 3 30	0 N58	15 45	27 38	15 59 22	18 3
5	TH	4 54 29	14 31 54	22 33	21 54 23	1 59	20 10	27 35	27 48 53	22 4
6	F	4 58 25	15 29 21	22 39	3♊43 11	2 55	23 45	27 32	9♊37 33	25 11
7	S	5 2 22	16 26 47	22 45	15 32 14	3 43	26 21	27 29	21 27 28	27 13
8	♋	5 6 18	17 24 12	22 51	27 23 28	4 22	27 47	27 26	3♋20 27	28 1
9	M	5 10 15	18 21 36	22 56	9♋18 38	4 49	27 55	27 23	15 18 12	27 30
10	T	5 14 11	19 18 59	23 1	21 19 23	5 4	26 45	27 19	27 22 26	25 41
11	W	5 18 8	20 16 22	23 5	3♌27 37	5 5	24 19	27 16	9♌35 13	22 41
12	TH	5 22 4	21 13 43	23 9	15 45 33	4 52	20 46	27 13	21 58 57	18 36
13	F	5 26 1	22 11 4	23 13	28 15 49	4 26	16 14	27 10	4♍36 31	13 39
14	S	5 29 58	23 8 23	23 16	11♍ 1 28	3 46	10 54	27 7	17 31 6	8 1
15	♋	5 33 54	24 5 42	23 19	24 5 48	2 53	4 N59	27 4	0♎45 58	1 N52
16	M	5 37 51	25 3 0	23 21	7♎31 57	1 49	1 S 19	27 0	14 24 0	4 S 33
17	T	5 41 47	26 0 16	23 21	22 22 20	0 N37	7 46	26 57	28 27 1	10 56
18	W	5 45 44	26 57 32	23 24	5♏37 58	0 S 39	14 1	26 54	12♏54 57	16 57
19	TH	5 49 40	27 54 48	23 26	20 37 33	1 55	19 40	26 51	27 45 7	22 6
20	F	5 53 37	28 52 2	23 26	5 ♐16 50	3 4	24 12	26 48	12 ♐51 40	25 53
21	S	5 57 33	29♊49 16	23 27	20 28 27	4 1	27 7	26 44	28 5 53	27 49
22	♋	6 1 30	0♋46 30	23 26	5♑42 37	4 41	28 0	26 41	13♑17 17	27 39
23	M	6 5 27	1 43 43	23 26	20 48 35	5 1	26 48	26 38	28 15 21	25 28
24	T	6 9 23	2 40 56	23 25	5♒36 33	5 1	23 43	26 35	12♒51 23	21 38
25	W	6 13 .20	3 38 9	23 24	19 59 16	4 41	19 15	26 32	26 59 49	16 39
26	TH	6 17 16	4 35 21	23 22	3♓52 54	4 5	13 53	26 29	10♓38 32	11 0
27	F	6 21 13	5 32 34	23 20	17 16 56	3 16	8 2	26 25	23 48 27	5 S 2
28	S	6 25 9	6 29 46	23 17	0♈13 32	2 19	2 S 2	26 22	6♈32 44	0 N56
29	♋	6 29 6	7 26 59	23 14	12 46 38	1 17	3 N52	26 19	18 55 53	6 44
30	M	6 33 2	8♋24 11	23 N11	25♈ 1 8	0 S 12	9 N30	26♈16	1 ♉ 3 1	12 N 9

D M	Mercury		Venus		Mars		Jupiter	
	Lat.	Dec.	Lat.	Dec.	Lat.	Dec.	Lat.	Dec.
	° ′	° ′ ° ′	° ′	° ′ ° ′	° ′	° ′ ° ′	° ′	° ′
1	1 N43	24 N55 25 N 7	1 N47	24 N34 24 N28	2 S 54	24 S 23 24 S 26	1 S 6	4 S 52
3	1 53	25 16 25 23	1 49	24 21 24 14	3 2	24 29 24 33	1 6	4 47
5	2 0	25 27 25 29	1 51	24 6 23 57	3 11	24 37 24 40	1 7	4 42
7	2 4	25 28 25 25	1 53	23 47 23 37	3 19	24 44 24 48	1 7	4 38
9	2 5	25 20 25 13	1 55	23 26 23 15	3 28	24 53 24 57	1 8	4 33
11	2 3	25 5 24 54	1 56	23 3 22 50	3 37	25 2 25 7	1 8	4 29
13	1 58	24 42 24 28	1 57	22 37 22 23	3 46	25 12 25 17	1 9	4 25
15	1 50	24 13 23 57	1 57	22 8 21 52	3 55	25 22 25 27	1 10	4 22
17	1 39	23 40 23 21	1 57	21 37 21 21	4 4	25 32 25 38	1 10	4 19
19	1 26	23 2 22 42	1 57	21 4 20 47	4 12	25 44 25 49	1 11	4 16
21	1 10	22 21 21 59	1 57	20 29 20 10	4 22	25 55 26 1	1 11	4 13
23	0 52	21 37 21 15	1 56	19 52 19 32	4 30	26 7 26 13	1 12	4 10
25	0 31	20 52 20 30	1 54	19 12 18 52	4 38	26 19 26 25	1 13	4 8
27	0 N 8	20 7 19 44	1 53	18 31 18 10	4 47	26 31 26 37	1 13	4 6
29	0 S 17	19 21 18 N59	1 51	17 48 17 N26	4 55	26 43 26 S 49	1 14	4 5
31	0 S 44	18 N36	1 N48	17 N 3	5 S 2	26 S 55	1 S 14	4 S 3

FIRST QUARTER—June 15, 0h. 0m. n.n. (24° ♍ 6′)

Full Moon—June 22, 3*h*. 42*m*. *a.m.* (0° ♑ 27′)

D M	☿ Long. ° ′	♀ Long. ° ′	♂ Long. ° ′	♃ Long. ° ′	♄ Long. ° ′	♅ Long. ° ′	♆ Long. ° ′	♇ Long. ° ′	☉	☿	♀	♂	♃	♄	♅	♆	♇
									Lunar Aspects								
𝕾	21 ♊ 56	13 ♋ 4	22 ♑ 46	20 ♓ 14	6 ♐ 5	20 ♐ 48	5 ♑ 5	5 ♏ 2						△		□	
2	23 58	14 16	22 51	20 22	6 ℞ 0	20 ℞ 45	5 ℞ 3	5 ℞ 1	⚹		□		⊻	⚼	△		
3	25 58	15 27	22 56	20 29	5 56	20 43	5 2	5 0	∠	⚹		□					
4	27 55	16 39	22 59	20 36	5 52	20 40	5 0	4 59	⊻	∠			∠		⚼	△	☍
5	29 ♊ 50	17 50	23 2	20 42	5 47	20 38	4 59	4 57			⚹	△	⚹			⚼	
6	1 ♋ 43	19 1	23 4	20 49	5 43	20 35	4 57	4 56		⊻	∠	⚼		☍			
7	3 33	20 13	23 6	20 55	5 38	20 33	4 56	4 55	☌		⊻		□		☍		⚼
𝕾	5 20	21 24	23 7	21 2	5 34	20 30	4 54	4 54									
9	7 6	22 35	23 ℞ 7	21 8	5 30	20 28	4 53	4 53		☌						☍	△
10	8 48	23 46	23 6	21 14	5 25	20 26	4 51	4 52	⊻		☌	☍	△	⚼			
11	10 28	24 57	23 4	21 19	5 21	20 23	4 50	4 51	∠				⚼	△	⚼		□
12	12 5	26 8	23 2	21 25	5 17	20 21	4 48	4 50	⚹	⊻					△	⚼	
13	13 40	27 18	22 59	21 31	5 13	20 18	4 47	4 49		∠	⊻						
14	15 12	28 29	22 55	21 36	5 9	20 16	4 45	4 48		⚹	∠	⚼		□		△	⚹
𝕾	16 41	29 ♋ 40	22 51	21 41	5 5	20 13	4 43	4 47	□		⚹	△	☍		□		∠
16	18 8	0 ♌ 50	22 45	21 46	5 1	20 11	4 42	4 46						⚹		□	⊻
17	19 32	2 1	22 39	21 51	4 57	20 8	4 40	4 45	△	□		□		∠	⚹		
18	20 53	3 11	22 33	21 55	4 53	20 6	4 39	4 44	⚼		□		⚼	⊻	∠	⚹	☌
19	22 11	4 22	22 25	22 0	4 49	20 3	4 37	4 43		△		⚹	△		⊻	∠	
20	23 26	5 32	22 17	22 4	4 45	20 1	4 35	4 42		⚼	△	∠		☌		⊻	⊻
21	24 39	6 42	22 8	22 8	4 41	19 59	4 34	4 42			⚼	⊻	□		☌		∠
𝕾	25 48	7 52	21 59	22 12	4 37	19 56	4 32	4 41	☍					⊻		☌	⚹
23	26 55	9 2	21 49	22 16	4 33	19 54	4 31	4 40		☍		●	⚹	∠	⊻		
24	27 58	10 12	21 38	22 19	4 30	19 51	4 29	4 39			☍		∠	⚹	∠	⊻	□
25	28 58	11 22	21 26	22 23	4 26	19 49	4 27	4 39	⚼			⊻	⊻		⚹	∠	
26	29 ♋ 55	12 32	21 14	22 26	4 23	19 47	4 26	4 38	△			∠		□		⚹	△
27	0 ♌ 48	13 42	21 2	22 29	4 19	19 44	4 24	4 37		⚼		⚹	☌		□		⚼
28	1 38	14 51	20 48	22 32	4 16	19 42	4 22	4 37		△	⚼			△		□	
𝕾	2 25	16 1	20 35	22 34	4 12	19 40	4 21	4 36	□		△						
30	3 ♌ 7	17 ♌ 10	20 ♑ 20	22 ♓ 37	4 ♐ 9	19 ♐ 37	4 ♑ 19	4 ♏ 36				□	⊻	⚼	△		

D M	Saturn Lat. ° ′	Saturn Dec. ° ′	Uranus Lat. ° ′	Uranus Dec. ° ′	Neptune Lat. ° ′	Neptune Dec. ° ′	Pluto Lat. ° ′	Pluto Dec. ° ′
1	2 N 1	19 S 20	0 S 5	23 S 13	1 N 7	22 S 14	16 N 58	2 N 50
3	2 1	19 19	0 5	23 12	1 7	22 14	16 58	2 50
5	2 1	19 17	0 5	23 12	1 7	22 14	16 57	2 50
7	2 1	19 16	0 5	23 12	1 7	22 15	16 56	2 50
9	2 1	19 15	0 5	23 11	1 7	22 15	16 55	2 50
11	2 0	19 13	0 5	23 11	1 7	22 15	16 54	2 50
13	2 0	19 12	0 5	23 11	1 7	22 15	16 53	2 49
15	2 0	19 11	0 5	23 10	1 7	22 15	16 53	2 49
17	2 0	19 10	0 6	23 10	1 7	22 15	16 52	2 49
19	1 59	19 9	0 6	23 10	1 7	22 15	16 51	2 48
21	1 59	19 8	0 6	23 9	1 7	22 15	16 50	2 48
23	1 59	19 6	0 6	23 9	1 7	22 15	16 49	2 48
25	1 58	19 5	0 6	23 9	1 7	22 16	16 48	2 47
27	1 58	19 4	0 6	23 8	1 7	22 16	16 47	2 46
29	1 58	19 4	0 6	23 8	1 6	22 16	16 45	2 46
31	1 N 57	19 S 3	0 S 6	23 S 8	1 N 6	22 S 16	16 N 44	2 N 45

Mutual Aspects

1. ☉ ± ♇. ☿ ▽ ♂.
2. ☉ **P** ♆. ♀ **P** ♂.
5. ♃ □ ♅.
7. ♀ ⚼ ♄, ▽ ♅.
8. ☉ ± ♂. ☿ ▽ ♄, ☍ ♆, △ ♇. ♀ △ ♃. ♂ **Stat.**
9. ♀ ☍ ♂. ♆ ⚹ ♇.
10. ♀ **P** ♅.
11. ☉ **P** ♀, ☍ ♅, ⚼ ♇. ☿ **P** ♂.
12. ☉ □ ♃, **P** ♅. ☿ ± ♄. ♀ ± ♅.
14. ☉ ▽ ♂.
15. ♀ **P** ♆.
17. ☉ ⊥ ♀. ☿ ⚼ ♄, ▽ ♅.
18. ☉ **P** ☿.
19. ☿ ☍ ♂, △ ♃, **P** ♅. ♀ △ ♄, ▽ ♆, □ ♇.
20. ♀ ⚼ ♅.
21. ☿ **P** ♆. ♀ ⚼ ♃. ♂ ⚹ ♃. ♄ ⊻ ♇.
22. ☿ ± ♅.
24. ♀ ± ♆. ♄ ⊻ ♆.
25. ♀ **P** ♄.
26. ☉ ▽ ♄, ☍ ♆, △ ♇.
30. ♀ ± ♃, **P** ♄.

Last Quarter—June 29, 0*h*. 53*m*. *a.m.* (7° ♈ 0′)

| 14 | | | | | | JULY, 1986 | | | | | | [RAPHAEL'S |

D M	D W	Sidereal Time	☉ Long.	☉ Dec.	☽ Long.	☽ Lat.	☽ Dec.	Node	MIDNIGHT	
									☽ Long.	☽ Dec.
		H. M. S.	° ′ ″	° ′	° ′ ″	° ′	° ′	° ′	° ′ ″	° ′
1	T	6 36 59	9♋21 24	23 N 7	7 ♉ 2 11	0 N51	14 N40	26 ♈13	12 ♉ 59 14	17 N 3
2	W	6 40 56	10 18 37	23 3	18 54 45	1 52	19 14	26 10	24 49 17	21 15
3	TH	6 44 52	11 15 50	22 58	0 ♊43 20	2 47	23 2	26 6	6 ♊37 20	24 34
4	F	6 48 49	12 13 4	22 53	12 31 42	3 35	25 51	26 3	18 26 46	26 51
5	S	6 52 45	13 10 17	22 47	24 22 52	4 14	27 33	26 0	0♋20 15	27 56
6	⊕	6 56 42	14 7 31	22 42	6♋19 74	4 42	27 59	25 57	12 19 41	27 42
7	M	7 0 38	15 4 44	22 35	18 22 54	4 57	27 5	25 54	24 26 26	26 9
8	T	7 4 35	16 1 58	22 29	0 ♌32 53	4 59	24 54	25 50	6 ♌41 31	23 22
9	W	7 8 31	16 59 12	22 22	12 52 27	4 48	21 33	25 47	19 5 48	19 29
10	TH	7 12 28	17 56 25	22 14	25 21 44	4 22	17 11	25 44	1 ♍40 23	14 41
11	F	7 16 25	18 53 39	22 7	8♍ 1 58	3 43	12 1	25 41	14 26 42	9 11
12	S	7 20 21	19 50 53	21 59	20 54 49	2 53	6 15	25 38	27 26 35	3 N12
13	⊕	7 24 18	20 48 6	21 50	4♎ 2 19	1 52	0 N 6	25 35	10♎42 18	3 S 2
14	M	7 28 14	21 45 20	21 41	17 26 49	0 N43	6 S 11	25 31	24 16 8	9 18
15	T	7 32 11	22 42 33	21 32	1 ♏10 28	0 S 29	12 20	25 28	8 ♏ 9 57	15 16
16	W	7 36 7	23 39 47	22 15	14 37 1	1 41	18 2	25 25	22 24 25	20 34
17	TH	7 40 4	24 37 1	21 12	29 39 6	2 49	22 50	25 22	6 ♐58 19	24 45
18	F	7 44 0	25 34 15	21 2	14 ♐21 28	3 47	26 17	25 19	21 47 50	27 21
19	S	7 47 57	26 31 29	20 51	29 16 30	4 30	27 56	25 16	6 ♑46 26	28 1
20	⊕	7 51 54	27 28 44	20 40	14♑16 30	4 55	27 34	25 12	21 45 28	26 37
21	M	7 55 50	28 25 59	20 29	29 12 10	4 59	25 12	25 9	6♒35 26	23 22
22	T	7 59 47	29♋23 14	20 17	13♒54 14	4 44	21 11	25 6	21 7 40	18 43
23	W	8 3 43	0 ♌20 30	20 5	28 15 1	4 11	16 0	25 3	5 ♓15 45	13 8
24	TH	8 7 40	1 17 47	19 52	12 ♓ 9 34	3 24	10 8	25 0	18 56 20	7 5
25	F	8 11 36	2 15 5	19 40	25 36 6	2 26	3 S 59	24 56	2 ♈ 9 4	0 S 54
26	S	8 15 33	3 12 23	19 27	8 ♈35 36	1 23	2 N 8	24 53	14 56 7	5 N 7
27	⊕	8 19 29	4 9 42	19 13	21 11 12	0 S 17	8 0	24 50	27 21 25	10 46
28	M	8 23 26	5 7 3	18 59	3 ♉27 25	0 N47	13 25	24 47	9 ♉29 52	15 54
29	T	8 27 23	6 4 24	18 45	15 29 27	1 49	18 13	24 44	21 26 50	20 21
30	W	8 31 19	7 1 46	18 31	27 22 39	2 45	22 15	24 41	3 ♊17 33	23 56
31	TH	8 35 16	7♌59 10	18 N16	9 ♊11 2	3 N33	25 N21	24 ♈37	15 ♊ 6 55	26 N30

D M	Mercury			Venus			Mars			Jupiter	
	Lat.	Dec.		Lat.	Dec.		Lat.	Dec.		Lat.	Dec.
	° ′	° ′	° ′	° ′	° ′	° ′	° ′	° ′	° ′	° ′	° ′
1	0 S 44	18 N36	18 N15	1 N48	17 N 3	16 N40	5 S 2	26 S 55	27 S 1	1 S 14	4 S 3
3	1 12	17 53	17 33	1 45	16 17	15 53	5 10	27 7	27 13	1 15	4 2
5	1 41	17 13	16 54	1 42	15 29	15 5	5 16	27 19	27 24	1 16	4 1
7	2 16	16 36	16 19	1 38	14 39	14 14	5 23	27 30	27 35	1 16	4 1
9	2 41	16 4	15 50	1 34	13 49	13 23	5 29	27 40	27 45	1 17	4 1
11	3 11	15 37	15 25	1 30	12 57	12 30	5 34	27 50	27 55	1 17	4 1
13	3 39	15 16	15 8	1 25	12 3	11 37	5 39	28 0	28 4	1 18	4 2
15	4 4	15 1	14 57	1 19	11 9	10 42	5 43	28 8	28 12	1 19	4 3
17	4 26	14 54	14 53	1 14	10 14	9 46	5 46	28 16	28 19	1 19	4 4
19	4 43	14 54	14 56	1 7	9 18	8 50	5 49	28 22	28 25	1 20	4 5
21	4 54	15 1	15 7	1 1	8 21	7 53	5 51	28 28	28 30	1 20	4 7
23	4 58	15 14	15 23	0 54	7 24	6 55	5 52	28 33	28 35	1 21	4 9
25	4 55	15 33	15 45	0 47	6 26	5 57	5 53	28 37	28 38	1 22	4 11
27	4 46	15 57	16 10	0 39	5 27	4 58	5 54	28 40	28 41	1 22	4 14
29	4 30	16 24	16 N38	0 31	4 28	3 N59	5 53	28 42	28 S 42	1 23	4 17
31	4 S 9	16 N52		0 N22	3 N29		5 S 52	28 S 43		1 S 23	4 S 20

FULL MOON—July 21, 10*h*. 40*m*. *a.m.* (28° ♑ 23′)

D M	☿ Long.	♀ Long.	♂ Long.	♃ Long.	♄ Long.	♅ Long.	♆ Long.	♇ Long.	☉	☿	♀	♂	♃	♄	♅	♆	♇
	° ′	° ′	° ′	° ′	° ′	° ′	° ′	° ′	Lunar Aspects								
1	3 ♌ 46	18 ♌ 20	20 ♑ 5	22 ♓ 39	4 ♐ 6	19 ♐ 35	4 ♑ 18	4 ♏ 35	✶	□			∠		⚼	△	☍
2	4 21	19 29	19 ℞ 50	22 41	4 ℞ 3	19 ℞ 33	4 ℞ 16	4 ℞ 35			□	△	✶			⚼	
3	4 52	20 38	19 34	22 43	3 59	19 31	4 14	4 35	∠	✶		⚼		☍			
4	5 19	21 47	19 18	22 45	3 56	19 28	4 13	4 34	⚺								
5	5 41	22 56	19 2	22 46	3 53	19 26	4 11	4 34		∠	✶		□		☍		⚼
S	5 59	24 5	18 45	22 48	3 51	19 24	4 10	4 33		⚺	∠					☍	△
7	6 12	25 14	18 28	22 49	3 48	19 22	4 8	4 33	☌			☍	△	⚼			
8	6 21	26 22	18 11	22 50	3 45	19 20	4 6	4 33		☌	⚺			△	⚼		□
9	6 25	27 31	17 54	22 50	3 42	19 18	4 5	4 33	⚺				⚼			⚼	
10	6 ℞ 24	28 39	17 36	22 51	3 40	19 16	4 3	4 33			☌				△		
11	6 19	29 ♌ 48	17 19	22 51	3 37	19 14	4 2	4 32	∠	⚺		⚼		□		△	✶
12	6 9	0 ♍ 56	17 1	22 51	3 35	19 12	4 0	4 32	✶	∠		△	☍		□		∠
S	5 54	2 4	16 44	22 ℞ 51	3 33	19 10	3 59	4 32		✶	⚺			✶		□	⚺
14	5 35	3 12	16 26	22 51	3 30	19 8	3 57	4 32	□		∠	□		∠	✶		
15	5 11	4 20	16 9	22 51	3 28	19 6	3 56	4 D 32		□	✶		⚼	⚺	∠	✶	☌
16	4 44	5 27	15 52	22 50	3 26	19 4	3 54	4 32				✶			⚺	∠	
17	4 13	6 35	15 35	22 49	3 24	19 2	3 53	4 32	△	△		∠	△	☌		⚺	⚺
18	3 38	7 42	15 18	22 48	3 22	19 0	3 51	4 32	⚼	⚼	□	⚺			☌		∠
19	3 1	8 50	15 2	22 47	3 21	18 58	3 50	4 32					□	⚺		☌	✶
S	2 22	9 57	14 46	22 46	3 19	18 57	3 48	4 33			△	●		∠	⚺		
21	1 41	11 4	14 30	22 44	3 17	18 55	3 47	4 33	☍	☍	⚼		✶	✶	∠	⚺	□
22	0 59	12 10	14 15	22 42	3 16	18 53	3 45	4 33				⚺	∠		✶	∠	
23	0 ♌ 17	13 17	14 1	22 40	3 14	18 52	3 44	4 33				∠	⚺	□		✶	△
24	29 ♋ 36	14 24	13 46	22 38	3 13	18 50	3 43	4 34	⚼	⚼	☍	✶			□		
25	28 56	15 30	13 33	22 36	3 12	18 48	3 41	4 34		△			☌				⚼
26	28 18	16 36	13 19	22 33	3 10	18 47	3 40	4 34	△			□		△		□	
S	27 43	17 42	13 7	22 30	3 9	18 45	3 38	4 35					⚺	⚼	△		
28	27 11	18 48	12 55	22 27	3 8	18 44	3 37	4 35	□	□	⚼		∠		⚼	△	☍
29	26 44	19 54	12 44	22 24	3 7	18 43	3 36	4 36			△	△				⚼	
30	26 21	20 59	12 33	22 21	3 7	18 41	3 35	4 36		✶		⚼	✶	☍			
31	26 ♋ 3	22 ♍ 5	12 ♑ 23	22 ♓ 17	3 ♐ 6	18 ♐ 40	3 ♑ 33	4 ♏ 37	✶	∠							

D M	Saturn Lat.	Saturn Dec.	Uranus Lat.	Uranus Dec.	Neptune Lat.	Neptune Dec.	Pluto Lat.	Pluto Dec.
	° ′	° ′	° ′	° ′	° ′	° ′	° ′	° ′
1	1 N57	19 S 3	0 S 6	23 S 8	1 N 6	22 S 16	16 N44	2 N45
3	1 57	19 2	0 6	23 7	1 6	22 16	16 43	2 44
5	1 57	19 1	0 6	23 7	1 6	22 16	16 42	2 43
7	1 56	19 1	0 6	23 7	1 6	22 16	16 41	2 42
9	1 56	19 0	0 6	23 6	1 6	22 17	16 40	2 42
11	1 56	18 59	0 6	23 6	1 6	22 17	16 39	2 41
13	1 55	18 59	0 6	23 6	1 6	22 17	16 38	2 40
15	1 55	18 59	0 6	23 5	1 6	22 17	16 36	2 38
17	1 54	18 58	0 6	23 5	1 6	22 17	16 35	2 37
19	1 54	18 58	0 6	23 5	1 6	22 17	16 34	2 36
21	1 53	18 58	0 6	23 5	1 6	22 17	16 33	2 35
23	1 53	18 58	0 6	23 4	1 6	22 17	16 32	2 34
25	1 52	18 58	0 6	23 4	1 6	22 18	16 31	2 32
27	1 52	18 58	0 6	23 4	1 6	22 18	16 29	2 31
29	1 52	18 58	0 6	23 4	1 6	22 18	16 28	2 30
31	1 N51	18 S 58	0 S 6	23 S 3	1 N 6	22 S 18	16 N27	2 N28

Mutual Aspects

1. ☉ **P** ♅. ☿ △ ♄. ♅ ∠ ♇.
2. ☉ ± ♄. ☿ ⚼ ♅, ⚻ ♆, □ ♇. ♀ ⚻ ♂, △ ♅, ⚼ ♆.
3. ♂ ⚺ ♅.
5. ♀ ⚻ ♃, **Q** ♇.
6. ♀ ± ♂. ♂ ∠ ♄.
9. ☿ **Stat.**
10. ☉ ☍ ♂, **P** ♆.
11. ☉ ⚼ ♄, ⚻ ♅.
12. ♃ **Stat.**
13. ♀ ⚼ ♂.
14. ♀ □ ♄. ♂ **Q** ♇.
15. ☉ △ ♃. ♀ △ ♆, ✶ ♇. ♇ **Stat.**
16. ☿ ⚺ ♀, □ ♇.
17. ☉ ± ♅. ☿ ⚼ ♅.
18. ☿ △ ♄, ⚻ ♆.
19. ☿ ⊥ ♀.
23. ☉ ☌ ☿.
24. ☿ ∠ ♀. ♀ △ ♂.
26. ☉ △ ♄, ⚻ ♆.
27. ☉ ⚼ ♅, □ ♇.
28. ☉ **P** ♄. ♀ □ ♅.
29. ♀ **P** ♃, ∠ ♇.
30. ☉ ⚼ ♃. ♀ **Q** ♄.
31. ♀ ☍ ♃.

LAST QUARTER—July 28, 3*h*. 34*m*. *p.m.* (5° ♉ 16′)

16							AUGUST, 1986			[RAPHAEL'S

									MIDNIGHT	
D M	D W	Sidereal Time	☉ Long.	☉ Dec.	☽ Long.	☽ Lat.	☽ Dec.	☽ Node	☽ Long.	☽ Dec.
		H. M. S.	° ' "	° '	° ' "	° '	° '	° '	° ' "	° '
1	F	8 39 12	8♌56 35	18 N 2	21♊ 2 26	4 N13	27 N21	24♈34	26♊59 9	27 N53
2	S	8 43 9	9 54 0	17 46	2♋57 26	4 41	28 6	24 31	8♋57 40	27 59
3	♋	8 47 5	10 51 27	17 31	15 0 7	4 58	27 32	24 28	21 5 1	26 44
4	M	8 51 2	11 48 55	17 15	27 12 32	5 1	25 38	24 25	3♌22 48	24 13
5	T	8 54 58	12 46 24	16 59	9♌35 54	4 50	22 30	24 21	15 51 53	20 31
6	W	8 58 55	13 43 53	16 42	22 10 44	4 24	18 17	24 18	28 32 27	15 50
7	Th	9 2 52	14 41 24	16 26	4♍57 2	3 46	13 12	24 15	11♍24 27	10 24
8	F	9 6 48	15 38 56	16 9	17 54 42	2 55	7 28	24 12	24 27 46	4 N25
9	S	9 10 45	16 36 28	15 52	1♎ 3 41	1 54	1 N19	24 9	7♎42 30	1 S 50
10	♋	9 14 41	17 34 1	15 34	14 24 18	0 N45	4 S 59	24 6	21 9 9	8 6
11	M	9 18 38	18 31 36	15 17	27 57 10	0 S 37	11 10	24 2	4♏48 27	14 7
12	T	9 22 34	19 29 11	14 59	11♏43 4	1 38	16 55	23 59	18 41 6	19 31
13	W	9 26 31	20 26 47	14 41	25 42 33	2 45	21 52	23 56	2♐47 21	23 55
14	Th	9 30 27	21 24 24	14 22	9♐55 21	3 43	25 37	23 53	17 6 20	26 55
15	F	9 34 24	22 22 2	14 4	24 19 54	4 28	27 47	23 50	1♑35 34	28 10
16	S	9 38 21	23 19 41	13 45	8♑52 47	4 56	28 4	23 47	16 10 48	27 24
17	♋	9 42 17	24 17 21	13 26	23 28 51	5 4	26 24	23 43	0≈46 5	24 53
18	M	9 46 14	25 15 2	13 6	8≈ 1 36	4 53	22 59	23 40	15 14 33	20 44
19	T	9 50 10	26 12 44	12 47	22 24 5	4 24	18 12	23 37	29 29 28	15 27
20	W	9 54 7	27 10 28	12 27	6♓30 3	3 39	12 31	23 34	13♓25 20	9 28
21	Th	9 58 3	28 8 13	12 7	20 14 55	2 42	6 21	23 31	26 58 36	3 S 12
22	F	10 2 0	29♌ 5 59	11 47	3♈36 18	1 37	0 S 3	23 27	10♈ 8 4	3 N 2
23	S	10 5 56	0♍ 3 47	11 27	16 34 50	0 S 29	6 N 4	23 24	22 54 39	8 59
24	♋	10 9 53	1 1 37	11 7	29 10 10	0 N38	11 47	23 21	5♉21 5	14 26
25	M	10 13 50	1 59 28	10 46	11♉27 57	1 43	16 54	23 18	17 31 20	19 11
26	T	10 17 46	2 57 20	10 25	23 31 52	2 41	21 16	23 15	29 30 10	23 6
27	W	10 21 43	3 55 16	10 4	5♊26 52	3 32	24 42	23 12	11♊22 39	26 1
28	Th	10 25 39	4 53 13	9 43	17 18 7	4 14	27 3	23 ˑ 8	23 13 53	27 46
29	F	10 29 36	5 51 12	9 22	29 10 32	4 44	28 11	23 5	5♋ 8 38	28 16
30	S	10 33 32	6 49 12	9 1	11♋ 8 41	5 3	28 0	23 2	17 11 9	27 25
31	♋	10 37 29	7♍47 15	8 N39	23♋16 26	5 N 8	26 N30	22♈59	29♋24 52	25 N15

D M	Mercury Lat.	Mercury Dec.	Mercury Dec.	Venus Lat.	Venus Dec.	Venus Dec.	Mars Lat.	Mars Dec.	Mars Dec.	Jupiter Lat.	Jupiter Dec.
	° '	° '	° '	° '	° '	° '	° '	° '	° '	° '	° '
1	3 S 56	17 N 7	17 N21	0 N18	2 N59	2 N29	5 S 52	28 S 43	28 S 43	1 S 23	4 S 22
3	3 28	17 35	17 49	0 N 9	1 59	1 30	5 50	28 43	28 42	1 24	4 25
5	2 58	18 2	18 14	0 S 1	1 N 0	0 N30	5 48	28 42	28 41	1 25	4 29
7	2 26	18 25	18 35	0 10	0 0	0 S 30	5 45	28 40	28 39	1 25	4 33
9	1 53	18 43	18 50	0 21	1 S 0	1 30	5 42	28 39	28 36	1 26	4 38
11	1 20	18 55	18 59	0 31	2 0	2 30	5 39	28 35	28 33	1 26	4 42
13	0 49	19 0	18 59	0 42	3 0	3 29	5 35	28 31	28 29	1 27	4 47
15	0 S 19	18 55	18 49	0 53	3 59	4 28	5 31	28 27	28 24	1 27	4 52
17	0 N 9	18 41	18 29	1 4	4 58	5 27	5 27	28 22	28 19	1 27	4 58
19	0 34	18 15	17 58	1 16	5 56	6 25	5 22	28 16	28 13	1 28	5 3
21	0 55	17 39	17 16	1 28	6 54	7 23	5 18	28 10	28 7	1 28	5 9
23	1 12	16 51	16 23	1 40	7 52	8 20	5 13	28 4	28 1	1 29	5 14
25	1 26	15 53	15 21	1 53	8 48	9 16	5 8	27 57	27 54	1 29	5 20
27	1 36	14 46	14 10	2 5	9 44	10 12	5 1	27 50	27 46	1 29	5 26
29	1 43	13 32	12 N52	2 18	10 39	11 S 7	4 58	27 42	27 S 38	1 29	5 32
31	1 N46	12 N10		2 S 31	11 S 34		4 S 52	27 S 34		1 S 30	5 S 39

Full Moon—August 19, 6*h*. 54*m*. *p.m*. (26° ♒ 29′)

D M	☿ Long.	♀ Long.	♂ Long.	♃ Long.	♄ Long.	♅ Long.	♆ Long.	♇ Long.	☉	☿	♀	♂	♃	♄	♅	♆	♇
	° ′	° ′	° ′	° ′	° ′	° ′	° ′	° ′	Lunar Aspects								
1	25♋51	23♍10	12♑14	22♓14	3♐ 5	18♐39	3♑32	4♏37	∠	⚺	□		□		☍		⚼
2	25 ℞ 45	24 15	12 ℞ 5	22 ℞ 10	3 ℞ 5	18 ℞ 37	3 ℞ 31	4 38								☍	△
𝔖	25 D44	25 20	11 58	22 6	3 4	18 36	3 30	4 38	⚺			☍		⚼			
4	25 51	26 24	11 51	22 2	3 4	18 35	3 28	4 39		☌	⚹		△	△			
5	26 3	27 29	11 45	21 57	3 4	18 34	3 27	4 40	☌		∠		⚼		⚼		□
6	26 23	28 33	11 39	21 53	3 4	18 33	3 26	4 41		⚺		⚼			△	⚼	
7	26 48	29♍37	11 35	21 48	3 D 4	18 32	3 25	4 41			⚺			□		△	⚹
8	27 21	0♎40	11 31	21 43	3 4	18 31	3 24	4 42	⚺	∠		△	☍		□		∠
9	28 0	1 44	11 28	21 38	3 4	18 30	3 23	4 43	∠	⚹	☌			⚹		□	⚺
𝔖	28 46	2 47	11 26	21 33	3 4	18 29	3 22	4 44	⚹			□		∠	⚹		
11	29♋38	3 50	11 25	21 27	3 5	18 28	3 21	4 45		□	⚺			⚺	∠	⚹	☌
12	0♌37	4 53	11 D25	21 22	3 5	18 27	3 20	4 46				⚹	⚼		⚺	∠	
13	1 42	5 55	11 26	21 16	3 6	18 27	3 19	4 47	□	△	∠	∠	△				
14	2 53	6 58	11 27	21 10	3 6	18 26	3 18	4 48			⚹	⚺		☌		⚺	⚺
15	4 9	8 0	11 29	21 4	3 7	18 25	3 17	4 49	△	⚼			□		☌		∠
16	5 31	9 1	11 32	20 58	3 8	18 25	3 16	4 50	⚼		□	●		⚺		☌	⚹
𝔖	6 58	10 3	11 36	20 52	3 9	18 24	3 15	4 51					⚹	∠	⚺		
18	8 30	11 4	11 41	20 46	3 10	18 24	3 14	4 52		☍	△	⚺	∠	⚹	∠	⚺	□
19	10 6	12 4	11 47	20 39	3 11	18 23	3 13	4 53	☍		⚼	∠	⚺		⚹	∠	
20	11 47	13 5	11 53	20 33	3 12	18 23	3 13	4 54				⚹		□		⚹	△
21	13 31	14 5	12 0	20 26	3 14	18 22	3 12	4 56					☌		□		⚼
22	15 18	15 5	12 8	20 19	3 15	18 22	3 11	4 57		⚼				△		□	
23	17 8	16 4	12 17	20 12	3 17	18 22	3 10	4 58	⚼	△	☍	□	⚺	⚼	△		
𝔖	19 0	17 3	12 26	20 5	3 18	18 22	3 10	4 59	△				∠		⚼	△	☍
25	20 55	18 2	12 36	19 58	3 20	18 22	3 9	5 1				△					
26	22 51	19 0	12 47	19 51	3 22	18 22	3 8	5 2		□		⚼	⚹			⚼	
27	24 48	19 58	12 59	19 44	3 24	18 21	3 8	5 4	□		⚼			☍			
28	26 45	20 55	13 11	19 36	3 26	18 D21	3 7	5 5			△		□		☍		⚼
29	28♌44	21 52	13 24	19 29	3 28	18 22	3 7	5 6		⚹						☍	△
30	0♍42	22 49	13 38	19 21	3 30	18 22	3 6	5 8	⚹	∠		☍					
𝔖	2♍40	23♎45	13♑53	19♓13	3♐32	18♐22	3♑ 6	5♏ 9	∠		□		△	⚼			

D M	Saturn Lat.	Saturn Dec.	Uranus Lat.	Uranus Dec.	Neptune Lat.	Neptune Dec.	Pluto Lat.	Pluto Dec.
	° ′	° ′	° ′	° ′	° ′	° ′	° ′	° ′
1	1 N51	18 S 58	0 S 6	23 S 3	1 N 6	22 S 18	16 N26	2 N27
3	1 50	18 58	0 6	23 3	1 6	22 18	16 25	2 26
5	1 50	18 59	0 6	23 3	1 6	22 18	16 24	2 24
7	1 49	18 59	0 6	23 3	1 6	22 18	16 23	2 23
9	1 49	19 0	0 6	23 3	1 6	22 19	16 22	2 21
11	1 48	19 0	0 6	23 2	1 5	22 19	16 21	2 20
13	1 48	19 1	0 6	23 2	1 5	22 19	16 20	2 18
15	1 48	19 2	0 6	23 2	1 5	22 19	16 19	2 16
17	1 47	19 2	0 6	23 2	1 5	22 19	16 17	2 15
19	1 47	19 3	0 6	23 2	1 5	22 19	16 16	2 13
21	1 46	19 4	0 6	23 2	1 5	22 19	16 15	2 11
23	1 46	19 5	0 6	23 2	1 5	22 19	16 14	2 9
25	1 45	19 6	0 6	23 2	1 5	22 19	16 13	2 8
27	1 45	19 7	0 6	23 2	1 5	22 20	16 12	2 6
29	1 44	19 9	0 6	23 2	1 5	22 20	16 11	2 4
31	1 N44	19 S 10	0 S 6	23 S 2	1 N 5	22 S 20	16 N10	2 N 2

Mutual Aspects

2. ☉ ± ♆. ♀ **P** ♇.
3. ☉ **P** ☿. ☿ ⚹ ♀, **Stat.**
4. ☉ ▿ ♂.
6. ♀ ⊥ ♇. ♄ **Stat.**
8. ☉ ∠ ♀, ± ♃.
10. ☉ ± ♂. ♀ ⚹ ♄.
11. ☉ △ ♅, ⚼ ♆. ♀ □ ♆.
12. ♀ ⚺ ♇, **P** ♇. ♂ **Stat.**
13. ♀ **Q** ♅.
14. ☉ ▿ ♃. ☿ △ ♄, ⚼ ♅, ▿ ♆.
15. ☉ **Q** ♇.
16. ☿ ⚼ ♃, □ ♇.
17. ♀ **P** ♃. 18. ☿ ± ♆.
19. ♀ □ ♂.
20. ☉ ⚼ ♂. ☿ ▿ ♂. ♄ ⚺ ♆.
21. ☿ ± ♃. 22. ☿ ⚹ ♀.
24. ☿ ± ♂, △ ♅, ⚼ ♆.
25. ☿ ▿ ♃. ♀ ∠ ♄, ⚹ ♅. ♃ ⚼ ♇.
26. ☉ □ ♄, △ ♆. ☿ **Q** ♇.
27. ☉ **P** ♀. ♀ ▿ ♃.
28. ☉ ⚹ ♇. ♀ **Q** ♆. ♅ **Stat.**
29. ☿ ⚼ ♂.
31. ☿ □ ♄, △ ♆.

Last Quarter—August 27, 8*h*. 38*m*. *a.m*. (3° ♊ 47′)

| 18 | | | | | SEPTEMBER, 1986 | | | | | | [RAPHAEL'S |

D M	D W	Sidereal Time	⊙ Long.	⊙ Dec.	☽ Long.	☽ Lat.	☽ Dec.	☽ Node	MIDNIGHT ☽ Long.	☽ Dec.
		H. M. S.	° ′ ″	° ′	° ′ ″	° ′	° ′	° ′	° ′ ″	° ′
1	M	10 41 25	8♍45 19	8 N17	5♌36 44	4 N59	23 N42	22♈56	11♌52 15	21 N52
2	T	10 45 22	9 43 25	7 55	18 11 33	4 36	19 45	22 53	24 34 43	17 24
3	W	10 49 19	10 41 32	7 34	1♍ 1 44	3 59	14 49	22 49	7♍32 36	12 4
4	TH	10 53 15	11 39 42	7 11	14 7 9	3 8	9 8	22 46	20 45 16	6 N 5
5	F	10 57 12	12 37 53	6 49	27 26 46	2 6	2 N56	22 43	4♎11 26	0 S 16
6	S	11 1 8	13 36 5	6 27	10♎59	2 0	N56	3 S 30	22 40	17 49 20	6 42
7	☉	11 5 5	14 34 20	6 5	24 42	0 S 19	9	52	22 37	1♏37 13	12 55
8	M	11 9 1	15 32 35	5 42	8♏34 22	1 33	15 50	22 33	15 33 23	18 33
9	T	11 12 58	16 30 53	5 19	22 34	2 42	21 2	22 30	29 36 21	23 13
10	W	11 16 54	17 29 12	4 57	6 ♐ 39 56	3 42	25 5	22 27	13 ♐ 44 41	26 33
11	TH	11 20 51	18 27 32	4 34	20 50 22	4 29	27 36	22 24	27 56 45	28 12
12	F	11 24 48	19 25 54	4 11	5♑ 3 34	5 0	28 20	22 21	12♑10 31	28 0
13	S	11 28 44	20 24 18	3 48	19 17 13	5 12	27 12	22 18	26 23 17	25 58
14	☉	11 32 41	21 22 43	3 25	3≈≈28 18	5 5	24 19	22 14	10≈≈31 46	22 19
15	M	11 36 37	22 21 10	3 2	17 33 15	4 40	20 1	22 11	24 32 15	17 27
16	T	11 40 34	23 19 38	2 39	1♓28 18	3 58	14 40	22 8	8♓21 0	11 43
17	W	11 44 30	24 18 8	2 16	15 9 56	3 4	8 40	22 5	21 54 47	5 S 33
18	TH	11 48 27	25 16 40	1 53	28 35 17	2 0	2 S 23	22 2	5♈11 17	0 N45
19	F	11 52 23	26 15 14	1 29	11♈42 39	0 S 50	3 N51	21 59	18 9 25	6 53
20	S	11 56 20	27 13 50	1 6	24 31 37	0 N20	9 49	21 55	0 ♉49 26	12 37
21	☉	12 0 17	28 12 28	0 43	7 ♉ 3 6	1 28	15 15	21 52	13 12 55	17 42
22	M	12 4 13	29♍11 8	0 N19	19 19 16	2 30	19 58	21 49	25 22 33	22 0
23	T	12 8 10	0♎ 9 50	0 S 4	1♊23 15	3 25	23 47	21 46	7♊21 53	25 18
24	W	12 12 6	1 8 35	0 27	13 19	4 10	26 32	21 43	19 15 12	27 28
25	TH	12 16 3	2 7 21	0 51	25 11	4 44	28 5	21 39	1♋ 7 6	28 23
26	F	12 19 59	3 6 10	1 14	7♋ 4 2	5 6	28 21	21 36	13 2 24	27 59
27	S	12 23 56	4 5 2	1 37	19 2 47	5 15	27 18	21 33	25 5 44	26 16
28	☉	12 27 52	5 3 55	2 1	1♌11 48	5 11	24 57	21 30	7♌21 26	23 19
29	M	12 31 49	6 2 51	2 24	13 35 6	4 51	21 24	21 27	19 53 8	19 13
30	T	12 35 46	7♎ 1 49	2 S 47	26♌15 51	4 N18	16 N48	21♈24	2♍43 29	14 N10

D M	Mercury Lat.	Dec.	Venus Lat.	Dec.	Mars Lat.	Dec.	Jupiter Lat.	Dec.
	° ′	° ′	° ′	° ′	° ′	° ′	° ′	° ′
1	1 N47	11 N28	2 S 38	12 S 0	4 S 50	27 S 30	1 S 30	5 S 42
3	1 46	10 0	10 N44 2 51	12 53	12 S 27	4 44 27 21	27 S 25	1 30	5 48
5	1 42	8 28	9 14 3 4	13 45	13 19	4 39 27 11	27 16	1 30	5 54
7	1 36	6 55	7 42 3 18	14 35	14 10	4 33 27 1	27 6	1 30	6 1
9	1 29	5 21	6 8 3 32	15 24	15 0	4 28 26 51	26 56	1 31	6 7
11	1 20	3 46	4 33 3 45	16 12	15 48	4 22 26 40	26 45	1 31	6 13
13	1 9	2 11	2 58 3 59	16 58	16 35	4 17 26 28	26 34	1 31	6 20
15	0 58	0 N37	1 N24 4 13	17 43	17 21	4 11 26 17	26 23	1 31	6 26
17	0 45	0 S 57	0 S 10 4 26	18 26	18 5	4 6 26 4	26 10	1 31	6 32
19	0 32	2 29	1 43 4 40	19 7	18 47	4 0 25 51	25 58	1 31	6 38
21	0 19	3 59	3 14 4 53	19 47	19 27	3 55 25 37	25 44	1 31	6 44
23	0 N 5	5 28	4 44 5 6	20 24	20 6	3 49 25 23	25 31	1 31	6 50
25	0 S 10	6 54	6 11 5 19	21 0	20 42	3 44 25 9	25 16	1 31	6 56
27	0 24	8 19	7 37 5 32	21 33	21 17	3 39 24 53	25 2	1 31	7 1
29	0 39	9 41	9 0 5 44	22 4	21 49	3 33 24 38	24 46	1 30	7 6
31	0 S 54	11 S 0	10 S 21 5 S 55	22 S 32	22 S 18	3 S 28 24 S 21	24 S 29	1 S 30	7 S 12

FULL MOON—September 18, *5h.* 34*m. a.m.* (25° ♓ 1′)

EPHEMERIS] **SEPTEMBER, 1986** 19

D M	☿ Long.	♀ Long.	♂ Long.	♃ Long.	♄ Long.	♅ Long.	♆ Long.	♇ Long.	☉	☿	♀	♂	♃	♄	♅	♆	♇
	° ′	° ′	° ′	° ′	° ′	° ′	° ′	° ′									
1	4♍39	24♎41	14♑ 8	19♓ 6	3♐35	18♐22	3♑ 5	5♏11	⊻	⊻			⚼	△	⚼		□
2	6 36	25 36	14 24	18℞58	3 37	18 22	3℞ 5	5 13							△	⚼	
3	8 33	26 30	14 40	18 50	3 40	18 23	3 4	5 14			*	⚼		□		△	*
4	10 29	27 25	14 57	18 42	3 42	18 23	3 4	5 16	☌	☌	∠	△	☍		□		∠
5	12 25	28 18	15 15	18 34	3 45	18 23	3 4	5 17			⊻			*		□	
6	14 19	29♎11	15 34	18 27	3 48	18 24	3 3	5 19	⊻	⊻		□					⊻
S	16 13	0♏ 4	15 53	18 19	3 51	18 24	3 3	5 21	∠		☌			∠	*		
8	18 5	0 56	16 12	18 11	3 54	18 25	3 3	5 22		∠			⚼	⊻	∠	*	☌
9	19 57	1 47	16 33	18 3	3 57	18 26	3 3	5 24	*	*		*	△		⊻	∠	
10	21 47	2 37	16 53	17 55	4 0	18 26	3 3	5 26			⊻	∠		☌		⊻	⊻
11	23 36	3 27	17 15	17 47	4 3	18 27	3 3	5 28	□	□	∠	⊻	□		☌		∠
12	25 24	4 17	17 37	17 39	4 7	18 28	3 2	5 30			*			⊻		☌	*
13	27 11	5 5	17 59	17 31	4 10	18 29	3 2	5 31	△			●	*	∠	⊻		
S	28♍57	5 53	18 22	17 23	4 14	18 29	3 2	5 33	⚼	△	□		∠	*	∠	⊻	□
15	0♎41	6 39	18 46	17 15	4 17	18 30	3 D 2	5 35		⚼		⊻	⊻		*	∠	
16	2 25	7 25	19 10	17 7	4 21	18 31	3 2	5 37			△	∠		□		*	△
17	4 8	8 11	19 34	16 59	4 25	18 32	3 2	5 39				*	☌		□		⚼
18	5 49	8 55	19 59	16 51	4 28	18 33	3 3	5 41	☍		⚼			△		□	
19	7 30	9 38	20 24	16 44	4 32	18 35	3 3	5 43		☍			⊻				
20	9 9	10 21	20 50	16 36	4 36	18 36	3 3	5 45				□		⚼	△		
S	10 48	11 2	21 17	16 28	4 40	18 37	3 3	5 47			☍		∠		⚼	△	☍
22	12 25	11 42	21 43	16 21	4 45	18 38	3 3	5 49	⚼			△	*			⚼	
23	14 1	12 21	22 10	16 13	4 49	18 40	3 4	5 51	△	⚼				☍			
24	15 37	12 59	22 38	16 6	4 53	18 41	3 4	5 53		△		⚼	□		☍		
25	17 12	13 36	23 6	15 58	4 57	18 42	3 4	5 55			⚼						⚼
26	18 45	14 12	23 34	15 51	5 2	18 44	3 5	5 57	□							☍	△
27	20 18	14 46	24 3	15 44	5 6	18 45	3 5	5 59		□	△	☍	△	⚼			
S	21 50	15 19	24 32	15 37	5 11	18 47	3 5	6 2	*				⚼	△	⚼		□
29	23 21	15 51	25 2	15 30	5 16	18 49	3 6	6 4			□				△	⚼	
30	24♎51	16♏21	25♑31	15♓23	5♐20	18♐50	3♑ 6	6♏ 6	∠	*							

D M	Saturn Lat.	Saturn Dec.	Uranus Lat.	Uranus Dec.	Neptune Lat.	Neptune Dec.	Pluto Lat.	Pluto Dec.
	° ′	° ′	° ′	° ′	° ′	° ′	° ′	° ′
1	1 N44	19 S 11	0 S 6	23 S 2	1 N 5	22 S 20	16 N10	2 N 1
3	1 43	19 12	0 6	23 2	1 5	22 20	16 9	1 59
5	1 43	19 13	0 6	23 2	1 4	22 20	16 8	1 57
7	1 42	19 15	0 6	23 2	1 4	22 20	16 7	1 55
9	1 42	19 16	0 6	23 2	1 4	22 20	16 6	1 53
11	1 41	19 18	0 6	23 2	1 4	22 20	16 5	1 52
13	1 41	19 20	0 6	23 3	1 4	22 20	16 4	1 50
15	1 41	19 21	0 6	23 3	1 4	22 21	16 4	1 48
17	1 40	19 23	0 6	23 3	1 4	22 21	16 3	1 46
19	1 40	19 25	0 6	23 3	1 4	22 21	16 2	1 44
21	1 39	19 27	0 6	23 3	1 4	22 21	16 1	1 42
23	1 39	19 29	0 6	23 4	1 4	22 21	16 1	1 40
25	1 39	19 31	0 6	23 4	1 4	22 21	16 0	1 38
27	1 38	19 33	0 6	23 4	1 3	22 21	15 59	1 36
29	1 38	19 35	0 6	23 4	1 3	22 21	15 59	1 34
31	1 N37	19 S 37	0 S 6	23 S 5	1 N 3	22 S 21	15 N58	1 N32

Mutual Aspects

1. ☿ **P** ♀, * ♇. ♀ ± ♃.
4. ♀ ⊥ ♄. 5. ☉ ☌ ☿.
6. ☿ ∠ ♀. ♃ □ ♅.
7. ☉ **P** ♃. ☿ △ ♂.
8. ☿ ☍ ♃, **P** ♃, □ ♅.
9. ☉ **P** ☿, △ ♂. ☿ ∠ ♇.
10. ☉ ☍ ♃. ☿ **Q** ♄. ♀ ⚼ ♃.
11. ☉ ∠ ♀, □ ♅. ♀ ∠ ♅, * ♆.
12. ♀ ⊻ ♄. ♂ * ♃, **Q** ♇.
13. ☉ ∠ ♇. ☿ **P** ♇.
14. ☿ ⊥ ♇. ♀ ☌ ♇. ♂ ⊻ ♅. ♆ **Stat.**
15. ☉ **Q** ♄. ☿ ⊥ ♀, ♀ **Q** ♂.
16. ☿ □ ♆. 17. ☿ * ♄. ♂ ∠ ♄.
18. ☉ **P** ☿, **P** ♇. ☿ **Q** ♅, ⊻ ♇, **P** ♇.
20. ♀ **P** ♄. 21. ☿ ⊻ ♀.
23. ☉ ⊥ ♇. ♀ ⊥ ♅.
24. ☿ ▿ ♃. 25. ☿ **P** ♃.
26. ☉ □ ♆. ☿ * ♅.
27. ☉ **P** ♇. ☿ ∠ ♄.
28. ☉ * ♄. ☿ ± ♃, **Q** ♆. ♀ △ ♃.
29. ☉ ⊻ ♇. ♂ ⊥ ♅.
30. ☉ **Q** ♅. ♀ **P** ♆.

LAST QUARTER—September, 26, *3h.* 17*m. a.m.* (2° ♋ 45′)

20								OCTOBER, 1986							[*RAPHAEL'S*	

D	D	Sidereal			⊙			⊙		☽		☽		☽		☽		MIDNIGHT			
M	W	Time			Long.			Dec.		Long.		Lat.		Dec.		Node		☽ Long.		☽ Dec.	

		H. M. S.	° ′ ″	° ′	° ′ ″	° ′	° ′	° ′ ″	° ′	° ′	° ′
1	W	12 39 42	8♎ 0 49	3 S 11	9♏16 8	3 N30	11 N20	21♈20	15♏53 52	8 N21
2	TH	12 43 39	8 59 51	3 34	22 36 38	2 30	5 N14	21 17	29 24 15	2 N 1
3	F	12 47 35	9 58 55	3 57	6♎16 30	1 20	1 S16	21 14	13♎13 2	4 S 34
4	S	12 51 32	10 58 2	4 20	20 13 27	0 N 4	7 51	21 11	27 17 15	11 4
5	☉	12 55 28	11 57 10	4 44	4♏23 55	1 S14	14 9	21 8	11♏32 53	17 5
6	M	12 59 25	12 56 21	5 7	18 43 32	2 28	19 46	21 5	25 55 18	22 11
7	T	13 3 21	13 55 33	5 30	3♐ 7 36	3 33	24 16	21 1	10♐19 54	25 59
8	W	13 7 18	14 54 47	5 53	17 31 40	4 25	27 15	20 58	24 42 26	28 5
9	TH	13 11 15	15 54 3	6 15	1♑51 48	5 0	28 25	20 55	8♑59 24	28 18
10	F	13 15 11	16 53 21	6 38	16 4 56	5 16	27 42	20 52	23 8 7	26 40
11	S	13 19 8	17 52 40	7 1	0♒ 8 45	5 13	25 13	20 49	7♒ 6 40	23 24
12	☉	13 23 4	18 52 1	7 24	14 1 41	4 52	21 16	20 45	20 53 42	18 52
13	M	13 27 1	19 51 24	7 46	27 42 37	4 14	16 14	20 42	4♓28 20	13 26
14	T	13 30 57	20 50 48	8 8	11♓10 48	3 23	10 30	20 39	17 49 56	7 28
15	W	13 34 54	21 50 15	8 31	24 25 43	2 22	4 S23	20 36	0♈58 5	1 S 16
16	TH	13 38 50	22 49 43	8 53	7♈27 21	1 14	1 N50	20 33	13 52 35	4 N53
17	F	13 42 47	23 49 13	9 15	20 14 44	0 S 4	7 51	20 30	26 33 32	10 44
18	S	13 46 44	24 48 45	9 37	2♉49 5	1 N 6	13 29	20 26	9♉ 1 28	16 4
19	☉	13 50 40	25 48 19	9 58	15 10 51	2 11	18 28	20 23	21 17 26	20 40
20	M	13 54 37	26 47 56	10 20	27 21 25	3 9	22 38	20 20	3♊23 6	24 20
21	T	13 58 33	27 47 34	10 41	9♊22 46	3 57	25 46	20 17	15 20 47	26 55
22	W	14 2 30	28 47 15	11 3	21 17 33	4 35	27 44	20 14	27 13 29	28 15
23	TH	14 6 26	29♎46 58	11 24	3♋ 9 4	5 2	28 26	20 10	9♋ 4 49	28 17
24	F	14 10 23	0♏46 43	11 45	15 1 13	5 15	27 49	20 7	20 58 52	27 1
25	S	14 14 19	1 46 31	12 6	26 58 18	5 15	25 54	20 4	3♌ 0 8	24 30
26	☉	14 18 16	2 46 20	12 26	9♌ 4 54	5 1	22 49	20 1	15 13 13	20 52
27	M	14 22 13	3 46 12	12 47	21 25 38	4 32	18 40	19 58	27 42 39	16 14
28	T	14 26 9	4 46 6	13 7	4♍ 4 46	3 51	13 36	19 55	10♍32 25	10 47
29	W	14 30 6	5 46 2	13 27	17 5 57	2 56	7 48	19 51	23 45 36	4 N41
30	TH	14 34 2	6 46 0	13 47	0♎31 31	1 50	1 N29	19 48	7♎23 44	1 S 48
31	F	14 37 59	7♏46 0	14 S 6	14♎22 8	0 N36	5 S 7	19♈45	21♎26 26	8 S 25

D	Mercury				Venus				Mars				Jupiter		
M	Lat.		Dec.		Lat.		Dec.		Lat.		Dec.		Lat.	Dec.	
	° ′	° ′	° ′		° ′	° ′	° ′		° ′	° ′	° ′		° ′	° ′	
1	0 S 54	11 S 0	11 S 39		5 S 55	22 S 32	22 S 46		3 S 28	24 S 21	24 S 13		1 S 30	7 S 12	
3	1 8	12 17	11 12 54		6 7	22 58	23 10		3 23	24 4	23 55		1 30	7 17	
5	1 23	13 30	14 6		6 17	23 22	23 32		3 18	23 46	23 37		1 30	7 21	
7	1 37	14 41	15 15		6 26	23 42	23 51		3 13	23 28	23 19		1 30	7 26	
9	1 50	15 48	16 20		6 35	23 59	24 6		3 8	23 9	22 59		1 29	7 30	
11	2 3	16 52	17 22		6 42	24 12	24 17		3 3	22 50	22 40		1 29	7 34	
13	2 15	17 51	18 20		6 47	24 22	24 25		2 58	22 29	22 19		1 29	7 38	
15	2 26	18 47	19 13		6 52	24 27	24 28		2 53	22 9	21 58		1 29	7 41	
17	2 37	19 38	20 1		6 54	24 28	24 27		2 48	21 47	21 36		1 28	7 44	
19	2 45	20 20	20 45		6 54	24 25	24 21		2 43	21 25	21 14		1 28	7 47	
21	2 53	21 4	21 23		6 52	24 16	24 10		2 38	21 1	20 51		1 28	7 50	
23	2 58	21 39	21 54		6 47	24 2	23 53		2 34	20 39	20 28		1 27	7 52	
25	3 1	22 7	22 19		6 39	23 43	23 31		2 29	20 16	20 3		1 27	7 54	
27	3 1	22 28	22 35		6 29	23 18	23 4		2 25	19 51	19 39		1 26	7 56	
29	2 58	22 40	22 42		6 15	22 48	22 S 32		2 20	19 26	19 S 13		1 26	7 57	
31	2 S 51	22 S 42			5 S 58	22 S 13			2 S 16	19 S 1			1 S 26	7 S 58	

FULL MOON—October 17, *7h. 22m. p.m.* (24° ♈ 7′)

D M	☿ Long.	♀ Long.	♂ Long.	♃ Long.	♄ Long.	♅ Long.	♆ Long.	♇ Long.	Lunar Aspects ☉	☿	♀	♂	♃	♄	♅	♆	♇
	° ′	° ′	° ′	° ′	° ′	° ′	° ′	° ′									
1	26♎20	16♏50	26♑ 2	15♓16	5♐25	18♐52	3♑ 7	6♏ 8	⊻	∠		⚼	☍	□		△	⚹
2	27 48	17 17	26 32	15℞ 9	5 30	18 54	3 8	6 10		⊻	⚹	△			□		∠
3	29♎16	17 43	27 3	15 3	5 35	18 56	3 8	6 13	●		∠			⚹		□	⊻
4	0♏42	18 7	27 34	14 56	5 40	18 57	3 9	6 15			⊻			∠	⚹		
𝕾	2 7	18 29	28 6	14 50	5 45	18 59	3 9	6 17		●		□	⚼	⊻	∠	⚹	☌
6	3 32	18 50	28 38	14 44	5 50	19 1	3 10	6 19	⊻		☌		△		⊻	∠	
7	4 55	19 9	29 10	14 38	5 55	19 3	3 11	6 22	∠	⊻		⚹		☌		⊻	⊻
8	6 18	19 25	29♑42	14 32	6 1	19 5	3 12	6 24	⚹	∠	⊻	∠	□		☌		∠
9	7 39	19 40	0♒15	14 26	6 6	19 7	3 12	6 26		⚹	∠	⊻		⊻		☌	⚹
10	9 0	19 53	0 48	14 21	6 11	19 9	3 13	6 28	□		⚹		⚹	∠	⊻		
11	10 19	20 4	1 21	14 16	6 17	19 12	3 14	6 31				☌	∠	⚹	∠	⊻	□
𝕾	11 37	20 12	1 55	14 10	6 22	19 14	3 15	6 33	△	□	□		⊻		⚹	∠	
13	12 53	20 18	2 29	14 5	6 28	19 16	3 16	6 36				⊻				⚹	
14	14 8	20 22	3 3	14 0	6 34	19 18	3 17	6 38	⚼	△			☌	□			△
15	15 22	20 24	3 37	13 56	6 39	19 21	3 18	6 40			△	∠			□		⚼
16	16 34	20℞23	4 12	13 51	6 45	19 23	3 19	6 43		⚼	⚼	⚹	⊻	△		□	
17	17 45	20 20	4 47	13 47	6 51	19 25	3 20	6 45	●●					⚼	△		
18	18 53	20 14	5 22	13 42	6 57	19 28	3 21	6 47				□	∠		⚼	△	☍
𝕾	20 0	20 6	5 57	13 38	7 2	19 30	3 22	6 50		☍	☍		⚹			⚼	
20	21 4	19 56	6 32	13 34	7 8	19 33	3 23	6 52									
21	22 6	19 43	7 8	13 31	7 14	19 35	3 24	6 55	⚼			△	□	☍			
22	23 5	19 28	7 44	13 27	7 20	19 38	3 25	6 57				⚼			☍		⚼
23	24 1	19 11	8 20	13 24	7 26	19 41	3 27	6 59	△		⚼					☍	△
24	24 54	18 51	8 56	13 21	7 33	19 43	3 28	7 2		⚼	△		△				
25	25 43	18 29	9 33	13 18	7 39	19 46	3 29	7 4	□	△			⚼	⚼			
𝕾	26 28	18 5	10 9	13 15	7 45	19 49	3 31	7 7				☍		△	⚼		□
27	27 9	17 38	10 46	13 13	7 51	19 51	3 32	7 9		□	□				△	⚼	
28	27 45	17 10	11 23	13 10	7 58	19 54	3 33	7 11	⚹					□		△	⚹
29	28 15	16 41	12 0	13 8	8 4	19 57	3 35	7 14	∠		⚹		☍		□		∠
30	28 39	16 9	12 38	13 6	8 10	20 0	3 36	7 16	⊻	⚹	∠	⚼				□	⊻
31	28♏57	15♏37	13♒15	13♓ 5	8♐17	20♐ 3	3♑37	7♏19		∠	⊻	△		⚹	⚹		

D M	Saturn Lat.	Saturn Dec.	Uranus Lat.	Uranus Dec.	Neptune Lat.	Neptune Dec.	Pluto Lat.	Pluto Dec.
	° ′	° ′	° ′	° ′	° ′	° ′	° ′	° ′
1	1 N37	19 S 37	0 S 6	23 S 5	1 N 3	22 S 21	15 N58	1 N32
3	1 37	19 39	0 6	23 5	1 3	22 21	15 58	1 31
5	1 37	19 41	0 6	23 5	1 3	22 21	15 57	1 29
7	1 36	19 43	0 6	23 6	1 3	22 21	15 57	1 27
9	1 36	19 45	0 6	23 6	1 3	22 21	15 56	1 25
11	1 36	19 47	0 6	23 6	1 3	22 21	15 56	1 23
13	1 35	19 50	0 6	23 7	1 3	22 21	15 56	1 21
15	1 35	19 52	0 6	23 7	1 3	22 21	15 55	1 20
17	1 35	19 54	0 6	23 8	1 3	22 22	15 55	1 18
19	1 34	19 56	0 6	23 8	1 3	22 22	15 55	1 16
21	1 34	19 59	0 6	23 8	1 2	22 22	15 54	1 14
23	1 34	20 1	0 6	23 9	1 2	22 22	15 54	1 13
25	1 34	20 3	0 6	23 9	1 2	22 22	15 54	1 11
27	1 33	20 5	0 6	23 10	1 2	22 22	15 54	1 10
29	1 33	20 8	0 6	23 10	1 2	22 22	15 54	1 8
31	1 N33	20 S 10	0 S 6	23 S 10	1 N 2	22 S 22	15 N54	1 N 6

Mutual Aspects

1. ☿ □ ♂. 2. ♃ **Q** ♆.
3. ☿ ⊥ ♄.
4. ☿ ⚼ ♃. ♀ **P** ♅, ∠ ♆.
6. ☉ ⊥ ♀. ☿ ∠ ♅, ⚹ ♆. ♀ **P** ♂.
7. ♀ ⊻ ♅.
8. ☉ ▿ ♃. ☿ ⊻ ♄, ☌ ♇. ♂ ∠ ♃.
9. ♂ **P** ♅. 12. ☉ ⚹ ♅.
13. ☉ ⊻ ♀, ± ♃, **P** ♃. ☿ ⊥ ♅. ♀ **Q** ♂.
14. ☉ **Q** ♆. ☿ △ ♃. ♂ ⊻ ♆, **P** ♆.
15. ☉ ∠ ♄. ♀ **Stat.** ♄ ⊻ ♇.
16. ♂ ∠ ♅.
18. ☿ **P** ♄, ∠ ♆.
19. ☿ ☌ ♀, ⊻ ♅.
21. ☿ **P** ♂. ♀ ⊻ ♅. ♂ ⚹ ♄, □ ♇.
22. ☉ ⚼ ♃. ♂ ⊥ ♃.
25. ☉ ⊥ ♄. ♀ ∠ ♆. ♂ ⊥ ♆.
26. ☿ **P** ♆. ♂ **P** ♄. 27. ☉ ⚹ ♆.
28. ☉ ∠ ♅. ☿ ⊥ ♆. ♀ **P** ♅.
29. ☿ **P** ♀.
31. ☉ ☌ ♇. ♀ **P** ♆. ♂ ⊻ ♃.

LAST QUARTER—October 25, *10h. 26m. p.m.* (2° ♌ 12′)

| 22 | | | | NOVEMBER, 1986 | | | | | [RAPHAEL'S | |

D M	D W	Sidereal Time	☉ Long.	☉ Dec.	☽ Long.	☽ Lat.	☽ Dec.	Node	MIDNIGHT ☽ Long.	☽ Dec.
		H. M. S.	° ′ ″	° ′	° ′ ″	° ′	° ′	° ′	° ′ ″	° ′
1	S	14 41 55	8♏46 3	14 S 26	28≏36 13	0 S 42	11 S 38	19♈42	5♏50 55	14 S 45
2	☉	14 45 52	9 46 7	14 45	13♏ 9 49	2 0	17 42	19 39	20 32 4	20 24
3	M	14 49 48	10 46 13	15 4	27 56 45	3 10	22 48	19 36	5♐22 51	24 50
4	T	14 53 45	11 46 21	15 22	12♐49 20	4 8	26 26	19 32	20 15 13	27 35
5	W	14 57 42	12 46 31	15 41	27 39 31	4 49	28 15	19 29	5♑ 1 21	28 23
6	Th	15 1 38	13 46 42	15 59	12♑19 58	5 11	28 2	19 26	19 34 45	27 12
7	F	15 5 35	14 46 55	16 16	26 45 11	5 12	25 55	19 23	3≈≈50 56	24 15
8	S	15 9 31	15 47 9	16 34	10≈≈51 46	4 55	22 14	19 20	17 47 37	19 56
9	☉	15 13 28	16 47 25	16 51	24 38 29	4 21	17 24	19 16	1♓24 28	14 41
10	M	15 17 24	17 47 42	17 8	8♓ 5 44	3 33	11 49	19 13	14 42 32	8 52
11	S	15 21 21	18 48 0	17 25	21 15 5	2 35	5 S 50	19 10	27 43 40	2 S 47
12	W	15 25 17	19 48 20	17 42	4♈ 8 34	1 30	0 N16	19 7	10♈30 4	3 N18
13	Th	15 29 14	20 48 41	17 58	16 48 23	0 S 22	6 16	19 4	23 3 49	9 10
14	F	15 33 11	21 49 4	18 13	29 16 33	0 N47	11 57	19 1	5♉26 48	14 35
15	S	15 37 7	22 49 28	18 29	11♉34 47	1 51	17 5	18 57	17 40 39	19 22
16	☉	15 41 4	23 49 54	18 44	23 44 35	2 50	21 28	18 54	29 46 44	23 19
17	M	15 45 0	24 50 22	18 59	5♊47 18	3 41	24 54	18 51	11♊46 27	26 12
18	T	15 48 57	25 50 51	19 13	17 44 22	4 21	27 13	18 48	23 41 17	27 54
19	W	15 52 53	26 51 22	19 27	29 37 26	4 50	28 17	18 45	5♋33 6	28 19
20	Th	15 56 50	27 51 55	19 41	11♋28 35	5 6	28 2	18 42	17 24 15	27 25
21	F	16 0 46	28 52 29	19 55	23 20 29	5 9	26 30	18 38	29 17 43	25 17
22	S	16 4 43	29♏53 5	20 8	5♌16 24	4 59	23 47	18 35	11♌17 3	22 1
23	☉	16 8 40	0♐53 42	20 20	17 20 12	4 35	20 1	18 32	23 26 25	17 47
24	M	16 12 36	1 54 22	20 33	29 36 17	3 59	15 20	18 29	5♍50 22	12 43
25	T	16 16 33	2 55 3	20 45	12♍ 9 16	3 10	9 56	18 26	18 33 34	7 0
26	W	16 20 29	3 55 45	20 56	25 3 45	2 11	3 N58	18 22	1≏40 20	0 N50
27	Th	16 24 26	4 56 29	21 7	8≏23 41	1 N 2	2 S 22	18 19	15 14 4	5 S 36
28	F	16 28 22	5 57 14	21 18	22 11 39	0 S 12	8 49	18 16	29 16 23	12 0
29	S	16 32 19	6 58 2	21 29	6♏28 5	1 28	15 3	18 13	13♏46 19	17 57
30	☉	16 36 15	7♐58 50	21 S 39	21♏10 28	2 S 40	20 S 37	18♈10	28♏39 40	23 S 0

D M	Mercury		Venus		Mars		Jupiter	
	Lat.	Dec.	Lat.	Dec.	Lat.	Dec.	Lat.	Dec.
	° ′	° ′	° ′	° ′	° ′	° ′	° ′	° ′
1	2 S 45	22 S 39	5 S 49	21 S 54	2 S 13	18 S 47	1 S 25	7 S 58
3	2 30	22 23	5 28	21 13 / 21 S 34	2 9	18 21 / 18 S 34	1 25	7 59
5	2 8	21 53	5 4	20 28 / 20 50	2 5	17 54 / 18 8	1 24	7 59
7	1 40	21 8	4 38	19 40 / 20 15	2 1	17 26 / 17 40	1 24	7 59
9	1 6	20 7	4 10	18 51 / 19 26	1 56	16 58 / 17 13	1 24	7 59
11	0 S 27	18 53	3 40	18 1 / 18 26	1 52	16 30 / 16 44	1 23	7 58
13	0 N15	17 32	3 9	17 12 / 17 36	1 48	16 1 / 16 15	1 23	7 57
15	0 54	16 11	2 39	16 25 / 16 48	1 44	15 31 / 15 46	1 22	7 55
17	1 29	15 2	2 8	15 40 / 16 2	1 40	15 1 / 15 16	1 22	7 54
19	1 56	14 10	1 37	14 59 / 15 19	1 36	14 31 / 14 46	1 21	7 52
21	2 15	13 39	1 8	14 22 / 14 40	1 33	14 0 / 14 15	1 21	7 49
23	2 26	13 29	0 40	13 50 / 14 5	1 29	13 29 / 13 44	1 20	7 47
25	2 31	13 37	0 S 13	13 22 / 13 35	1 25	12 57 / 13 13	1 20	7 44
27	2 30	14 0	0 N13	12 58 / 13 9	1 22	12 25 / 12 41	1 19	7 41
29	2 25	14 35	0 36	12 40 / 12 48	1 18	11 52 / 12 9	1 19	7 37
31	2 N17	15 S 17	0 N59	12 25 / 12 S 32	1 S 15	11 S 20 / 11 S 36	1 S 19	7 S 33

FIRST QUARTER—November 8, 9h. 11m. p.m. (16° ≈ 10′)

FULL MOON—November 16, 0*h.* 12*m.* *p.m.* (23° ♉ 50′)

D M	☿ Long.	♀ Long.	♂ Long.	♃ Long.	♄ Long.	♅ Long.	♆ Long.	♇ Long.	☉	☿	♀	♂	♃	♄	♅	♆	♇
	° ′	° ′	° ′	° ′	° ′	° ′	° ′	° ′									
1	29♏ 7	15♏ 3	13♒53	13♓ 3	8♐23	20♐ 6	3♑39	7♏21		⊻			Q	∠	∠	✶	
S	29℞10	14℞28	14 31	13℞ 2	8 30	20 9	3 40	7 24	☌		☌	□	△	⊻	⊻	∠	☌
3	29 3	13 52	15 9	13 1	8 36	20 12	3 42	7 26		●						⊻	
4	28 48	13 16	15 47	13 0	8 43	20 15	3 44	7 28	⊻		⊻	✶	□	☌			⊻
5	28 23	12 40	16 25	12 59	8 50	20 18	3 45	7 31	∠	⊻	∠	∠			☌	☌	∠
6	27 49	12 3	17 4	12 58	8 56	20 21	3 47	7 33	✶	∠	✶	⊻	✶	⊻			✶
7	27 4	11 27	17 42	12 58	9 3	20 24	3 48	7 36		✶			∠	∠	⊻	⊻	
8	26 11	10 51	18 21	12D58	9 10	20 27	3 50	7 38	□		□		⊻	✶	∠		□
S	25 8	10 16	19 0	12 58	9 16	20 30	3 52	7 41		□		☌			✶	∠	
10	23 59	9 42	19 39	12 59	9 23	20 34	3 53	7 43			△		☌	□		✶	△
11	22 43	9 9	20 18	12 59	9 30	20 37	3 55	7 45	△	△	Q	⊻			□		Q
12	21 24	8 37	20 57	13 0	9 37	20 40	3 57	7 48	Q	Q		∠		△		□	
13	20 4	8 7	21 36	13 1	9 43	20 43	3 59	7 50				✶	⊻		△		
14	18 45	7 39	22 16	13 2	9 50	20 47	4 0	7 53					∠	Q		△	
15	17 30	7 12	22 55	13 3	9 57	20 50	4 2	7 55		☍	☍		✶		Q		☍
S	16 21	6 48	23 35	13 5	10 4	20 53	4 4	7 57	☍			□				Q	
17	15 21	6 26	24 15	13 7	10 11	20 57	4 6	8 0						☍			
18	14 31	6 6	24 54	13 9	10 18	21 0	4 8	8 2			Q		□		☍		Q
19	13 52	5 48	25 34	13 11	10 25	21 3	4 9	8 4		Q		△				☍	
20	13 25	5 33	26 14	13 13	10 32	21 7	4 11	8 7	Q	△	△	Q	△				△
21	13 9	5 20	26 54	13 16	10 39	21 10	4 13	8 9					Q	Q			
22	13D 5	5 10	27 35	13 18	10 46	21 14	4 15	8 11	△		□			△	Q		□
S	13 12	5 2	28 15	13 21	10 53	21 17	4 17	8 14		□					△	Q	
24	13 29	4 57	28 55	13 25	11 0	21 21	4 19	8 16	□		✶	☍				△	
25	13 55	4 54	29♒35	13 28	11 7	21 24	4 21	8 18		✶			☍	□			✶
26	14 29	4D54	0♓16	13 31	11 14	21 28	4 23	8 20		∠	∠				□		∠
27	15 12	4 56	0 56	13 35	11 21	21 31	4 25	8 23	✶		⊻			✶		□	⊻
28	16 0	5 1	1 37	13 39	11 28	21 35	4 27	8 25	∠	⊻		Q	Q	∠	✶		
29	16 55	5 7	2 18	13 43	11 36	21 38	4 29	8 27	⊻		☌	△	△	⊻	∠	✶	☌
S	17♏55	5♏17	2♓58	13♓48	11♐43	21♐42	4♑31	8♏29		☌					⊻	∠	

D M	Saturn Lat.	Saturn Dec.	Uranus Lat.	Uranus Dec.	Neptune Lat.	Neptune Dec.	Pluto Lat.	Pluto Dec.
	° ′	° ′	° ′	° ′	° ′	° ′	° ′	° ′
1	1 N33	20 S 11	0 S 6	23 S 11	1 N 2	22 S 22	15 N54	1 N 6
3	1 32	20 13	0 6	23 11	1 2	22 22	15 54	1 4
5	1 32	20 16	0 6	23 12	1 2	22 22	15 54	1 3
7	1 32	20 18	0 6	23 12	1 2	22 22	15 54	1 1
9	1 32	20 20	0 6	23 13	1 2	22 22	15 54	1 0
11	1 32	20 22	0 6	23 13	1 2	22 21	15 54	0 59
13	1 31	20 24	0 6	23 13	1 2	22 21	15 54	0 57
15	1 31	20 27	0 6	23 14	1 2	22 21	15 54	0 56
17	1 31	20 29	0 6	23 14	1 1	22 21	15 55	0 55
19	1 31	20 31	0 6	23 15	1 1	22 21	15 55	0 54
21	1 31	20 33	0 6	23 15	1 1	22 21	15 55	0 53
23	1 30	20 35	0 6	23 16	1 1	22 21	15 55	0 52
25	1 30	20 37	0 6	23 16	1 1	22 21	15 56	0 51
27	1 30	20 39	0 6	23 17	1 1	22 21	15 56	0 50
29	1 30	20 41	0 6	23 17	1 1	22 21	15 57	0 49
31	1 N30	20 S 43	0 S 6	23 S 18	1 N 1	22 S 21	15 N57	0 N48

Mutual Aspects

1. ☉ ⊻ ♄.
2. ☿ **Stat.** ♀ □ ♂, ⊥ ♅.
3. ☿ **P** ♆. 4. ♀ △ ♃.
5. ☉ ☌ ♀, △ ♃. ♀ **P** ♄.
6. ☿ ⊥ ♆. 7. ☉ ⊥ ♅.
8. ♃ **Stat.**
9. ☉ **P** ♂. ☿ **P** ♄. ♂ ∠ ♆.
10. ♀ ⊻ ♄. 11. ☉ ∠ ♆.
12. ☉ **P** ♀. ☿ □ ♂. ♂ ✶ ♅.
13. ☉ ☌ ☿, **P** ☿, ⊻ ♅. ☿ ⊻ ♅. ♂ **Q** ♄.
14. ☿ **P** ♀, ∠ ♆. ♀ ☌ ♇.
15. ☉ □ ♂.
17. ☿ **P** ♂, ⊥ ♅.
18. ♀ ∠ ♅. 20. ☉ ⊥ ♆.
21. ☿ △ ♃. 22. ☿ **Stat.**
23. ☿ **P** ♂.
24. ☉ **P** ♄. ☿ **P** ♀, △ ♃. ♀ ⊥ ♄.
26. ☉ ⊻ ♆. ♀ **Stat.**
27. ☉ ⊻ ♀. ☿ ⊥ ♅.

LAST QUARTER—November 24, 4*h.* 50*m.* *p.m.* (2° ♍ 7′)

NEW MOON—Dec. 1, 4h. 43m. p.m. (9° ♐ 12′) and Dec. 31, 3h. 10m. a.m. (9° ♑ 8′)

D M	D W	Sidereal Time	⊙ Long.	⊙ Dec.	☽ Long.	☽ Lat.	☽ Dec.	☽ Node	☽ Long. MIDNIGHT	☽ Dec. MIDNIGHT
		H. M. S.	° ′ ″	° ′	° ′ ″	° ′	° ′	° ′	° ′ ″	° ′
1	M	16 40 12	8 ♐ 59 40	21 S 48	6 ♐ 12 53	3 S 42	25 S 0	18 ♈ 7	13 ♐ 48 55	26 S 34
2	T	16 44 9	10 0 32	21 57	21 26 27	4 30	27 39	18 3	29 4 3	28 13
3	W	16 48 5	11 1 24	22 6	6 ♑ 40 22	4 58	28 14	18 0	14 ♑ 14 6	27 44
4	TH	16 52 2	12 2 18	22 14	21 44 1	5 6	28 43	17 57	29 9 7	25 15
5	F	16 55 58	13 3 12	22 22	6 ≈ 28 35	4 53	28 22	17 54	13 ≈ 41 50	21 10
6	S	16 59 55	14 4 7	22 30	20 48 27	4 21	18 41	17 51	27 48 16	15 59
7	☉	17 3 51	15 5 2	22 37	4 ✕ 41 18	3 35	13 8	17 48	11 ✕ 27 42	10 10
8	M	17 7 48	16 5 58	22 43	18 7 45	2 39	7 8	17 44	24 41 50	4 S 3
9	T	17 11 44	17 6 55	22 49	1 ♈ 10 23	1 35	0 S 59	17 41	7 ♈ 33 55	2 N 3
10	W	17 15 41	18 7 53	22 55	13 52 56	0 S 29	5 N 2	17 38	20 7 57	7 57
11	TH	17 19 38	19 8 51	23 0	26 19 27	0 N 38	10 45	17 35	2 ♉ 27 54	13 26
12	F	17 23 34	20 9 50	23 5	8 ♉ 33 46	1 41	15 57	17 32	14 37 27	18 19
13	S	17 27 31	21 10 50	23 9	20 39 19	2 39	20 29	17 28	26 39 40	22 25
14	☉	17 31 27	22 11 50	23 13	2 ♉ 38 48	3 29	24 7	17 25	8 ♊ 36 58	25 33
15	M	17 35 24	23 12 51	23 16	14 34 22	4 10	26 41	17 22	20 31 12	27 32
16	T	17 39 20	24 13 52	23 19	26 27 38	4 39	28 3	17 19	2 ♋ 23 51	28 15
17	W	17 43 17	25 14 55	23 21	8 ♋ 19 58	4 57	28 7	17 16	14 16 12	27 39
18	TH	17 47 13	26 15 58	23 20	20 12 41	5 1	26 53	17 13	26 9 40	25 48
19	F	17 51 10	27 17 1	23 25	2 ♌ 7 21	4 52	24 26	17 9	8 ♌ 6 2	22 48
20	S	17 55 7	28 18 6	23 26	14 6 0	4 31	20 55	17 6	20 7 37	18 48
21	☉	17 59 3	29 ♐ 19 11	23 26	26 11 17	3 57	16 30	17 3	2 ♍ 17 26	14 1
22	M	18 3 0	0 ♑ 20 17	23 27	8 ♍ 26 34	3 11	11 22	17 0	14 39 11	8 35
23	T	18 6 56	1 21 23	23 26	20 55 51	2 16	5 N 41	16 57	27 17 6	2 N 41
24	W	18 10 53	2 22 30	23 25	3 ≏ 43 31	1 13	0 S 22	16 54	10 ≏ 15 39	3 S 28
25	TH	18 14 49	3 23 38	23 24	16 53 59	0 N 4	6 35	16 50	23 38 59	9 41
26	F	18 18 46	4 24 47	23 22	0 ♏ 30 59	1 S 8	12 43	16 47	7 ♏ 30 13	15 39
27	S	18 22 42	5 25 56	23 20	14 36 45	2 18	18 25	16 44	21 50 25	20 58
28	☉	18 26 39	6 27 6	23 17	29 10 54	3 21	23 15	16 41	6 ♐ 37 35	25 6
29	M	18 30 36	7 28 16	23 14	14 ♐ 9 40	4 12	26 40	16 38	21 46 3	27 42
30	T	18 34 32	8 29 27	23 10	29 25 28	4 46	28 13	16 34	7 ♑ 6 30	28 10
31	W	18 38 29	9 ♑ 30 38	23 S 6	14 ♑ 47 39	5 S 0	27 S 35	16 ♈ 31	22 ♑ 27 21	26 S 29

D M	Mercury Lat.	Mercury Dec.	Venus Lat.	Venus Dec.	Mars Lat.	Mars Dec.	Jupiter Lat.	Jupiter Dec.
	° ′	° ′ ′	° ′	° ′ ′	° ′	° ′ ′	° ′	° ′
1	2 N17	15 S 17	0 N59	12 S 25	1 S 15	11 S 20	1 S 19	7 S 33
3	2 6	16 4	15 S 40	1 19	12 16	12 S 20	1 11	10 46	11 S 3	1 18	7 29
5	1 54	16 54	16 29	1 38	12 10	12 12	1 8	10 13	10 30	1 18	7 25
7	1 40	17 45	17 19	1 56	12 8	12 9	1 4	9 39	9 56	1 17	7 20
9	1 26	18 36	18 10	2 11	12 10	12 9	1 1	9 5	9 22	1 17	7 15
11	1 11	19 25	19 1	2 26	12 15	12 12	0 58	8 31	8 48	1 16	7 10
13	0 56	20 13	19 49	2 39	12 23	12 19	0 55	7 57	8 14	1 16	7 5
15	0 41	20 58	20 36	2 50	12 34	12 29	0 52	7 22	7 39	1 15	6 59
17	0 26	21 39	21 19	3 0	12 48	12 41	0 48	6 47	7 30	1 15	6 53
19	0 N12	22 17	21 59	3 3	13 3	12 55	0 46	6 12	6 55	1 15	6 47
21	0 S 3	22 51	22 35	3 17	13 21	13 12	0 43	5 37	5 19	1 14	6 40
23	0 17	23 21	23 7	3 24	13 40	13 30	0 40	5 2	4 44	1 14	6 34
25	0 30	23 46	23 34	3 29	14 1	13 50	0 37	4 26	4 9	1 13	6 27
27	0 43	24 6	23 57	3 34	14 22	14 11	0 34	3 51	3 33	1 13	6 20
29	0 56	24 22	24 15	3 37	14 45	14 33	0 31	3 15	2 S 58	1 13	6 12
31	1 S 7	24 S 32	24 S 28	3 N40	15 S 8	14 S 56	0 S 29	2 S 40		1 S 12	6 S 5

FIRST QUARTER—December 8, 8h. 1m. a.m. (15° ✕ 56′)

FULL MOON—December 16, *7h. 4m. a.m.* (24° ♊ 1′)

D M	☿ Long. ° ′	♀ Long. ° ′	♂ Long. ° ′	♃ Long. ° ′	♄ Long. ° ′	♅ Long. ° ′	♆ Long. ° ′	♇ Long. ° ′	Lunar Aspects ☉	☿	♀	♂	♃	♄	♅	♆	♇
1	18♏59	5♏28	3♓39	13♓52	11♐50	21♐45	4♑33	8♏31	☌		⊻	□		☌		⊻	⊻
2	20 7	5 42	4 20	13 57	11 57	21 49	4 36	8 34		⊻	∠		□		☌		∠
3	21 19	5 57	5 1	14 2	12 4	21 53	4 38	8 36	⊻	∠	✱	✱	✱	⊻		☌	✱
4	22 33	6 15	5 42	14 7	12 11	21 56	4 40	8 38	∠	✱		∠		∠	⊻		
5	23 50	6 35	6 23	14 12	12 18	22 0	4 42	8 40	✱		□	⊻	∠	✱	∠	⊻	□
6	25 9	6 56	7 4	14 17	12 25	22 4	4 44	8 42		□			⊻		✱	∠	
𝕾	26 30	7 20	7 46	14 23	12 33	22 7	4 46	8 44			△	☌				✱	△
8	27 52	7 45	8 27	14 29	12 40	22 11	4 48	8 46	□		⚼		☌	□	□		⚼
9	29♏16	8 12	9 8	14 35	12 47	22 14	4 51	8 48		△						□	
10	0♐41	8 41	9 49	14 41	12 54	22 18	4 53	8 50	△	⚼		⊻	⊻	△			
11	2 6	9 11	10 31	14 47	13 1	22 22	4 55	8 52				∠	∠	⚼	△		
12	3 33	9 43	11 12	14 53	13 8	22 25	4 57	8 54	⚼		☍	✱			⚼	△	☍
13	5 1	10 16	11 54	15 0	13 15	22 29	4 59	8 56					✱			⚼	
𝕾	6 29	10 51	12 35	15 7	13 22	22 33	5 2	8 58		☍							
15	7 58	11 27	13 17	15 14	13 29	22 36	5 4	9 0				□	□	☍			
16	9 27	12 5	13 58	15 21	13 36	22 40	5 6	9 2	☍		⚼				☍		⚼
17	10 56	12 44	14 40	15 28	13 43	22 44	5 8	9 4			△					☍	△
18	12 26	13 24	15 21	15 36	13 50	22 47	5 11	9 5				△	△				
19	13 57	14 5	16 3	15 43	13 57	22 51	5 13	9 7		⚼		⚼	⚼	⚼	⚼		
20	15 28	14 48	16 45	15 51	14 4	22 55	5 15	9 9	⚼	△	□			△			□
𝕾	16 59	15 31	17 26	15 59	14 11	22 58	5 17	9 11	△						△	⚼	
22	18 30	16 16	18 8	16 7	14 18	23 2	5 20	9 12						□		△	✱
23	20 1	17 1	18 50	16 15	14 25	23 5	5 22	9 14		□	✱	☍	☍		□		∠
24	21 33	17 48	19 31	16 24	14 32	23 9	5 24	9 16	□		∠					□	⊻
25	23 5	18 36	20 13	16 32	14 39	23 13	5 26	9 17			⊻			✱	✱		
26	24 38	19 24	20 55	16 41	14 46	23 16	5 29	9 19	✱	✱		⚼	⚼	∠		✱	
27	26 10	20 13	21 37	16 49	14 53	23 20	5 31	9 21	∠	∠	☌		△	⊻	∠	∠	☌
𝕾	27 43	21 4	22 18	16 58	14 59	23 23	5 33	9 22		⊻		△			⊻	⊻	
29	29♐17	21 54	23 0	17 7	15 6	23 27	5 36	9 24	⊻				□	☌			⊻
30	0♑50	22 46	23 42	17 17	15 13	23 31	5 38	9 25		☌	⊻	□			☌	☌	∠
31	2♑24	23♏39	24♓24	17♓26	15♐20	23♐34	5♑40	9♏27	☌		∠		✱	⊻			✱

D M	Saturn Lat. ° ′	Saturn Dec. ° ′	Uranus Lat. ° ′	Uranus Dec. ° ′	Neptune Lat. ° ′	Neptune Dec. ° ′	Pluto Lat. ° ′	Pluto Dec. ° ′
1	1 N30	20 S 43	0 S 6	23 S 18	1 N 1	22 S 21	15 N57	0 N48
3	1 30	20 45	0 6	23 18	1 1	22 21	15 58	0 47
5	1 30	20 47	0 6	23 19	1 1	22 21	15 58	0 46
7	1 30	20 49	0 7	23 19	1 1	22 21	15 59	0 45
9	1 30	20 51	0 7	23 19	1 1	22 20	15 59	0 45
11	1 29	20 53	0 7	23 20	1 1	22 20	16 0	0 44
13	1 29	20 55	0 7	23 20	1 1	22 20	16 1	0 44
15	1 29	20 57	0 7	23 21	1 1	22 20	16 1	0 43
17	1 29	20 58	0 7	23 21	1 1	22 20	16 2	0 43
19	1 29	21 0	0 7	23 22	1 1	22 20	16 3	0 42
21	1 29	21 2	0 7	23 22	1 1	22 20	16 3	0 42
23	1 29	21 3	0 7	23 22	1 1	22 19	16 4	0 42
25	1 29	21 5	0 7	23 23	1 1	22 19	16 5	0 42
27	1 29	21 7	0 7	23 23	1 1	22 19	16 6	0 41
29	1 29	21 8	0 7	23 24	1 1	22 19	16 7	0 41
31	1 N29	21 S 10	0 S 7	23 S 24	1 N 1	22 S 19	16 N 8	0 N41

Mutual Aspects

1. ☉ ⊻ ♇. ♂ **Q** ♅.
2. ☿ ∠ ♆. ♂ ✱ ♆.
3. ☿ ⊻ ♅.
4. ☉ ⊥ ♀, ☌ ♄. ♀ ⊥ ♄.
5. ☉ **P** ♆.
6. ☉ □ ♃. ♀ △ ♂, ∠ ♅.
7. ☉ ⊥ ♇.
8. ♂ △ ♇.
9. ☿ ⊥ ♆.
10. ♀ ☌ ♇.
13. ☿ ⊻ ♆.
14. ☉ ☌ ♅.
15. ☿ **P** ♄. ♂ □ ♄.
16. ☉ ∠ ♇. ☿ ⊻ ♇.
17. ☉ **P** ♅. ♂ **P** ♃.
18. ♂ ☌ ♃.
19. ☿ ⊻ ♀, ☌ ♄, **P** ♆. ♀ ⊻ ♄.
20. ☿ □ ♃, ⊥ ♇.
21. ♂ **Q** ♆.
22. ☿ □ ♂. ♀ △ ♃.
23. ☉ **P** ☿. ☿ **P** ♅. ♀ ⊥ ♅.
25. ☿ ☌ ♅.
26. ☉ ∠ ♀, **Q** ♃, **P** ♅. ☿ ∠ ♇.
27. ☉ ☌ ♆. ☿ ⊥ ♀. ♀ ∠ ♆.
30. ♂ □ ♅.
31. ☉ ✱ ♇. ♀ ⊻ ♅. ♂ ⚼ ♇.

LAST QUARTER—December 24, *9h. 17m. a.m.* (2° ♎ 16′)

DAILY MOTIONS OF THE PLANETS, 1986

JANUARY

D	☉ (° ′ ″)	☽ (° ′ ″)	☽ Dec. (° ′)	☿ (° ′)	♀ (° ′)	♂ (′)
1	1 1 9	13 22 49	5 58	1 27	1 15	37
2	1 1 9	13 36 45	6 18	1 28	1 15	37
3	1 1 9	13 51 49	6 22	1 28	1 16	37
4	1 1 10	14 7 27	6 7	1 29	1 16	37
5	1 1 10	14 22 30	5 30	1 29	1 16	36
6	1 1 10	14 35 13	4 26	1 30	1 16	37
7	1 1 11	14 43 25	2 55	1 30	1 16	37
8	1 1 10	14 45 4	1 4	1 31	1 16	36
9	1 1 10	14 38 52	0 53	1 31	1 15	36
10	1 1 10	14 24 46	2 40	1 32	1 15	36
11	1 1 10	14 4 6	4 4	1 32	1 15	36
12	1 1 9	13 39 9	5 1	1 33	1 15	36
13	1 1 8	13 12 41	5 34	1 33	1 15	36
14	1 1 8	12 47 18	5 47	1 34	1 15	36
15	1 1 7	12 25 4	5 46	1 34	1 15	36
16	1 1 6	12 7 24	5 34	1 35	1 15	36
17	1 1 6	11 55 5	5 13	1 35	1 15	36
18	1 1 5	11 48 24	4 42	1 36	1 15	36
19	1 1 4	11 47 15	4 1	1 36	1 15	36
20	1 1 3	11 51 11	3 9	1 37	1 15	36
21	1 1 2	11 59 27	2 5	1 37	1 15	36
22	1 1 1	12 11 7	0 51	1 38	1 15	36
23	1 1 0	12 25 3	0 32	1 38	1 15	36
24	1 0 59	12 40 0	1 56	1 39	1 15	36
25	1 0 59	12 54 48	3 15	1 40	1 15	36
26	1 0 58	13 8 30	4 24	1 40	1 15	36
27	1 0 57	13 20 31	5 19	1 41	1 15	36
28	1 0 56	13 30 43	5 58	1 42	1 15	36
29	1 0 55	13 39 24	6 19	1 42	1 15	36
30	1 0 55	13 47 5	6 23	1 43	1 15	36
31	1 0 54	13 54 19	6 9	1 44	1 15	36

FEBRUARY

D	☉ (° ′ ″)	☽ (° ′ ″)	☽ Dec. (° ′)	☿ (° ′)	♀ (° ′)	♂ (′)
1	1 0 53	14 1 25	5 34	1 44	1 15	35
2	1 0 52	14 8 11	4 37	1 45	1 15	35
3	1 0 52	14 13 55	3 16	1 46	1 15	35
4	1 0 51	14 17 25	1 36	1 46	1 15	35
5	1 0 50	14 17 20	0 14	1 47	1 15	35
6	1 0 49	14 12 27	2 2	1 48	1 15	35
7	1 0 48	14 2 13	3 34	1 48	1 15	35
8	1 0 46	13 46 56	4 43	1 49	1 15	35
9	1 0 45	13 27 44	5 27	1 49	1 15	35
10	1 0 44	13 6 24	5 50	1 49	1 15	35
11	1 0 42	12 44 55	5 56	1 49	1 15	35
12	1 0 41	12 25 11	5 47	1 49	1 15	35
13	1 0 39	12 8 45	5 27	1 49	1 15	35
14	1 0 37	11 56 44	4 57	1 49	1 15	35
15	1 0 36	11 49 52	4 17	1 48	1 15	35
16	1 0 34	11 48 29	3 27	1 47	1 15	35
17	1 0 32	11 52 32	2 26	1 46	1 15	35
18	1 0 30	12 1 42	1 15	1 44	1 15	34
19	1 0 29	12 15 16	0 5	1 42	1 15	34
20	1 0 27	12 32 15	1 29	1 39	1 15	34
21	1 0 25	12 51 16	2 51	1 36	1 15	34
22	1 0 23	13 10 46	4 7	1 32	1 15	34
23	1 0 21	13 29 8	5 10	1 28	1 15	34
24	1 0 20	13 44 55	5 57	1 23	1 15	34
25	1 0 18	13 57 9	6 27	1 17	1 15	34
26	1 0 16	14 5 27	6 36	1 11	1 15	34
27	1 0 15	14 10 2	6 24	1 4	1 15	34
28	1 0 13	14 11 33	5 50	0 57	1 15	34

MARCH

D	☉ (° ′ ″)	☽ (° ′ ″)	☽ Dec. (° ′)	☿ (° ′)	♀ (° ′)	♂ (′)
1	1 0 12	14 10 47	4 53	0 49	1 15	34
2	1 0 10	14 8 24	3 35	0 40	1 15	33
3	1 0 9	14 4 45	1 58	0 32	1 15	33
4	1 0 7	13 59 50	0 11	0 23	1 15	33
5	1 0 6	13 53 21	1 34	0 13	1 15	33
6	1 0 4	13 44 54	3 7	0 4	1 15	33
7	1 0 2	13 34 10	4 21	0 5	1 15	33
8	1 0 1	13 21 10	5 12	0 14	1 15	33
9	0 59 59	13 6 16	5 44	0 22	1 15	33
10	0 59 57	12 50 13	5 57	0 30	1 15	33
11	0 59 55	12 34 2	5 40	0 37	1 15	33
12	0 59 53	12 18 53	5 39	0 43	1 15	32
13	0 59 51	12 5 53	5 12	0 48	1 15	32
14	0 59 49	11 56 3	4 34	0 52	1 15	32
15	0 59 47	11 50 12	3 46	0 55	1 15	32
16	0 59 44	11 48 57	2 48	0 56	1 15	32
17	0 59 42	11 52 41	1 40	0 56	1 14	32
18	0 59 40	12 1 28	0 23	0 55	1 14	32
19	0 59 38	12 15 8	0 58	0 53	1 14	32
20	0 59 35	12 33 6	2 0	0 50	1 14	31
21	0 59 32	12 54 23	3 38	0 46	1 14	31
22	0 59 31	13 17 34	4 47	0 42	1 14	31
23	0 59 28	13 40 50	5 44	0 37	1 14	31
24	0 59 26	14 2 10	6 24	0 31	1 14	31
25	0 59 24	14 19 39	6 45	0 26	1 14	31
26	0 59 22	14 31 45	6 43	0 20	1 14	31
27	0 59 20	14 37 43	6 17	0 14	1 14	30
28	0 59 18	14 37 32	5 24	0 8	1 14	30
29	0 59 17	14 31 58	4 5	0 2	1 14	30
30	0 59 15	14 22 14	2 26	0 4	1 14	30
31	0 59 13	14 9 39	0 36	0 9	1 14	30

APRIL

D	☉ (° ′ ″)	☽ (° ′ ″)	☽ Dec. (° ′)	☿ (° ′)	♀ (° ′)	♂ (′)
1	0 59 12	13 55 26	1 12	0 14	1 14	30
2	0 59 10	13 40 33	2 47	0 19	1 14	29
3	0 59 8	13 25 36	3 0	0 24	1 14	29
4	0 59 6	13 10 58	4 58	0 29	1 14	29
5	0 59 4	12 56 49	5 33	0 33	1 14	29
6	0 59 2	12 43 17	5 10	0 37	1 14	29
7	0 59 0	12 30 30	5 40	0 41	1 14	28
8	0 58 58	12 18 42	5 44	0 45	1 14	28
9	0 58 56	12 8 12	5 22	0 48	1 14	28
10	0 58 54	11 59 28	4 49	0 51	1 14	28
11	0 58 52	11 53 0	0 4	0 54	1 14	28
12	0 58 50	11 49 22	3 8	0 57	1 14	27
13	0 58 48	11 49 7	2 1	1 0	1 14	27
14	0 58 46	11 52 46	0 48	1 3	1 13	27
15	0 58 44	12 0 42	0 31	1 6	1 13	27
16	0 58 41	12 13 9	1 51	1 8	1 14	26
17	0 58 39	12 30 2	3 7	1 11	1 13	26
18	0 58 37	12 51 0	4 17	1 13	1 13	26
19	0 58 35	13 15 9	5 17	1 15	1 13	26
20	0 58 32	13 41 5	6 4	1 17	1 13	25
21	0 58 30	14 6 52	6 36	1 19	1 13	25
22	0 58 28	14 30 5	6 49	1 21	1 13	25
23	0 58 26	14 48 18	6 37	1 24	1 13	24
24	0 58 24	14 59 22	5 57	1 25	1 13	24
25	0 58 23	15 2 1	4 47	1 27	1 13	24
26	0 58 21	14 56 10	3 9	1 29	1 13	23
27	0 58 20	14 42 54	1 14	1 31	1 13	23
28	0 58 18	14 24 11	0 44	1 33	1 13	23
29	0 58 16	14 2 21	2 28	1 35	1 13	22
30	0 58 15	13 39 36	3 50	1 37	1 13	22

MAY — JUNE

D	⊙	☽	☽Dec.	☿	♀	♂	D	⊙	☽	☽Dec.	☿	♀	♂
1	0 58 13	13 17 40	4 48	1 39	1 13	22	1	0 57 30	12 16 36	5 46	2 2	1 11	5
2	0 58 12	12 57 42	5 26	1 41	1 13	21	2	0 57 29	12 4 15	5 29	2 0	1 11	4
3	0 58 10	12 40 22	5 45	1 42	1 13	21	3	0 57 28	11 55 51	5 2	1 57	1 11	4
4	0 58 9	12 25 50	5 51	1 44	1 13	21	4	0 57 28	11 50 53	4 25	1 55	1 11	3
5	0 58 7	12 14 2	5 44	1 46	1 13	20	5	0 57 27	11 48 48	3 36	1 53	1 11	2
6	0 58 6	12 4 44	5 26	1 48	1 13	20	6	0 57 26	11 49 3	2 36	1 50	1 11	1
7	0 58 4	11 57 43	4 57	1 50	1 13	19	7	0 57 25	11 51 15	1 25	1 48	1 11	1
8	0 58 3	11 52 47	4 16	1 52	1 13	19	8	0 57 24	11 55 9	0 9	1 45	1 11	0
9	0 58 1	11 49 53	3 24	1 54	1 13	18	9	0 57 23	12 0 45	1 1	1 43	1 11	1
10	0 57 59	11 49 6	2 20	1 55	1 13	18	10	0 57 22	12 8 14	2 26	1 40	1 11	2
11	0 57 58	11 50 39	1 8	1 57	1 13	17	11	0 57 21	12 17 56	3 34	1 37	1 11	2
12	0 57 56	11 54 53	0 9	1 59	1 13	17	12	0 57 21	12 30 16	4 32	1 35	1 11	3
13	0 57 54	12 2 12	1 28	2 1	1 12	16	13	0 57 20	12 45 40	5 19	1 32	1 11	4
14	0 57 53	12 13 2	2 43	2 3	1 12	16	14	0 57 19	13 4 20	5 55	1 29	1 11	4
15	0 57 51	12 27 41	3 51	2 4	1 12	15	15	0 57 18	13 26 8	6 18	1 27	1 11	5
16	0 57 49	12 46 16	4 50	2 6	1 12	15	16	0 57 17	13 50 24	6 27	1 24	1 10	6
17	0 57 47	13 8 34	5 38	2 7	1 12	14	17	0 57 16	14 15 38	6 15	1 21	1 10	7
18	0 57 46	13 33 49	6 15	2 8	1 12	14	18	0 57 15	14 39 35	5 39	1 18	1 10	7
19	0 57 44	14 0 39	6 36	2 10	1 12	13	19	0 57 15	14 59 17	4 32	1 15	1 10	8
20	0 57 42	14 26 59	6 38	2 10	1 12	13	20	0 57 14	15 11 37	2 54	1 12	1 10	9
21	0 57 41	14 50 2	6 16	2 11	1 12	12	21	0 57 14	15 14 10	0 54	1 9	1 10	10
22	0 57 40	15 6 53	5 23	2 12	1 12	12	22	0 57 13	15 5 58	1 13	1 6	1 10	10
23	0 57 38	15 14 55	3 57	2 12	1 11	11	23	0 57 13	14 47 58	3 4	1 3	1 10	11
24	0 57 37	15 12 42	2 5	2 12	1 11	11	24	0 57 13	14 22 43	4 28	1 0	1 10	11
25	0 57 36	15 0 28	0 0	2 11	1 11	10	25	0 57 13	13 53 38	5 22	0 57	1 10	12
26	0 57 35	14 40 0	1 58	2 11	1 12	9	26	0 57 12	13 24 2	5 10	0 53	1 10	13
27	0 57 34	14 14 14	3 42	2 10	1 12	9	27	0 57 12	12 56 36	6 0	0 50	1 10	13
28	0 57 33	13 46 17	4 42	2 9	1 12	8	28	0 57 13	12 33 6	6 5	0 46	1 10	14
29	0 57 32	13 18 56	5 24	2 7	1 12	7	29	0 57 13	12 14 30	5 37	0 43	1 9	14
30	0 57 31	12 54 11	5 46	2 6	1 12	7	30	0 57 13	12 1 3	5 11	0 39	1 9	15
31	0 57 31	12 33 14	5 52	2 4	1 12	6							

JULY — AUGUST

D	⊙	☽	☽Dec.	☿	♀	♂	D	⊙	☽	☽Dec.	☿	♀	♂
1	0 57 13	11 52 35	4 34	0 35	1 9	15	1	0 57 26	11 55 0	0 45	0 6	1 5	8
2	0 57 13	11 48 35	3 47	0 31	1 9	16	2	0 57 27	12 2 40	0 34	0 0	1 5	8
3	0 57 13	11 48 22	2 50	0 27	1 9	16	3	0 57 28	12 12 25	0 54	0 6	1 5	7
4	0 57 13	11 51 10	1 42	0 22	1 9	16	4	0 57 29	12 23 22	3 58	0 13	1 4	6
5	0 57 14	11 56 15	0 26	0 18	1 9	17	5	0 57 30	12 34 49	4 13	0 19	1 4	5
6	0 57 14	12 2 57	0 54	0 13	1 9	17	6	0 57 31	12 46 18	5 5	0 26	1 4	4
7	0 57 14	12 10 48	2 11	0 9	1 9	17	7	0 57 32	12 57 39	5 44	0 33	1 4	4
8	0 57 14	12 19 34	3 22	0 4	1 9	17	8	0 57 32	13 8 59	6 9	0 39	1 3	3
9	0 57 14	12 29 17	4 22	0 1	1 8	18	9	0 57 33	13 20 37	6 18	0 46	1 3	2
10	0 57 14	12 40 14	5 10	0 5	1 8	18	10	0 57 34	13 32 52	6 11	0 52	1 3	1
11	0 57 14	12 52 50	5 46	0 10	1 8	18	11	0 57 35	13 45 54	5 45	0 59	1 3	0
12	0 57 14	13 7 31	6 9	0 15	1 8	17	12	0 57 36	13 59 29	5 7	1 5	1 3	1
13	0 57 14	13 24 30	6 17	0 19	1 8	17	13	0 57 37	14 12 48	4 5	1 11	1 2	1
14	0 57 14	13 43 39	6 9	0 24	1 8	17	14	0 57 38	14 24 32	3 10	1 16	1 2	2
15	0 57 14	14 4 9	5 41	0 28	1 8	17	15	0 57 39	14 32 53	1 17	1 22	1 2	3
16	0 57 14	14 24 29	4 48	0 31	1 8	17	16	0 57 40	14 36 5	0 40	1 27	1 1	4
17	0 57 14	14 42 21	3 27	0 34	1 7	17	17	0 57 41	14 32 45	2 25	1 32	1 1	5
18	0 57 14	14 55 2	1 40	0 37	1 7	16	18	0 57 42	14 22 29	4 47	1 36	1 1	6
19	0 57 15	15 0 0	0 23	0 39	1 7	16	19	0 57 43	14 5 58	5 41	1 40	1 0	6
20	0 57 15	14 55 41	2 22	0 41	1 7	16	20	0 57 45	13 44 52	6 10	1 44	1 0	7
21	0 57 15	14 42 4	4 1	0 42	1 7	15	21	0 57 46	13 21 23	6 17	1 47	1 0	8
22	0 57 16	14 20 47	5 11	0 42	1 7	15	22	0 57 48	12 57 47	5 5	1 50	0 59	9
23	0 57 17	13 54 33	5 52	0 41	1 7	14	23	0 57 50	12 36 5	5 43	1 52	0 59	9
24	0 57 17	13 26 32	6 9	0 40	1 6	13	24	0 57 51	12 17 47	5 7	1 56	0 59	10
25	0 57 18	12 59 30	7 0	0 38	1 6	13	25	0 57 53	12 3 55	4 22	1 56	0 58	11
26	0 57 19	12 35 36	5 52	0 35	1 6	13	26	0 57 55	11 55 1	3 26	1 57	0 58	12
27	0 57 20	12 16 13	5 25	0 32	1 6	12	27	0 57 57	11 51 14	2 21	1 58	0 57	13
28	0 57 21	12 2 2	4 48	0 28	1 6	11	28	0 57 59	11 52 26	1 8	1 58	0 57	13
29	0 57 22	11 53 12	4 2	0 23	1 6	11	29	0 58 1	11 58 9	0 10	1 58	0 57	14
30	0 57 24	11 49 28	3 6	0 18	1 5	10	30	0 58 2	12 7 44	1 31	1 58	0 56	15
31	0 57 25	11 50 19	2 0	0 12	1 5	9	31	0 58 4	12 20 18	2 48	1 58	0 56	15

SEPTEMBER

D	☉ (° ′ ″)	☽ (° ′ ″)	☽ Dec. (° ′)	☿ (° ′)	♀ (° ′)	♂ (′)
1	0 58 6	12 34 49	3 57	1 58	0 55	16
2	0 58 8	12 50 12	4 56	1 57	0 55	17
3	0 58 9	13 5 25	5 41	1 56	0 54	17
4	0 58 11	13 19 37	6 12	1 55	0 54	18
5	0 58 13	13 32 16	6 26	1 54	0 53	18
6	0 58 14	13 43 7	6 22	1 53	0 52	19
7	0 58 16	13 52 13	5 58	1 52	0 52	20
8	0 58 17	13 59 45	5 12	1 51	0 51	20
9	0 58 19	14 5 50	4 3	1 50	0 51	21
10	0 58 21	14 10 25	2 32	1 49	0 50	21
11	0 58 22	14 13 13	0 44	1 48	0 49	22
12	0 58 24	14 13 39	1 8	1 47	0 48	22
13	0 58 25	14 11 5	2 53	1 46	0 48	23
14	0 58 27	14 4 57	4 19	1 45	0 47	24
15	0 58 28	13 55 4	5 21	1 44	0 46	24
16	0 58 30	13 41 37	6 0	1 43	0 45	24
17	0 58 32	13 25 22	6 17	1 42	0 44	25
18	0 58 34	13 7 22	6 15	1 40	0 43	25
19	0 58 36	12 48 58	5 57	1 39	0 42	26
20	0 58 38	12 31 29	5 26	1 38	0 41	26
21	0 58 40	12 16 9	4 43	1 37	0 40	27
22	0 58 42	12 3 59	3 49	1 36	0 39	27
23	0 58 45	11 55 46	2 45	1 36	0 38	28
24	0 58 47	11 52 1	1 33	1 35	0 37	28
25	0 58 49	11 53 0	0 16	1 34	0 36	28
26	0 58 51	11 58 45	1 4	1 33	0 34	29
27	0 58 54	12 9 1	2 11	1 32	0 33	29
28	0 58 56	12 23 18	3 33	1 31	0 32	29
29	0 58 58	12 40 46	4 36	1 30	0 30	30
30	0 59 0	13 0 17	5 28	1 29	0 29	30

OCTOBER

D	☉ (° ′ ″)	☽ (° ′ ″)	☽ Dec. (° ′)	☿ (° ′)	♀ (° ′)	♂ (′)
1	0 59 2	13 20 29	6 7	1 28	0 27	31
2	0 59 4	13 39 52	6 30	1 27	0 26	31
3	0 59 6	13 56 57	6 35	1 26	0 24	31
4	0 59 8	14 10 28	6 18	1 25	0 22	32
5	0 59 10	14 19 37	5 37	1 24	0 21	32
6	0 59 12	14 24 4	4 30	1 23	0 19	32
7	0 59 14	14 24 3	2 59	1 22	0 17	32
8	0 59 16	14 20 8	1 10	1 21	0 15	33
9	0 59 18	14 13 8	0 44	1 20	0 13	33
10	0 59 19	14 3 50	2 29	1 19	0 11	33
11	0 59 21	13 52 56	3 57	1 18	0 8	34
12	0 59 23	13 40 56	5 2	1 17	0 6	34
13	0 59 25	13 28 11	5 44	1 15	0 4	34
14	0 59 26	13 14 55	6 7	1 14	0 2	34
15	0 59 28	13 1 20	6 12	1 12	0 1	35
16	0 59 30	12 47 41	6 2	1 10	0 3	35
17	0 59 32	12 34 21	5 37	1 9	0 6	35
18	0 59 34	12 21 47	5 0	1 7	0 8	35
19	0 59 36	12 10 34	4 10	1 4	0 10	35
20	0 59 39	12 1 20	3 8	1 2	0 13	36
21	0 59 41	11 54 47	1 58	0 59	0 15	36
22	0 59 43	11 51 32	0 42	0 56	0 18	36
23	0 59 45	11 52 9	0 37	0 53	0 20	36
24	0 59 47	11 57 5	1 51	0 49	0 22	36
25	0 59 50	12 6 36	3 6	0 45	0 24	37
26	0 59 52	12 20 43	4 9	0 41	0 26	37
27	0 59 54	12 39 9	5 4	0 36	0 28	37
28	0 59 56	13 1 10	5 48	0 30	0 30	37
29	0 59 58	13 25 34	6 19	0 24	0 31	37
30	1 0 0	13 50 37	6 35	0 18	0 33	38
31	1 0 2	14 14 5	6 32	0 10	0 34	38

NOVEMBER

D	☉ (° ′ ″)	☽ (° ′ ″)	☽ Dec. (° ′)	☿ (° ′)	♀ (° ′)	♂ (′)
1	1 0 4	14 33 36	6 3	0 2	0 35	38
2	1 0 6	14 46 56	5 6	0 6	0 36	38
3	1 0 8	14 52 35	3 39	0 15	0 36	38
4	1 0 10	14 50 10	1 48	0 25	0 36	38
5	1 0 11	14 40 28	0 13	0 35	0 36	38
6	1 0 13	14 25 13	2 7	0 44	0 36	39
7	1 0 14	14 6 35	3 41	0 54	0 36	39
8	1 0 16	13 46 43	4 50	1 2	0 35	39
9	1 0 17	13 27 16	5 35	1 10	0 34	39
10	1 0 18	13 9 21	5 59	1 16	0 33	39
11	1 0 20	12 53 30	7 1	1 19	0 32	39
12	1 0 21	12 39 49	6 0	1 20	0 30	39
13	1 0 23	12 28 9	5 40	1 19	0 28	39
14	1 0 24	12 18 14	5 8	1 15	0 26	40
15	1 0 26	12 9 48	4 23	1 8	0 24	40
16	1 0 28	12 2 43	3 26	1 0	0 22	40
17	1 0 29	11 57 4	2 19	0 50	0 20	40
18	1 0 31	11 53 4	1 4	0 39	0 18	40
19	1 0 33	11 51 10	0 15	0 27	0 15	40
20	1 0 34	11 51 54	1 32	0 16	0 13	40
21	1 0 36	11 55 55	2 43	0 4	0 10	40
22	1 0 37	12 3 48	3 46	0 7	0 8	40
23	1 0 39	12 16 44	4 40	0 17	0 5	40
24	1 0 41	12 33 0	5 24	0 26	0 3	40
25	1 0 42	12 54 29	5 58	0 35	0 0	40
26	1 0 44	13 19 55	6 20	0 42	0 2	41
27	1 0 46	13 47 58	6 27	0 49	0 5	41
28	1 0 47	14 16 26	6 14	0 55	0 7	41
29	1 0 49	14 42 23	5 34	1 0	0 9	41
30	1 0 50	15 2 26	4 23	1 4	0 11	41

DECEMBER

D	☉ (° ′ ″)	☽ (° ′ ″)	☽ Dec. (° ′)	☿ (° ′)	♀ (° ′)	♂ (′)
1	1 0 51	15 13 33	2 39	1 8	0 14	41
2	1 0 52	15 13 56	0 35	1 11	0 16	41
3	1 0 53	15 3 38	1 31	1 14	0 18	41
4	1 0 54	14 44 35	3 21	1 17	0 20	41
5	1 0 55	14 19 51	4 41	1 19	0 22	41
6	1 0 56	13 52 51	5 33	1 21	0 23	41
7	1 0 56	13 26 27	6 0	1 22	0 25	41
8	1 0 57	13 2 39	6 8	1 24	0 27	41
9	1 0 57	12 42 33	6 2	1 25	0 29	41
10	1 0 58	12 26 30	5 43	1 26	0 30	41
11	1 0 59	12 14 20	5 13	1 27	0 32	41
12	1 1 0	12 5 17	4 31	1 28	0 33	41
13	1 1 0	11 59 29	3 38	1 28	0 35	41
14	1 1 1	11 55 34	2 35	1 29	0 36	42
15	1 1 2	11 53 17	1 22	1 29	0 38	42
16	1 1 2	11 52 20	0 4	1 30	0 39	42
17	1 1 3	11 52 43	1 14	1 30	0 40	42
18	1 1 4	11 54 40	2 27	1 30	0 41	42
19	1 1 4	11 58 39	3 11	1 31	0 42	42
20	1 1 5	12 5 17	4 25	1 31	0 44	42
21	1 1 6	12 15 17	5 8	1 31	0 45	42
22	1 1 6	12 29 17	5 41	1 32	0 46	42
23	1 1 7	12 47 40	6 3	1 32	0 47	42
24	1 1 8	13 10 28	6 13	1 32	0 48	42
25	1 1 9	13 37 0	6 8	1 32	0 48	42
26	1 1 9	14 5 45	5 42	1 33	0 49	42
27	1 1 10	14 34 9	4 50	1 33	0 50	42
28	1 1 10	14 58 46	3 26	1 33	0 51	42
29	1 1 11	15 15 48	1 32	1 33	0 52	42
30	1 1 11	15 22 11	0 37	1 34	0 52	42
31	1 1 11	15 16 31	2 42	1 34	0 53	42

JANUARY

D.M.		
2	5.08 A.M.	⊕ In Perihelion.
3	5.19 A.M.	☿ in ☊.
3	7.21 A.M.	☽ on Equator.
8	7.26 A.M.	☽ in Perigee.
9	1.06 P.M.	☽ Max. Dec. 27 °S. 39′.
13	1.10 P.M.	☿ in Aphelion.
16	3.12 A.M.	☽ on Equator.
19	4.05 P.M.	♀ Sup. ☌ ☉.
20	1.24 A.M.	☽ in Apogee.
23	2.59 P.M.	☽ Max. Dec. 27 °N. 41′.
27	5.20 A.M.	♀ in Aphelion.
30	11.48 A.M.	☽ on Equator.

FEBRUARY

D.M.		
1	1.11 A.M.	☿ Sup ☌ ☉.
4	4.09 P.M.	☽ in Perigee.
5	8.56 P.M.	☽ Max. Dec. 27 °S. 46′.
12	11.26 A.M.	☽ on Equator.
16	10.24 P.M.	☽ in Apogee.
19	10.46 P.M.	☽ Max. Dec. 27° N. 52′.
21	9.14 P.M.	☿ in ☊.
26	0.49 P.M.	☿ in Perihelion.
26	6.00 P.M.	☽ on Equator.
28	4.00 P.M.	☿ Gt. Elong. 18° E.

MARCH

D.M.		
1	9.36 A.M.	☽ in Perigee.
5	2.35 A.M.	☽ Max. Dec. 27 °S. 58′.
11	7.46 P.M.	☽ on Equator.
16	6.50 P.M.	☽ in Apogee.
16	7.34 P.M.	☿ Inf. ☌ ☉.
19	7.00 A.M.	☽ Max. Dec. 28 °N. 04′.
20	10.03 P.M.	☉ Enters ♈, *Equinox*
26	2.59 A.M.	☽ on Equator.
26	0.45 P.M.	♂ in ☋.
28	1.57 P.M.	☽ in Perigee.

APRIL

D.M.		
1	4.35 A.M.	☿ in ☋.
1	7.53 A.M.	☽ Max. Dec. 28 °S. 07′.
8	3.02 A.M.	☽ on Equator.
9	6.08 A.M.	☉ Partial Eclipse.
11	0.27 P.M.	☿ in Aphelion.
13	11.59 A.M.	☽ in Apogee.
13	3.00 P.M.	☿ Gt. Elong. 28 °W.
15	2.42 P.M.	☽ Max. Dec. 28 °N. 09′.
15	7.07 P.M.	♀ in ☊.
22	1.30 P.M.	☽ on Equator.
24	0.46 P.M.	☽ Total Eclipse.
25	5.41 P.M.	☽ in Perigee.
28	2.54 P.M.	☽ Max. Dec. 28 °S. 08′.

MAY

D.M.		
5	8.59 A.M.	☽ on Equator.
10	10.36 P.M.	☽ in Apogee.
12	9.12 P.M.	☽ Max. Dec. 28 °N. 06′.
19	3.04 P.M.	♀ in Perihelion.
19	11.24 P.M.	☽ on Equator.
20	8.30 P.M.	☿ in ☊.
23	1.24 A.M.	☿ Sup ☌ ☉.
24	3.04 P.M.	☽ in Perigee.
25	0.04 P.M.	☿ in Perihelion.
26	0.01 A.M.	☽ Max. Dec. 28 °S. 04′.

JUNE

D.M.		
1	2.17 P.M.	☽ on Equator.
7	1.57 A.M.	☽ in Apogee.
9	2.40 P.M.	☽ Max. Dec. 28 °N. 01′.
16	7.05 A.M.	☽ on Equator.
21	4.30 P.M.	☉ Enters ♋, *Solstice.*
21	0.52 P.M.	☽ in Perigee.
22	10.09 A.M.	☽ Max. Dec. 28 °S. 01′.
25	8.00 P.M.	☿ Gt. Elong. 25 °E.
28	3.50 A.M.	☿ in ☋.
28	8.12 P.M.	☽ on Equator.

JULY

D.M.		
4	8.06 A.M.	☽ in Apogee.
5	10.20 A.M.	⊕ in Aphelion.

JULY—*contd.*

D.M.		
6	7.53 A.M.	☽ Max. Dec. 28 °N. 00′.
8	11.42 A.M.	☿ in Aphelion.
13	0.24 P.M.	☽ on Equator.
19	7.33 P.M.	☽ in Perigee.
19	7.40 P.M.	☽ Max. Dec. 28 °S. 03′.
23	11.10 A.M.	☿ Inf. ☌ ☉.
26	3.35 A.M.	☽ on Equator.
31	9.21 P.M.	☽ in Apogee.

AUGUST

D.M.		
2	1.49 P.M.	☽ Max. Dec. 28 °N. 06′.
5	8.22 A.M.	♀ in ☋.
9	5.03 P.M.	☽ on Equator.
11	4.00 P.M.	☿ Gt. Elong. 19 °W.
16	3.30 A.M.	☽ Max. Dec. 28 °S. 11′.
16	4.38 P.M.	☽ in Perigee.
16	7.46 P.M.	☿ in ☊.
21	11.20 A.M.	☿ in Perihelion.
22	0.13 P.M.	☽ on Equator.
27	9.00 A.M.	♀ Gt. Elong. 46 °E.
28	2.43 P.M.	☽ in Apogee.
29	8.54 P.M.	☽ Max. Dec. 28 °N. 16′.

SEPTEMBER

D.M.		
5	5.32 P.M.	☿ Sup. ☌ ☉.
5	11.01 P.M.	☽ on Equator.
8	10.11 P.M.	♀ in Aphelion.
12	0.02 A.M.	☽ in Perigee.
12	9.27 A.M.	☽ Max. Dec. 28 °S. 21′.
18	9.08 P.M.	☽ on Equator.
23	7.59 A.M.	☉ Enters ♎, *Equinox.*
24	3.05 A.M.	☿ in ☋.
25	10.01 A.M.	☽ in Apogee.
25	1.38 P.M.	♂ in Perihelion.
26	4.49 A.M.	☽ Max. Dec. 28 °N. 25′.

OCTOBER

D.M.		
1	10.00 A.M.	♀ Gt. Brilliance
3	7.24 A.M.	☽ on Equator.
3	6.55 P.M.	☉ Annular-Total Eclipse.
4	10.57 A.M.	☿ in Aphelion.
7	9.56 A.M.	☽ in Perigee.
9	2.48 P.M.	☽ Max. Dec. 28 °S. 26′.
16	4.56 A.M.	☽ on Equator.
17	7.22 P.M.	☽ Total Eclipse.
21	10.00 P.M.	☿ Gt. Elong. 24 °E.
23	5.35 A.M.	☽ in Apogee.
23	0.41 P.M.	☽ Max. Dec. 28 °N. 26′.
30	5.27 P.M.	☽ on Equator.

NOVEMBER

D.M.		
4	2.34 A.M.	☽ in Perigee.
5	10.16 A.M.	♀ Inf. ☌ ☉.
5	9.29 P.M.	☽ Max. Dec. 28 °S. 24′.
12	10.56 A.M.	☽ on Equator.
12	7.01 P.M.	☿ in ☊.
13	4.19 A.M.	☿ Inf. ☌ ☉ (Transit).
17	10.35 A.M.	☿ in Perihelion.
19	7.31 P.M.	☽ Max. Dec. 28 °N. 20′.
19	10.14 P.M.	☽ in Apogee.
26	11.50 A.M.	♀ in ☊.
27	3.08 A.M.	☽ on Equator.
30	3.00 A.M.	☿ Gt. Elong. 20 °W.

DECEMBER

D.M.		
2	10.37 A.M.	☽ in Perigee.
3	6.32 A.M.	☽ Max. Dec. 28 °S. 18′.
9	3.54 P.M.	☽ on Equator.
11	8.00 P.M.	♀ Gt. Brilliance.
17	1.12 A.M.	☽ Max. Dec. 28 °N. 15′.
17	5.05 A.M.	☽ in Apogee.
21	2.21 A.M.	☿ in ☋.
22	4.02 A.M.	☉ Enters ♑, *Solstice.*
24	10.34 A.M.	☽ on Equator.
30	8.49 A.M.	♀ in Perihelion.
30	5.12 P.M.	☽ Max. Dec. 28 °S. 16′.
30	11.19 P.M.	☽ in Perigee.
31	10.12 A.M.	☿ in Aphelion.

TABLES OF HOUSES FOR LONDON, Latitude 51° 32′ N.

Sidereal Time H. M. S.	10 (♈)	11 (♉)	12 (♊)	Ascen (♋)	2 (♌)	3 (♍)
0 0 0	0	9	22	26 36	12	3
0 3 40	1	10	23	27 17	13	3
0 7 20	2	11	24	27 56	14	4
0 11 0	3	12	25	28 42	15	5
0 14 41	4	13	25	29 17	15	6
0 18 21	5	14	26	29 55	16	7
0 22 2	6	15	27	0 ♌ 34	17	8
0 25 42	7	16	28	1 14	18	8
0 29 23	8	17	29	1 55	18	9
0 33 4	9	18	♋	2 33	19	10
0 36 45	10	19	1	3 14	20	11
0 40 26	11	20	1	3 54	20	12
0 44 8	12	21	2	4 33	21	13
0 47 50	13	22	3	5 12	22	14
0 51 32	14	23	4	5 52	23	15
0 55 14	15	24	5	6 30	23	15
0 58 57	16	25	6	7 9	24	16
1 2 40	17	26	6	7 50	25	17
1 6 23	18	27	7	8 30	26	18
1 10 7	19	28	8	9 9	26	19
1 13 51	20	29	9	9 48	27	19
1 17 35	21	♊	10	10 28	28	20
1 21 20	22	1	10	11 8	28	21
1 25 6	23	2	11	11 48	29	22
1 28 52	24	3	12	12 28	♍	23
1 32 38	25	4	13	13 8	1	24
1 36 25	26	5	14	13 48	1	25
1 40 12	27	6	14	14 28	2	25
1 44 0	28	7	15	15 8	3	26
1 47 48	29	8	16	15 48	4	27
1 51 37	30	9	17	16 28	4	28

Sidereal Time H. M. S.	10 (♉)	11 (♊)	12 (♋)	Ascen (♌)	2 (♍)	3 (♍)
1 51 37	0	9	17	16 28	4	28
1 55 27	1	10	18	17 8	5	29
1 59 17	2	11	19	17 48	6	♎
2 3 8	3	12	19	18 28	7	1
2 6 59	4	13	20	19 9	8	2
2 10 51	5	14	21	19 49	9	2
2 14 44	6	15	22	20 29	9	3
2 18 37	7	16	22	21 10	10	4
2 22 31	8	17	23	21 51	11	5
2 26 25	9	18	24	22 32	11	6
2 30 20	10	19	25	23 14	12	7
2 34 16	11	20	25	23 55	13	8
2 38 13	12	21	26	24 36	14	9
2 42 10	13	22	27	25 17	15	10
2 46 8	14	23	28	25 58	15	11
2 50 7	15	24	29	26 40	16	12
2 54 7	16	25	29	27 22	17	12
2 58 7	17	26	♌	28 4	18	13
3 2 8	18	27	1	28 46	18	14
3 6 9	19	27	2	29 29	19	15
3 10 12	20	28	3	0 ♍ 12	20	16
3 14 15	21	29	3	0 54	21	17
3 18 19	22	♋	4	1 36	22	18
3 22 23	23	1	5	2 20	22	19
3 26 29	24	2	6	3 2	23	20
3 30 35	25	3	7	3 45	24	21
3 34 41	26	4	7	4 28	25	22
3 38 49	27	5	8	5 11	26	23
3 42 57	28	6	9	5 54	27	24
3 47 6	29	7	10	6 38	27	25
3 51 15	30	8	11	7 21	28	25

Sidereal Time H. M. S.	10 (♊)	11 (♋)	12 (♌)	Ascen (♍)	2 (♍)	3 (♎)
3 51 15	0	8	11	7 21	28	25
3 55 25	1	9	12	8 5	29	26
3 59 36	2	10	12	8 49	♎	27
4 3 48	3	10	13	9 33	1	28
4 8 0	4	11	14	10 17	2	29
4 12 13	5	12	15	11 2	2	♏
4 16 26	6	13	16	11 46	3	1
4 20 40	7	14	17	12 30	4	2
4 24 55	8	15	17	13 15	5	3
4 29 10	9	16	18	14 0	6	4
4 33 26	10	17	19	14 45	7	5
4 37 42	11	18	20	15 30	8	6
4 41 59	12	19	21	16 15	8	7
4 46 16	13	20	21	17 0	9	8
4 50 34	14	21	22	17 45	10	9
4 54 52	15	22	23	18 30	11	10
4 59 10	16	23	24	19 16	12	11
5 3 29	17	24	25	20 3	13	12
5 7 49	18	25	26	20 49	14	13
5 12 9	19	25	27	21 35	14	14
5 16 29	20	26	28	22 20	15	14
5 20 49	21	27	28	23 6	16	15
5 25 9	22	28	29	23 51	17	16
5 29 30	23	29	♏	24 37	18	17
5 33 51	24	♌	1	25 23	19	18

Sidereal Time H. M. S.	10 (♋)	11 (♌)	12 (♍)	Ascen (♎)	2 (♎)	3 (♏)
6 0 0	0	6	6	0 0	24	24
6 4 22	1	7	7	0 47	25	25
6 8 43	2	8	8	1 33	26	26
6 13 5	3	9	9	2 19	27	27
6 17 26	4	10	10	3 5	27	28
6 21 48	5	11	10	3 51	28	29
6 26 9	6	12	11	4 37	29	♐
6 30 30	7	13	12	5 23	♏	1
6 34 51	8	14	13	6 9	1	2
6 39 11	9	15	14	6 55	2	3
6 43 31	10	16	15	7 40	2	4
6 47 51	11	16	16	8 26	3	4
6 52 11	12	17	16	9 12	4	5
6 56 31	13	18	17	9 58	5	6
7 0 50	14	19	18	10 43	6	7
7 5 8	15	20	19	11 28	7	8
7 9 26	16	21	20	12 14	8	9
7 13 44	17	22	21	12 59	8	10
7 18 1	18	23	22	13 45	9	11
7 22 18	19	24	23	14 30	10	12
7 26 34	20	25	24	15 15	11	13
7 30 50	21	26	25	16 0	12	14
7 35 5	22	27	26	16 45	13	15
7 39 20	23	28	26	17 30	13	16
7 43 34	24	29	27	18 15	14	17
7 47 47	25	♍	28	18 59	15	18
7 52 0	26	1	29	19 43	16	19
7 56 12	27	2	29	20 27	17	20
8 0 24	28	3	♎	21 11	18	20
8 4 35	29	4	1	21 56	18	21
8 8 45	30	5	2	22 40	19	22

Sidereal Time H. M. S.	10 (♌)	11 (♍)	12 (♎)	Ascen (♎)	2 (♏)	3 (♐)
8 8 45	0	5	2	22 40	19	22
8 12 54	1	5	3	23 24	20	23
8 17 3	2	6	3	24 7	21	24
8 21 11	3	7	4	24 50	22	25
8 25 19	4	8	5	25 34	23	26
8 29 26	5	9	6	26 18	23	27
8 33 31	6	10	7	27 1	24	28
8 37 37	7	11	8	27 44	25	29
8 41 41	8	12	8	28 26	26	♐
8 45 45	9	13	9	29 9	27	1
8 49 48	10	14	10	29 50	27	2
8 53 51	11	15	11	0 ♏ 32	28	3
8 57 52	12	16	12	1 15	29	4
9 1 53	13	17	12	1 58	♐	4
9 5 53	14	18	13	2 39	1	5
9 9 53	15	18	14	3 21	1	6
9 13 52	16	19	15	4 3	2	7
9 17 50	17	20	16	4 44	3	8
9 21 47	18	21	16	5 26	3	9
9 25 44	19	22	17	6 7	4	10
9 29 40	20	23	18	6 48	5	11
9 33 35	21	24	18	7 29	5	12
9 37 29	22	25	19	8 9	6	13
9 41 23	23	26	20	8 50	7	14
9 45 16	24	27	21	9 31	8	15
9 49 8	25	28	22	10 11	9	16
9 53 1	26	28	23	10 51	9	17
9 56 52	27	29	23	11 32	10	18
10 0 43	28	♎	24	12 12	11	19
10 4 33	29	1	25	12 53	12	20
10 8 2	30	2	26	13 33	13	21

Sidereal Time H. M. S.	10 (♍)	11 (♎)	12 (♎)	Ascen (♏)	2 (♐)	3 (♑)
10 8 23	0	2	26	13 33	13	20
10 12 12	1	3	26	14 14	14	21
10 16 0	2	4	27	14 53	15	22
10 19 48	3	5	28	15 33	15	23
10 23 35	4	5	29	16 13	16	24
10 27 22	5	6	29	16 52	17	25
10 31 8	6	7	♏	17 32	18	26
10 34 54	7	8	1	18 12	19	27
10 38 40	8	9	2	18 52	20	28
10 42 25	9	10	2	19 31	20	29
10 46 9	10	11	3	20 11	21	♑
10 49 53	11	11	4	20 50	22	1
10 53 37	12	12	4	21 30	23	2
10 57 20	13	13	5	22 9	24	3
11 1 3	14	14	6	22 49	24	4
11 4 46	15	15	7	23 28	25	5
11 8 28	16	16	7	24 8	26	6
11 12 10	17	17	8	24 47	27	8
11 15 52	18	17	9	25 27	28	9
11 19 34	19	18	10	26 6	29	10
11 23 15	20	19	10	26 45	♑	11
11 26 56	21	20	11	27 25	0	12
11 30 37	22	21	12	28 5	1	13
11 34 18	23	22	13	28 44	2	14
11 37 58	24	23	13	29 24	3	15
11 41 39	25	23	14	0 ♐ 3	4	16
11 45 19	26	24	15	0 43	5	17
11 49 0	27	25	15	1 23	6	18
11 52 40	28	26	16	2 3	6	19
11 56 20	29	27	17	2 43	7	20
12 0 0	30	27	17	3 23	8	21

Upper half

Sidereal Time (H. M. S.)	10 ♎	11 ♎	12 ♏	Ascen ♐	2 ♑	3 ♒
12 0 0	0	27	17	3 23	8	21
12 3 40	1	28	18	4 4	9	23
12 7 20	2	29	19	4 45	10	24
12 11 0	3	♏	20	5 26	11	25
12 14 41	4	1	20	6 7	12	26
12 18 21	5	1	21	6 48	13	27
12 22 2	6	2	22	7 29	14	28
12 25 42	7	3	23	8 10	15	29
12 29 23	8	4	23	8 51	16	♓
12 33 4	9	5	24	9 33	17	2
12 36 45	10	6	25	10 15	18	4
12 40 26	11	6	25	10 57	19	5
12 44 8	12	7	26	11 40	20	6
12 47 50	13	8	27	12 22	21	8
12 51 32	14	9	28	13 4	22	9
12 55 14	15	10	28	13 47	23	9
12 58 57	16	11	29	14 30	24	11
13 2 40	17	11	♐	15 14	25	11
13 6 23	18	12	1	15 59	26	12
13 10 7	19	13	1	16 44	27	13
13 13 51	20	14	2	17 29	28	15
13 17 35	21	15	3	18 14	29	16
13 21 20	22	16	4	19 0	♒	18
13 25 6	23	16	4	19 45	1	18
13 28 52	24	17	5	20 31	2	20
13 32 38	25	18	6	21 18	4	21
13 36 25	26	19	7	22 6	5	22
13 40 12	27	20	7	22 54	6	23
13 44 0	28	21	8	23 42	7	25
13 47 48	29	21	9	24 31	8	26

Sidereal Time (H. M. S.)	10 ♏	11 ♏	12 ♐	Ascen ♐	2 ♒	3 ♓
13 51 37	0	22	10	25 20	10	27
13 55 27	1	23	11	26 10	11	28
13 59 17	2	24	11	27 2	12	♈
14 3 8	3	25	12	27 53	14	1
14 6 59	4	26	13	28 45	15	2
14 10 51	5	26	14	29 36	16	4
14 14 44	6	27	15	0♑ 29	18	5
14 18 37	7	28	15	1 23	19	6
14 22 31	8	29	16	2 18	20	8
14 26 25	9	♐	17	3 14	22	9
14 30 20	10	1	18	4 11	23	10
14 34 16	11	2	19	5 9	25	11
14 38 13	12	2	20	6 7	26	13
14 42 10	13	3	20	7 6	27	14
14 46 8	14	4	21	8 6	28	15
14 50 7	15	5	22	9 8	29	16
14 54 7	16	6	23	10 11	♈	18
14 58 7	17	7	24	11 15	1	19
15 2 8	18	8	25	12 20	3	20
15 6 9	19	9	26	13 25	4	21
15 10 12	20	10	27	14 35	5	23
15 14 15	21	10	27	15 43	7	24
15 18 19	22	11	28	16 52	8	25
15 22 23	23	12	29	18 3	10	26
15 26 29	24	13	♑	19 16	11	27
15 30 35	25	14	1	20 32	12	29
15 34 41	26	15	2	21 48	14	♉
15 38 49	27	16	3	23 8	15	1
15 42 57	28	17	4	24 29	16	2
15 47 51	29	18	5	25 51	17	3

Sidereal Time (H. M. S.)	10 ♐	11 ♐	12 ♑	Ascen ♑	2 ♓	3 ♉
15 51 15	0	18	6	27 15	26	6
15 55 25	1	19	7	28 42	28	7
15 59 36	2	20	8	0♒ 11	♈	9
16 3 48	3	21	9	1 42	2	10
16 8 0	4	22	10	3 16	3	11
16 12 13	5	23	11	5 23	5	12
16 16 26	6	24	12	6 32	7	14
16 20 40	7	25	13	7 25	8	15
16 24 55	8	26	14	9 57	11	16
16 29 10	9	27	16	11 44	12	17
16 33 26	10	28	17	13 34	14	18
16 37 42	11	29	18	15 26	16	20
16 41 59	12	♑	19	17 20	18	21
16 46 16	13	1	20	19 18	20	22
16 50 34	14	2	21	21 22	21	23
16 54 52	15	3	22	23 29	23	25
16 59 10	16	4	24	25 39	25	26
17 3 29	17	5	25	27 55	27	27
17 7 49	18	6	26	0♓ 26	♉	28
17 12 9	19	7	27	2	19	29
17 16 29	20	8	29	4 40	2	♊
17 20 49	21	9	♒	7	3	1
17 25 9	22	10	1	9 26	5	2
17 29 30	23	11	3	11 54	7	3
17 33 51	24	12	4	14 24	8	5
17 38 12	25	13	5	17	10	6
17 42 34	26	14	7	19 33	11	7
17 46 55	27	15	8	22	13	8
17 51 17	28	16	10	24 40	14	9
17 55 38	29	17	11	27 20	16	10
18 0 0	♑	18	13	0 0	17	11

Lower half

Sidereal Time (H. M. S.)	10 ♑	11 ♑	12 ♒	Ascen ♈	2 ♉	3 ♊
18 0 0	0	18	13	0 0	17	11
18 4 22	1	20	14	2 39	19	13
18 8 43	2	21	16	5 19	20	14
18 13 5	3	22	17	7 55	22	15
18 17 26	4	23	19	10 29	23	16
18 21 48	5	24	20	13 2	25	18
18 26 9	6	25	22	15 36	26	19
18 30 30	7	26	23	18 7	28	20
18 34 51	8	27	25	20 41	29	21
18 39 11	9	29	27	23 6	♊	23
18 43 31	10	♒	28	25	2	24
18 47 51	11	1	♈	27 42	3	25
18 52 11	12	2	2	29 57	5	26
18 56 31	13	3	3	2♊ 8	6	27
19 0 50	14	4	5	4 26	8	29
19 5 8	15	6	7	6 30	9	♋
19 9 26	16	7	9	8 36	11	1
19 13 44	17	8	10	10 40	12	2
19 18 1	18	9	12	12 39	14	3
19 22 18	19	10	14	14 35	15	4
19 26 34	20	12	16	16	17	5
19 30 50	21	13	18	17 14	18	6
19 35 5	22	14	19	21	19	7
19 39 20	23	15	21	23	21	8
19 43 34	24	16	23	24	22	9
19 47 47	25	18	25	9 9	24	9
19 52 0	26	19	27	45 20	26	11
19 56 12	27	20	28	18 21	27	12
20 0 24	28	21	♈	49 22	18	1
20 4 35	29	23	2	1♊ 11	23	11
20 8 45	♒	24	4	2 45	24	12

Sidereal Time (H. M. S.)	10 ♒	11 ♒	12 ♈	Ascen ♊	2 ♋	3 ♋
20 8 45	0	24	4	2 45	24	12
20 12 54	1	25	6	4 9	25	12
20 17 3	2	27	7	5 53	27	13
20 21 11	3	28	9	6 53	28	14
20 25 19	4	29	11	8 12	29	15
20 29 26	5	♓	13	9	27	♋
20 33 31	6	2	14	10 43	♋	17
20 37 37	7	3	16	11 58	1	18
20 41 41	8	4	18	13 9	2	19
20 45 45	9	6	19	14	3	20
20 49 48	10	7	21	15 25	3	21
20 53 51	11	8	23	16 32	4	21
20 57 52	12	9	24	17 39	5	22
21 1 53	13	11	26	18 44	6	23
21 5 53	14	12	28	19 48	7	24
21 9 53	15	13	29	20 51	8	25
21 13 52	16	15	♉	21 53	9	26
21 17 50	17	17	2	22 53	10	27
21 21 47	18	17	4	23 52	10	28
21 25 44	19	19	6	24 50	11	29
21 29 40	20	20	7	25 48	12	♌
21 33 35	21	22	8	26 44	13	1
21 37 29	22	23	10	27 40	14	2
21 41 23	23	24	11	28 34	15	3
21 45 16	24	25	13	29 29	15	3
21 49 9	25	26	14	0♋ 22	16	4
21 53 1	26	27	15	1 15	17	4
21 56 52	27	29	16	2 7	18	5
22 0 43	28	♈	18	2 59	18	6
22 4 33	29	2	19	3 48	19	7
22 8 23	♓	3	20	4 38	20	8

Sidereal Time (H. M. S.)	10 ♓	11 ♈	12 ♉	Ascen ♋	2 ♋	3 ♌
22 8 23	0	3	20	4 38	20	8
22 12 12	1	4	21	5 28	21	8
22 16 0	2	6	23	6 23	22	9
22 19 48	3	7	24	7 24	23	10
22 23 35	4	8	25	7 25	23	10
22 27 22	5	9	26	9 26	24	11
22 31 8	6	10	28	10 28	25	13
22 34 54	7	12	29	11 29	26	14
22 38 40	8	13	♊	11	11	2
22 42 25	9	14	1	11	11	14
22 46 9	10	15	2	12	31	16
22 49 53	11	17	3	13	13	16
22 53 37	12	18	4	14	14	29
22 57 20	13	19	5	14	45	♌ 19
23 1	14	20	6	15	24	20
23 4 46	15	21	7	16	11	2♌
23 8 28	16	23	8	16	54	2
23 12 10	17	24	9	17	37	3 22
23 15 52	18	25	10	18	20	4 23
23 19 34	19	26	11	19	♌	5 24
23 23 15	20	27	12	19	45	5 24
23 26 56	21	29	13	20	26	6 25
23 30 37	22	♉	14	21	6	7 26
23 34 18	23	1	15	21	50	7 27
23 38 6	24	2	16	22	30	8 28
23 41 39	25	3	17	23	12	9 28
23 45 19	26	4	18	23	53	10 ♍
23 49 0	27	5	19	24	32	10 ♍
23 52 40	28	6	20	25	15	11 1
23 56 20	29	8	21	25	56	12 2
24 0 0	♈	9	22	26	36	13 3

TABLES OF HOUSES FOR LIVERPOOL, Latitude 53° 25' N.

Sidereal Time.	10 ♈	11 ♉	12 ♊	Ascen ♋	2 ♌	3 ♍
H. M. S.	°	°	°	° '	°	°
0 0 0	0	9	24	28 12	14	3
0 3 40	1	10	25	28 51	14	4
0 7 20	2	12	25	29 30	15	4
0 11 0	3	13	26	0♌ 9	16	5
0 14 41	4	14	27	0 48	17	6
0 18 21	5	15	28	1 27	17	7
0 22 2	6	16	29	2 6	18	8
0 25 42	7	17	♋	2 44	19	9
0 29 23	8	18	1	3 22	19	10
0 33 4	9	19	1	4 1	20	10
0 36 45	10	20	2	4 39	21	11
0 40 26	11	21	3	5 18	22	12
0 44 8	12	22	4	5 56	22	13
0 47 50	13	23	5	6 34	23	14
0 51 32	14	24	6	7 13	24	14
0 55 14	15	25	6	7 51	24	15
0 58 57	16	26	7	8 30	25	16
1 2 40	17	27	8	9 8	26	17
1 6 23	18	28	9	9 47	26	18
1 10 7	19	29	10	10 25	27	19
1 13 51	20	♊	11	11 4	28	19
1 17 35	21	1	11	11 43	28	20
1 21 20	22	2	12	12 21	29	21
1 25 6	23	3	13	13 0♍	0	22
1 28 52	24	4	14	13 39	1	23
1 32 38	25	5	15	14 17	1	24
1 36 25	26	6	15	14 56	2	25
1 40 12	27	7	16	15 35	3	25
1 44 0	28	8	17	16 14	3	26
1 47 48	29	9	18	16 53	4	27
1 51 37	30	10	18	17 32	5	28

Sidereal Time.	10 ♉	11 ♊	12 ♋	Ascen ♌	2 ♍	3 ♍
H. M. S.	°	°	°	° '	°	°
1 51 37	0	10	18	17 32	5	28
1 55 27	1	11	19	18 11	6	29
1 59 17	2	12	20	18 51	6	♎
2 3 8	3	13	21	19 30	7	1
2 6 59	4	14	22	20 9	8	2
2 10 51	5	15	22	20 49	9	2
2 14 44	6	16	23	21 28	9	3
2 18 37	7	17	24	22 8	10	4
2 22 31	8	18	25	22 48	11	5
2 26 25	9	19	25	23 28	12	6
2 30 20	10	20	26	24 8	12	7
2 34 16	11	21	27	24 48	13	8
2 38 13	12	22	28	25 28	14	9
2 42 10	13	23	29	26 8	15	10
2 46 8	14	24	29	26 49	15	10
2 50 7	15	25	♌	27 29	16	11
2 54 7	16	26	1	28 10	17	12
2 58 7	17	27	2	28 51	18	13
3 2 8	18	28	2	29 32	19	14
3 6 9	19	29	3	0♍13	19	15
3 10 12	20	29	4	0 54	20	16
3 14 15	21	♋	5	1 36	21	17
3 18 19	22	1	5	2 17	22	18
3 22 23	23	2	6	2 59	23	19
3 26 29	24	3	7	3 41	23	20
3 30 35	25	4	8	4 23	24	21
3 34 41	26	5	9	5 5	25	22
3 38 49	27	6	10	5 47	26	22
3 42 57	28	7	10	6 29	27	23
3 47 6	29	8	11	7 12	27	24
3 51 15	30	9	12	7 55	28	25

Sidereal Time.	10 ♊	11 ♋	12 ♌	Ascen ♍	2 ♍	3 ♎
H. M. S.	°	°	°	° '	°	°
3 51 15	0	9	12	7 55	28	25
3 55 25	1	10	13	8 37	29	26
3 59 36	2	11	13	9 20	♎	27
4 3 48	3	12	14	10 3	1	28
4 8 0	4	12	15	10 46	2	29
4 12 13	5	13	16	11 30	2	♏
4 16 26	6	14	17	12 13	3	1
4 20 40	7	15	18	12 56	4	2
4 24 55	8	16	18	13 40	5	3
4 29 10	9	17	19	14 24	6	4
4 33 26	10	18	20	15 8	7	5
4 37 42	11	19	21	15 52	7	6
4 41 59	12	20	21	16 36	8	6
4 46 16	13	21	22	17 20	9	7
4 50 34	14	22	23	18 4	10	8
4 54 52	15	23	24	18 48	11	9
4 59 10	16	24	25	19 32	12	10
5 3 29	17	24	26	20 17	12	11
5 7 49	18	25	26	21 1	13	12
5 12 9	19	26	27	21 46	14	13
5 16 29	20	27	28	22 31	15	14
5 20 49	21	28	29	23 16	16	15
5 25 9	22	29	♍	24 0	17	16
5 29 30	23	♌	1	24 45	18	17
5 33 51	24	1	1	25 30	18	18
5 38 12	25	2	2	26 15	19	19
5 42 34	26	3	3	27 0	20	20
5 46 55	27	4	4	27 45	21	21
5 51 17	28	5	5	28 30	22	22
5 55 38	29	6	6	29 15	23	22
6 0 0	30	7	7	30 0	23	23

Sidereal Time.	10 ♋	11 ♌	12 ♍	Ascen ♎	2 ♎	3 ♏
H. M. S.	°	°	°	° '	°	°
6 0 0	0	7	7	0 0	23	23
6 4 22	1	8	7	0 45	24	24
6 8 43	2	9	8	1 30	25	25
6 13 5	3	9	9	2 15	26	26
6 17 26	4	10	10	3 0	27	27
6 21 48	5	11	11	3 45	28	28
6 26 9	6	12	12	4 30	29	29
6 30 30	7	13	12	5 15	29	♐
6 34 51	8	14	13	6 0	♏	1
6 39 11	9	15	14	6 44	1	2
6 43 31	10	16	15	7 29	2	3
6 47 51	11	17	16	8 14	3	4
6 52 11	12	18	17	8 59	4	5
6 56 31	13	19	18	9 43	4	6
7 0 50	14	20	18	10 27	5	6
7 5 8	15	21	19	11 11	6	7
7 9 26	16	22	20	11 56	7	8
7 13 44	17	23	21	12 40	8	9
7 18 1	18	24	22	13 24	8	10
7 22 18	19	24	23	14 8	9	11
7 26 34	20	25	23	14 52	10	12
7 30 50	21	26	24	15 36	11	13
7 35 5	22	27	25	16 20	12	14
7 39 20	23	28	26	17 4	13	15
7 43 34	24	29	27	17 47	13	16
7 47 47	25	♍	28	18 30	14	17
7 52 0	26	1	28	19 13	15	18
7 56 12	27	2	29	19 57	16	18
8 0 24	28	3	♎	20 40	17	19
8 4 35	29	4	1	21 23	17	20
8 8 45	30	5	2	22 5	18	21

Sidereal Time.	10 ♌	11 ♍	12 ♎	Ascen ♎	2 ♏	3 ♐
H. M. S.	°	°	°	° '	°	°
8 8 45	0	5	2	22 5	18	21
8 12 54	1	6	2	22 48	19	22
8 17 3	2	7	3	23 30	20	23
8 21 11	3	8	4	24 13	20	24
8 25 19	4	8	5	24 54	21	25
8 29 26	5	9	6	25 37	22	26
8 33 31	6	10	7	26 19	23	27
8 37 37	7	11	7	27 1	24	28
8 41 41	8	12	8	27 43	25	29
8 45 45	9	13	9	28 24	25	♑
8 49 48	10	14	10	29 6	26	1
8 53 51	11	15	11	29 47	27	1
8 57 52	12	16	11	0♏28	28	2
9 1 53	13	17	12	1 9	28	3
9 5 53	14	18	13	1 50	29	4
9 9 53	15	19	14	2 31	♐	5
9 13 52	16	19	15	3 11	1	6
9 17 50	17	20	15	3 52	1	7
9 21 47	18	21	16	4 32	2	8
9 25 44	19	22	17	5 12	3	9
9 29 40	20	23	18	5 52	4	10
9 33 35	21	24	18	6 32	5	11
9 37 29	22	25	19	7 12	5	12
9 41 23	23	26	20	7 52	6	13
9 45 16	24	27	21	8 32	7	14
9 49 49	25	27	21	9 12	8	15
9 53 1	26	28	22	9 51	8	16
9 56 12	27	29	23	10 30	9	17
10 0 43	28	♎	24	11 9	10	17
10 4 33	29	1	24	11 49	11	18
10 8 23	30	2	25	12 28	11	19

Sidereal Time.	10 ♍	11 ♎	12 ♎	Ascen ♏	2 ♐	3 ♑
H. M. S.	°	°	°	° '	°	°
10 8 23	0	2	25	12 28	11	19
10 12 12	1	3	26	13 6	12	20
10 16 0	2	4	27	13 45	13	21
10 19 48	3	4	27	14 24	14	22
10 23 35	4	5	28	15 4	15	23
10 27 22	5	6	29	15 43	15	24
10 31 8	6	7	29	16 21	16	25
10 34 54	7	8	♏	17 0	17	26
10 38 40	8	9	1	17 39	18	27
10 42 25	9	10	1	18 18	18	28
10 46 9	10	10	2	18 55	19	29
10 49 53	11	11	3	19 34	20	♒
10 53 37	12	12	4	20 13	21	1
10 57 20	13	13	4	20 52	22	2
11 1 3	14	14	5	21 30	22	3
11 4 46	15	15	6	22 8	23	5
11 8 28	16	16	7	22 46	24	6
11 12 10	17	16	7	23 25	25	7
11 15 52	18	17	8	24 4	26	8
11 19 18	19	18	9	24 42	26	9
11 23 15	20	19	9	25 21	27	10
11 26 56	21	20	10	25 59	28	11
11 30 37	22	20	11	26 38	28	12
11 34 18	23	21	12	27 17	29	13
11 37 58	24	22	12	27 54	♑	14
11 41 39	25	23	13	28 33	1	15
11 45 19	26	24	14	29 11	2	16
11 49 0	27	25	14	29 50	2	17
11 52 40	28	26	15	0♐30	3	18
11 56 20	29	26	16	1 9	5	20
12 0 0	30	27	16	1 48	6	21

TABLES OF HOUSES FOR LIVERPOOL, Latitude 53° 25' N

Panel A

Sidereal Time H.M.S.	10 ♎	11 ♎	12 ♏	Ascen ♐ ° '	2 ♑	3 ♒
12 0 0	0	27	16	1 48	6	21
12 3 40	1	28	17	2 27	7	22
12 7 20	2	29	18	3 6	8	23
12 11 0	3	♏	18	3 46	9	24
12 14 41	4	0	19	4 25	10	25
12 18 21	5	1	20	5 6	10	26
12 22 2	6	2	21	5 46	11	28
12 25 42	7	3	21	6 26	12	29
12 29 23	8	4	22	7 6	13	♓
12 33 4	9	4	23	7 46	14	1
12 36 45	10	5	24	8 27	15	2
12 40 26	11	6	24	9 8	16	3
12 44 8	12	7	25	9 49	17	5
12 47 50	13	8	26	10 30	18	6
12 51 32	14	9	26	11 12	19	7
12 55 14	15	9	27	11 54	20	8
12 58 57	16	10	28	12 36	21	10
13 2 40	17	11	28	13 19	22	11
13 6 23	18	12	29	14 2	23	12
13 10 7	19	13	♐	14 45	25	13
13 13 51	20	13	1	15 28	26	15
13 17 35	21	14	1	16 12	27	16
13 21 20	22	15	2	16 56	28	17
13 25 6	23	16	3	17 41	29	18
13 28 52	24	17	4	18 26	♒	19
13 32 38	25	17	4	19 11	1	21
13 36 25	26	18	5	19 57	3	22
13 40 12	27	19	6	20 44	4	23
13 44 0	28	20	7	21 31	5	24
13 47 48	29	21	7	22 18	7	26
13 51 37	30	21	8	23 6	8	27

Panel B

Sidereal Time H.M.S.	10 ♏	11 ♏	12 ♐	Ascen ♐ ° '	2 ♒	3 ♓
13 51 37	0	21	8	23 6	8	27
13 55 27	1	22	9	23 55	9	28
13 59 17	2	23	10	24 43	10	♈
14 3 8	3	24	10	25 33	12	1
14 6 59	4	25	11	26 23	13	2
14 10 51	5	26	12	27 14	15	4
14 14 44	6	26	13	28 6	16	5
14 18 37	7	27	13	28 59	18	6
14 22 31	8	28	14	29 52	19	8
14 26 25	9	29	15	0 ♑ 46	20	9
14 30 20	10	♐	16	1 41	22	10
14 34 16	11	1	17	2 36	23	11
14 38 13	12	2	18	3 33	25	13
14 42 10	13	2	18	4 30	26	14
14 46 8	14	3	19	5 29	28	16
14 50 7	15	4	20	6 29	29	17
14 54 7	16	5	21	7 31	♓ 1	18
14 58 7	17	6	22	8 32	2	19
15 2 8	18	7	23	9 35	3	21
15 6 9	19	8	23	10 40	5	22
15 10 12	20	9	24	11 45	6	23
15 14 15	21	10	25	12 51	7	24
15 18 19	22	11	26	13 57	9	25
15 22 23	23	12	27	15 3	10	26
15 26 29	24	12	28	16 10	11	28
15 30 35	25	13	29	17 18	13	29
15 34 41	26	14	0 ♑	18 28	14	♉
15 38 49	27	15	1	19 39	16	1
15 42 57	28	16	2	20 52	17	2
15 47 6	29	17	3	22 8	18	3
15 51 15	30	17	4	24 15	26	7

Panel C

Sidereal Time H.M.S.	10 ♐	11 ♐	12 ♑	Ascen ♑ ° '	2 ♓	3 ♉
15 51 15	0	17	4	24 15	26	7
15 55 25	1	18	5	25 41	28	8
15 59 36	2	19	6	27 10	♈	9
16 3 48	3	20	7	28 41	2	10
16 8 0	4	21	8	0 ♒ 14	4	12
16 12 13	5	22	9	1 50	5	13
16 16 26	6	23	10	3 30	7	14
16 20 40	7	24	11	5 13	9	15
16 24 55	8	25	12	6 58	11	17
16 29 10	9	26	13	8 46	13	18
16 33 26	10	27	14	10 38	15	19
16 37 42	11	28	15	12 32	16	20
16 41 59	12	29	16	14 31	18	22
16 46 16	13	♑	18	16 13	20	23
16 50 34	14	1	19	18 31	22	24
16 54 52	15	2	20	20 50	24	25
16 59 10	16	3	21	23 4	26	26
17 3 29	17	4	22	25 4	27	27
17 7 49	18	5	24	27 42	29	29
17 12 9	19	6	25	0 ♓ 8	♉	♊
17 16 29	20	7	26	2 37	3	1
17 20 49	21	8	28	5 10	5	3
17 25 9	22	9	29	7 46	6	4
17 29 30	23	11	♒	10 24	8	5
17 33 51	24	11	2	13 7	10	6
17 38 12	25	12	3	15 52	11	7
17 42 34	26	13	4	18 38	13	8
17 46 55	27	14	6	21 27	15	10
17 51 17	28	15	7	24 17	16	11
17 55 38	29	16	9	27 8	18	12
18 0 0	30	17	11	30 0	19	13

Panel D

Sidereal Time H.M.S.	10 ♑	11 ♑	12 ♒	Ascen ♈ ° '	2 ♉	3 ♊
18 0 0	0	17	11	0 0	19	13
18 4 22	1	18	12	2 52	21	14
18 8 43	2	20	14	5 43	23	15
18 13 5	3	21	15	8 33	24	16
18 17 26	4	22	17	11 22	25	17
18 21 48	5	23	19	14	8 27	18
18 26 9	6	24	20	16 53	28	19
18 30 30	7	25	♒	19 37	♊	20
18 34 51	8	26	22	14	1 21	20
18 39 11	9	27	25	45	9	20 21
18 43 31	10	29	27	27	23	4 22
18 47 51	11	♒	28	29	52	5 24
18 52 11	12	1	♈	2 8 18	6 25	19
18 56 31	13	2	2	4 39	8	2 21
19 0 0	14	4	4	6 56	9	27
19 5 8	15	5	6	9 53	13	23
19 9 26	16	6	8	11 20	14	2 24
19 13 44	17	7	10	13 27	17	5 26
19 18 1	18	8	11	15 29	14	18
19 22 18	19	9	13	17 28	15	2 21
19 26 34	20	11	15	19 26	♋	8 28
19 30 50	21	12	17	21 33	35	14 15
19 35 5	22	13	19	23 22	0 ♋ 16	
19 39 20	23	15	21	24 47	1 17	
19 43 34	24	16	23	26 20	3 18	
19 47 47	25	17	25	28 10	21	8
19 52 0	26	18	26	29 46	22	9
19 56 12	27	20	28	1 ♉ 11	19	23
20 0 24	28	21	♈	2 50	24	11
20 4 35	29	22	2	4 19	25	12
20 8 45	30	23	4	5 45	26	13

Panel E

Sidereal Time H.M.S.	10 ♒	11 ♒	12 ♈	Ascen ♊ ° '	2 ♊	3 ♋
20 8 45	0	23	4	5 45	26	13
20 12 54	1	25	6	7 9	27	14
20 17 3	2	26	8	8 31	28	14
20 21 11	3	27	9	9 50	29	15
20 25 19	4	29	11	11 7	♋	16
20 29 26	5	♓	13	12 23	1	17
20 33 31	6	1	15	13 37	2	18
20 37 37	7	3	17	14 49	3	19
20 41 41	8	4	19	15 59	4	20
20 45 45	9	5	20	17 8	5	20
20 49 48	10	7	22	18 15	6	22
20 53 51	11	8	24	19 21	7	22
20 57 52	12	10	25	20 25	7	23
21 1 53	13	11	27	21 28	8	24
21 5 53	14	12	29	22 30	9	25
21 9 53	15	13	♈	23 31	10	18
21 13 52	16	14	2	24 31	11	27
21 17 50	17	16	4	25 26	12	28
21 21 47	18	17	5	26 27	12	28
21 25 44	19	18	7	27 24	13	29
21 29 40	20	20	8	28 14	15	♌
21 33 35	21	21	10	29 14	15	1
21 37 29	22	22	12	0 ♋ 8	16	2
21 41 23	23	24	12	1 1	17	3
21 45 16	24	25	15	2 46	18	4
21 49 9	25	26	15	2 46	18	4
21 53 1	26	28	17	3 37	19	5
21 56 52	27	29	18	4 27	20	6
22 0 43	28	♈	20	5 17	20	7
22 4 33	29	2	21	6 5	21	8
22 8 23	30	3	22	6 54	22	8

Panel F

Sidereal Time H.M.S.	10 ♓	11 ♈	12 ♉	Ascen ♋ ° '	2 ♋	3 ♌
22 8 23	0	3	22	6 54	22	8
22 12 12	1	4	23	7 42	23	9
22 16 0	2	5	25	8 29	23	10
22 19 48	3	7	26	9 16	24	11
22 23 35	4	8	27	10 3	25	12
22 27 22	5	9	29	10 49	26	13
22 31 8	6	11	♊	11 34	26	13
22 34 54	7	12	1	12 19	27	14
22 38 40	8	13	2	13 3	28	15
22 42 25	9	14	3	13 48	29	16
22 46 9	10	16	4	14 32	♌	17
22 49 53	11	17	5	15 15	1	18
22 53 37	12	18	7	16 0	1	19
22 57 20	13	19	8	16 41	2	19
23 1 3	14	20	9	17 24	3	20
23 4 46	15	22	10	18 6	3	21
23 8 28	16	23	11	18 48	4	21
23 12 10	17	24	12	19 30	5	22
23 15 52	18	25	13	20 11	5	23
23 19 27	19	27	14	20 52	6	24
23 23 15	20	28	15	21 33	6	25
23 26 56	21	29	16	22 14	7	26
23 30 50	22	♉	17	22 54	8	26
23 34 18	23	1	18	23 34	8	27
23 38 4	24	2	19	24 14	9	28
23 41 39	25	4	19	24 54	10	29
23 45 19	26	5	20	25 35	11	♍
23 49 0	27	6	22	26 22	11	1
23 52 40	28	7	22	26 54	12	1
23 56 20	29	8	23	27 33	13	2
24 0 0	30	9	24	28 12	14	3

TABLES OF HOUSES FOR NEW YORK, Latitude 40° 43′ N.

Top section — Panel 1

Sidereal Time H. M. S.	10 ♈	11 ♉	12 ♊	Ascen ♋ °	′	2 ♌	3 ♍
0 0 0	0	6	15	18	53	8	1
0 3 40	1	7	16	19	38	9	2
0 7 20	2	8	17	20	23	10	3
0 11 0	3	9	18	21	12	11	4
0 14 41	4	11	19	21	55	12	5
0 18 21	5	12	20	22	40	12	5
0 22 2	6	13	21	23	24	13	6
0 25 42	7	14	22	24	8	14	7
0 29 23	8	15	23	24	54	15	8
0 33 4	9	16	23	25	37	15	9
0 36 45	10	17	24	26	22	16	10
0 40 26	11	18	25	27	5	17	11
0 44 8	12	19	26	27	50	18	12
0 47 50	13	20	27	28	33	19	13
0 51 32	14	21	28	29	18	19	13
0 55 14	15	22	28	♌0	3	20	14
0 58 57	16	23	29	0	46	21	15
1 2 40	17	24	♋0	1	31	22	16
1 6 23	18	25	1	2	14	22	17
1 10 7	19	26	2	2	58	23	18
1 13 51	20	27	3	3	43	24	19
1 17 35	21	28	3	4	27	25	20
1 21 20	22	29	4	5	12	25	21
1 25 6	23	♊0	5	5	56	26	22
1 28 52	24	1	6	6	40	27	22
1 32 38	25	2	7	7	25	28	23
1 36 25	26	2	8	8	9	29	24
1 40 12	27	3	9	8	53	29	25
1 44 0	28	4	10	9	38	♍0	26
1 47 48	29	5	10	10	24	1	27
1 51 37	♉0	6	11	11	8	2	28

Top section — Panel 2

Sidereal Time H. M. S.	10 ♉	11 ♊	12 ♋	Ascen ♌ °	′	2 ♍	3 ♎
1 51 37	0	6	11	11	8	2	28
1 55 27	1	7	12	11	53	3	29
1 59 17	2	8	13	12	38	4	♎0
2 3 8	3	9	14	13	22	5	1
2 6 59	4	10	15	14	8	5	2
2 10 51	5	11	15	14	53	6	3
2 14 44	6	12	16	15	39	7	4
2 18 37	7	13	17	16	24	8	4
2 22 31	8	14	18	17	10	9	5
2 26 25	9	15	19	17	56	10	6
2 30 20	10	16	20	18	41	10	7
2 34 16	11	17	20	19	27	11	8
2 38 13	12	18	21	20	14	12	9
2 42 10	13	19	22	21	0	13	10
2 46 8	14	19	23	21	47	14	11
2 50 7	15	20	24	22	33	15	12
2 54 7	16	21	25	23	20	16	13
2 58 7	17	22	25	24	7	17	14
3 2 8	18	23	26	24	54	17	15
3 6 9	19	24	27	25	42	18	16
3 10 12	20	25	28	26	29	19	17
3 14 15	21	26	29	27	17	20	18
3 18 19	22	27	♌0	28	4	21	19
3 22 23	23	28	1	28	52	22	20
3 26 29	24	29	1	29	40	23	21
3 30 35	25	♋0	2	♍0	29	24	22
3 34 41	26	1	3	1	17	24	23
3 38 49	27	2	4	2	6	25	24
3 42 57	28	3	5	2	55	26	25
3 47 6	29	4	6	3	43	27	26
3 51 15	♊0	5	7	4	32	28	27

Top section — Panel 3

Sidereal Time H. M. S.	10 ♊	11 ♋	12 ♌	Ascen ♍ °	′	2 ♎	3 ♏
3 51 15	0	5	7	4	32	28	27
3 55 25	1	6	8	5	22	29	28
3 59 36	2	6	8	6	10	♎0	29
4 3 48	3	7	9	7	0	1	♏0
4 8 0	4	8	10	7	49	2	1
4 12 13	5	9	11	8	40	3	2
4 16 26	6	10	12	9	30	4	3
4 20 40	7	11	13	10	19	4	4
4 24 55	8	12	14	11	10	5	5
4 29 10	9	13	15	12	0	6	6
4 33 26	10	14	16	12	51	7	7
4 37 42	11	15	16	13	41	8	8
4 41 59	12	16	17	14	32	9	9
4 46 16	13	17	18	15	23	10	10
4 50 34	14	18	19	16	14	11	11
4 54 52	15	19	20	17	5	12	12
4 59 10	16	20	21	17	56	13	13
5 3 29	17	21	22	18	47	14	14
5 7 49	18	22	23	19	39	15	15
5 12 9	19	23	24	20	30	16	16
5 16 29	20	24	25	21	22	17	17
5 20 49	21	25	25	22	13	18	18
5 25 9	22	26	26	23	5	18	19
5 29 30	23	27	27	23	57	19	20
5 33 51	24	28	28	24	49	20	21
5 38 12	25	29	29	25	40	21	22
5 42 34	26	♍0	♍0	26	32	22	22
5 46 55	27	1	1	27	24	23	23
5 51 17	28	2	2	28	16	24	24
5 55 38	29	3	3	29	8	25	25
6 0 0	♋0	4	4	♎0	0	26	26

Bottom section — Panel 1

Sidereal Time H. M. S.	10 ♋	11 ♌	12 ♍	Ascen ♎ °	′	2 ♎	3 ♏
6 0 0	0	4	4	0	26	26	26
6 4 22	1	5	5	0	52	27	27
6 8 43	2	6	6	1	44	28	28
6 13 5	3	6	7	2	35	29	29
6 17 26	4	7	8	3	28	♏0	♐0
6 21 48	5	8	9	4	20	1	1
6 26 9	6	9	10	5	11	2	2
6 30 30	7	10	11	6	3	3	3
6 34 51	8	11	12	6	55	3	4
6 39 11	9	12	13	7	47	4	5
6 43 31	10	13	14	8	38	5	6
6 47 51	11	14	15	9	30	6	7
6 52 11	12	15	16	10	21	7	8
6 56 31	13	16	16	11	13	8	9
7 0 50	14	17	17	12	4	9	10
7 5 8	15	18	18	12	55	10	11
7 9 26	16	19	19	13	46	11	12
7 13 44	17	20	20	14	37	12	13
7 18 1	18	21	21	15	28	13	14
7 22 18	19	22	22	16	19	14	15
7 26 34	20	23	23	17	9	14	16
7 30 50	21	24	23	18	0	15	17
7 35 5	22	25	24	18	50	16	18
7 39 20	23	26	25	19	41	17	19
7 43 34	24	27	26	20	30	18	20
7 47 47	25	28	27	21	20	19	21
7 52 0	26	29	28	22	11	20	22
7 56 12	27	♍0	29	23	0	21	23
8 0 24	28	1	♎0	23	50	21	24
8 4 35	29	2	1	24	38	22	24
8 8 45	♌0	3	2	25	28	23	25

Bottom section — Panel 2

Sidereal Time H. M. S.	10 ♌	11 ♍	12 ♎	Ascen ♏ °	′	2 ♏	3 ♐
8 8 45	0	3	2	25	28	23	25
8 12 54	1	4	3	26	17	24	26
8 17 3	2	5	4	27	5	25	27
8 21 11	3	6	5	27	54	26	28
8 25 19	4	7	6	28	43	27	29
8 29 26	5	8	7	29	31	28	♑0
8 33 31	6	9	7	♏0	20	28	1
8 37 37	7	10	8	1	9	♐0	1
8 41 41	8	11	9	1	56	1	2
8 45 45	9	12	10	2	43	2	3
8 49 48	10	13	11	3	31	2	5
8 53 51	11	14	12	4	18	3	6
8 57 52	12	15	12	5	6	4	7
9 1 53	13	16	13	5	53	5	8
9 5 53	14	17	14	6	40	5	9
9 9 53	15	18	15	7	27	6	10
9 13 52	16	19	16	8	13	7	10
9 17 50	17	20	17	9	0	8	11
9 21 47	18	21	18	9	46	9	12
9 25 44	19	22	19	10	33	10	13
9 29 40	20	23	19	11	19	10	14
9 33 35	21	24	20	12	4	11	15
9 37 29	22	24	21	12	50	12	16
9 41 23	23	25	22	13	36	13	17
9 45 16	24	26	23	14	21	14	18
9 49 9	25	27	24	15	7	15	19
9 53 1	26	28	24	15	52	15	20
9 56 52	27	29	25	16	38	16	21
10 0 43	28	♎0	26	17	22	17	22
10 4 33	29	1	27	18	7	18	23
10 8 23	♍0	2	28	18	52	19	24

Bottom section — Panel 3

Sidereal Time H. M. S.	10 ♍	11 ♎	12 ♏	Ascen ♐ °	′	2 ♑	3 ♒
10 8 23	0	2	28	18	52	19	24
10 12 12	1	3	29	19	36	20	25
10 16 0	2	4	29	20	20	22	26
10 19 48	3	5	♏0	21	7	21	27
10 23 35	4	6	1	21	51	22	28
10 27 22	5	7	1	22	35	23	28
10 31 8	6	7	2	23	23	24	♒0
10 34 54	7	8	3	24	4	25	1
10 38 40	8	9	4	24	48	25	1
10 42 25	9	10	5	25	33	26	2
10 46 9	10	11	6	26	17	27	3
10 49 53	11	12	7	27	2	28	4
10 53 37	12	13	7	27	46	29	5
10 57 20	13	14	8	28	29	♑0	6
11 1 3	14	15	9	29	13	1	7
11 4 46	15	16	10	29	57	1	8
11 8 28	16	17	11	♐0	42	2	9
11 12 10	17	17	11	1	27	3	10
11 15 52	18	18	12	2	10	4	11
11 19 34	19	19	13	2	55	5	12
11 23 15	20	20	14	3	38	6	13
11 26 56	21	21	14	4	23	7	14
11 30 37	22	22	15	5	6	7	15
11 34 18	23	23	16	5	52	8	16
11 37 58	24	23	17	6	36	9	17
11 41 39	25	24	18	7	20	10	18
11 45 19	26	25	18	8	5	11	19
11 49 0	27	26	19	8	48	12	20
11 52 40	28	27	20	9	37	13	22
11 56 20	29	28	21	10	21	14	23
12 0 0	♎0	29	21	11	7	15	24

TABLES OF HOUSES FOR NEW YORK, Latitude 40° 43' N.

(Upper tables)

Sidereal Time H. M. S.	10 ♎	11 ♎	12 ♏	Ascen ♐ °	'	2 ♑	3 ♒
12 0 0	0	29	21	11	7	15	24
12 3 40	1	♏	22	11	52	16	25
12 7 20	2	1	23	12	37	17	26
12 11 0	3	1	24	13	19	17	27
12 14 41	4	2	25	14	7	18	28
12 18 21	5	3	25	14	52	19	29
12 22 2	6	4	26	15	38	20	♓
12 25 42	7	5	27	16	23	21	1
12 29 23	8	6	28	17	11	22	2
12 33 4	9	6	28	17	58	23	3
12 36 45	10	7	29	18	45	24	4
12 40 26	11	8	♐	19	32	25	5
12 44 8	12	9	1	20	20	26	7
12 47 50	13	10	2	21	8	27	8
12 51 32	14	11	2	21	57	28	9
12 55 14	15	12	3	22	43	29	10
12 58 57	16	13	4	23	33	♒	11
13 2 40	17	13	5	24	22	1	12
13 6 23	18	14	6	25	11	2	13
13 10 7	19	15	7	26	1	3	15
13 13 51	20	16	7	26	51	5	16
13 17 35	21	17	8	27	40	6	17
13 21 20	22	18	9	28	32	7	18
13 25 6	23	19	10	29	23	8	19
13 28 52	24	19	10	0 ♑	14	9	20
13 32 38	25	20	11	1	7	10	21
13 36 25	26	21	12	2	0	11	23
13 40 12	27	22	13	2	52	12	24
13 44 0	28	23	13	3	46	13	25
13 47 48	29	24	14	4	41	15	26
13 51 37	30	25	15	5	35	16	27

Sidereal Time H. M. S.	10 ♏	11 ♏	12 ♐	Ascen ♑ °	'	2 ♒	3 ♓
13 51 37	0	25	15	5	35	16	27
13 55 27	1	25	16	6	30	17	29
13 59 17	2	26	17	7	27	18	♈
14 3 8	3	27	18	8	23	20	1
14 6 59	4	28	18	9	20	21	2
14 10 51	5	29	19	10	18	22	3
14 14 44	6	♐	20	11	16	23	5
14 18 37	7	1	21	12	15	24	6
14 22 31	8	2	22	13	15	26	7
14 26 25	9	2	23	14	16	27	8
14 30 20	10	3	24	15	17	28	9
14 34 16	11	4	24	16	19	♓	11
14 38 13	12	5	25	17	23	1	12
14 42 10	13	6	26	18	27	2	13
14 46 8	14	7	27	19	32	4	14
14 50 7	15	8	28	20	37	5	16
14 54 7	16	9	29	21	44	6	17
14 58 7	17	10	♑	22	51	8	18
15 2 8	18	10	1	23	59	9	19
15 6 9	19	11	2	25	9	11	20
15 10 12	20	12	2	26	19	12	22
15 14 15	21	13	4	27	31	14	23
15 18 19	22	14	5	28	43	15	24
15 22 23	23	15	6	29	57	16	25
15 26 29	24	16	6	1 ♒	14	18	26
15 30 30	25	17	7	2	28	19	28
15 34 41	26	18	8	3	46	21	29
15 38 49	27	19	9	5	5	22	♉
15 42 57	28	20	10	6	25	24	1
15 47 15	29	21	11	7	46	25	3
15 51 15	30	21	13	9	8	27	4

Sidereal Time H. M. S.	10 ♐	11 ♐	12 ♑	Ascen ♒ °	'	2 ♓	3 ♉
15 51 15	0	21	13	9	8	27	4
15 55 25	1	22	14	10	31	28	5
15 59 36	2	23	15	11	56	♈	6
16 3 48	3	24	16	13	23	1	7
16 8 0	4	25	17	14	50	3	9
16 12 13	5	26	18	16	9	4	10
16 16 26	6	27	19	17	50	6	11
16 20 40	7	28	20	19	22	7	12
16 24 55	8	29	21	20	56	9	13
16 29 10	9	♑	22	22	30	11	15
16 33 26	10	1	23	24	7	12	16
16 37 42	11	2	24	25	44	14	17
16 41 59	12	3	26	27	23	15	18
16 46 16	13	4	27	29	4	17	19
16 50 34	14	5	28	0 ♓	45	18	20
16 54 52	15	6	29	2	27	20	22
16 59 10	16	7	♒	4	11	21	23
17 3 29	17	8	2	5	56	23	24
17 7 49	18	9	3	7	43	24	25
17 12 9	19	10	4	9	30	26	26
17 16 29	20	11	5	11	18	27	27
17 20 49	21	12	7	13	8	29	28
17 25 9	22	13	8	14	57	♉	♊
17 29 30	23	14	9	16	48	2	1
17 33 51	24	15	10	18	41	3	2
17 38 12	25	16	11	20	33	5	3
17 42 34	26	17	13	22	25	6	4
17 46 55	27	19	14	24	19	7	5
17 51 17	28	20	16	26	12	9	6
17 55 38	29	21	17	28	7	10	7
18 0 0	30	22	18	0 ♈	0	12	9

(Lower tables)

Sidereal Time H. M. S.	10 ♑	11 ♑	12 ♒	Ascen ♈ °	'	2 ♉	3 ♊
18 0 0	0	22	18	0	0	12	9
18 4 22	1	23	20	1	53	13	10
18 8 43	2	24	21	3	48	14	11
18 13 5	3	25	23	5	41	16	12
18 17 26	4	26	24	7	37	17	13
18 21 48	5	27	25	9	27	18	14
18 26 9	6	28	27	11	19	20	15
18 30 30	7	29	28	13	12	21	16
18 34 51	8	♒	♓	15	3	22	17
18 39 11	9	2	1	16	52	23	18
18 43 31	10	3	3	18	42	25	19
18 47 51	11	4	4	20	30	26	20
18 52 11	12	5	5	22	17	27	21
18 56 31	13	6	7	24	4	29	22
19 0 50	14	7	9	25	49	♊	24
19 5 8	15	9	10	27	33	1	24
19 9 26	16	10	12	29	15	2	25
19 13 44	17	11	13	0 ♉	56	3	26
19 18 1	18	12	15	2	37	4	27
19 22 18	19	13	16	4	16	6	28
19 26 34	20	14	18	5	53	7	29
19 30 50	21	16	19	7	30	8	♋
19 35 5	22	17	21	9	4	9	1
19 39 20	23	18	22	10	38	10	2
19 43 34	24	19	24	12	10	11	3
19 47 47	25	20	25	13	41	12	4
19 52 0	26	21	27	15	10	13	5
19 56 12	27	23	29	16	37	14	6
20 0 24	28	24	♈	18	4	15	7
20 4 35	29	25	2	19	29	16	8
20 8 45	30	26	3	20	52	17	9

Sidereal Time H. M. S.	10 ♒	11 ♒	12 ♈	Ascen ♉ °	'	2 ♊	3 ♋
20 8 45	0	26	3	20	52	17	9
20 12 54	1	27	5	22	14	18	9
20 17 3	2	29	6	23	35	19	10
20 21 11	3	♓	8	24	55	20	11
20 25 19	4	1	9	26	14	21	12
20 29 26	5	2	11	27	32	22	13
20 33 31	6	3	12	28	46	23	14
20 37 37	7	5	14	0 ♊	0	24	15
20 41 41	8	6	15	1	17	25	16
20 45 45	9	7	16	2	29	26	16
20 49 48	10	8	18	3	41	27	18
20 53 51	11	10	19	4	51	28	19
20 57 52	12	11	21	6	1	29	20
21 1 53	13	12	22	7	9	♋	20
21 5 53	14	13	24	8	16	1	21
21 9 53	15	14	25	9	23	2	22
21 13 52	16	16	26	10	30	3	23
21 17 50	17	17	28	11	37	4	24
21 21 47	18	18	29	12	43	5	25
21 25 44	19	19	0 ♉	13	48	6	26
21 29 40	20	20	2	14	53	7	26
21 33 35	21	22	3	15	56	8	27
21 37 29	22	23	4	16	59	9	28
21 41 23	23	24	6	18	2	10	29
21 45 16	24	25	7	19	4	11	♌
21 49 9	25	27	8	20	6	12	1
21 53 1	26	28	10	21	6	13	2
21 56 52	27	29	11	22	7	14	3
22 0 43	28	♈	12	23	6	15	4
22 4 33	29	1	13	24	5	16	4
22 8 23	30	3	14	24	25	17	5

Sidereal Time H. M. S.	10 ♓	11 ♈	12 ♉	Ascen ♊ °	'	2 ♋	3 ♌
22 8 23	0	3	14	24	25	15	5
22 12 12	1	4	15	25	19	16	6
22 16 0	2	5	17	26	14	17	7
22 19 48	3	6	18	27	8	17	8
22 23 35	4	7	19	28	2	18	9
22 27 22	5	8	20	28	53	19	10
22 31 8	6	10	21	29	46	20	11
22 34 54	7	11	22	0 ♋	37	21	11
22 38 40	8	12	23	1	28	22	12
22 42 25	9	13	24	2	20	22	13
22 46 9	10	14	25	3	9	23	14
22 49 53	11	15	27	4	0	24	15
22 53 37	12	17	28	4	49	25	16
22 57 20	13	18	29	5	38	25	17
23 1 3	14	19	♊	6	27	26	17
23 4 46	15	20	1	7	17	27	18
23 8 28	16	21	2	8	5	28	19
23 12 10	17	22	4	8	52	29	21
23 15 52	18	23	5	9	40	♌	21
23 19 34	19	24	6	10	28	1	23
23 23 15	20	25	8	11	15	1	23
23 26 56	21	26	9	12	2	2	24
23 30 37	22	27	10	12	49	3	25
23 34 18	23	29	12	13	36	4	26
23 38 0	24	♉	13	14	22	5	27
23 41 39	25	1	15	15	8	5	27
23 45 19	26	2	16	15	53	6	28
23 49 0	27	3	18	16	41	7	29
23 52 40	28	4	18	17	23	7	29
23 56 20	29	5	19	18	8	8	♍
24 0 0	30	6	20	18	53	9	1

125

PROPORTIONAL LOGARITHMS FOR FINDING THE PLANETS' PLACES
DEGREES OR HOURS

Min.	0	1	2	3	4	5	6	7	8	9	10	11	12	13	14	15	Min.
0	3.1584	1.3802	1.0792	9031	7781	6812	6021	5351	4771	4260	3802	3388	3010	2663	2341	2041	0
1	3.1584	1.3730	1.0756	9007	7763	6798	6009	5341	4762	4252	3795	3382	3004	2657	2336	2036	1
2	2.8573	1.3660	1.0720	8983	7745	6784	5997	5330	4753	4244	3788	3375	2998	2652	2330	2032	2
3	2.6812	1.3590	1.0685	8959	7728	6769	5985	5320	4744	4236	3780	3368	2992	2646	2325	2027	3
4	2.5563	1.3522	1.0649	8935	7710	6755	5973	5310	4735	4228	3773	3362	2986	2640	2320	2022	4
5	2.4594	1.3454	1.0614	8912	7692	6741	5961	5300	4726	4220	3766	3355	2980	2635	2315	2017	5
6	2.3802	1.3388	1.0580	8888	7674	6726	5949	5289	4717	4212	3759	3349	2974	2629	2310	2012	6
7	2.3133	1.3323	1.0546	8865	7657	6712	5937	5279	4708	4204	3752	3342	2968	2624	2305	2008	7
8	2.2553	1.3258	1.0511	8842	7639	6698	5925	5269	4699	4196	3745	3336	2962	2618	2300	2003	8
9	2.2041	1.3195	1.0478	8819	7622	6684	5913	5259	4690	4188	3737	3329	2956	2613	2295	1998	9
10	2.1584	1.3133	1.0444	8796	7604	6670	5902	5249	4682	4180	3730	3323	2950	2607	2289	1993	10
11	2.1170	1.3071	1.0411	8773	7587	6656	5890	5239	4673	4172	3723	3316	2944	2602	2284	1988	11
12	2.0792	1.3010	1.0378	8751	7570	6642	5878	5229	4664	4164	3716	3310	2938	2596	2279	1984	12
13	2.0444	1.2950	1.0345	8728	7552	6628	5866	5219	4655	4156	3709	3303	2933	2591	2274	1979	13
14	2.0122	1.2891	1.0313	8706	7535	6614	5855	5209	4646	4148	3702	3297	2927	2585	2269	1974	14
15	1.9823	1.2833	1.0280	8683	7518	6600	5843	5199	4638	4141	3695	3291	2921	2580	2264	1969	15
16	1.9542	1.2775	1.0248	8661	7501	6587	5832	5189	4629	4133	3688	3284	2915	2574	2259	1965	16
17	1.9279	1.2719	1.0216	8639	7484	6573	5820	5179	4620	4125	3681	3278	2909	2569	2254	1960	17
18	1.9031	1.2663	1.0185	8617	7467	6559	5809	5169	4611	4117	3674	3271	2903	2564	2249	1955	18
19	1.8796	1.2607	1.0153	8595	7451	6546	5797	5159	4603	4109	3667	3265	2897	2558	2244	1950	19
20	1.8573	1.2553	1.0122	8573	7434	6532	5786	5149	4594	4102	3660	3258	2891	2553	2239	1946	20
21	1.8361	1.2499	1.0091	8552	7417	6519	5774	5139	4585	4094	3653	3252	2885	2547	2234	1941	21
22	1.8159	1.2445	1.0061	8530	7401	6505	5763	5129	4577	4086	3646	3246	2880	2542	2229	1936	22
23	1.7966	1.2393	1.0030	8509	7384	6492	5752	5120	4568	4079	3639	3239	2874	2536	2223	1932	23
24	1.7781	1.2341	1.0000	8487	7368	6478	5740	5110	4559	4071	3632	3233	2868	2531	2218	1927	24
25	1.7604	1.2289	0.9970	8466	7351	6465	5729	5100	4551	4063	3625	3227	2862	2526	2213	1922	25
26	1.7434	1.2239	0.9940	8445	7335	6451	5718	5090	4542	4055	3618	3220	2856	2520	2208	1917	26
27	1.7270	1.2188	0.9910	8424	7318	6438	5706	5081	4534	4048	3611	3214	2850	2515	2203	1913	27
28	1.7112	1.2139	0.9881	8403	7302	6425	5695	5071	4525	4040	3604	3208	2845	2509	2198	1908	28
29	1.6960	1.2090	0.9852	8382	7286	6412	5684	5061	4516	4032	3597	3201	2839	2504	2193	1903	29
30	1.6812	1.2041	0.9823	8361	7270	6398	5673	5051	4508	4025	3590	3195	2833	2499	2188	1899	30
31	1.6670	1.1993	0.9794	8341	7254	6385	5662	5042	4499	4017	3583	3189	2827	2493	2183	1894	31
32	1.6532	1.1946	0.9765	8320	7238	6372	5651	5032	4491	4010	3576	3183	2821	2488	2178	1889	32
33	1.6398	1.1899	0.9737	8300	7222	6359	5640	5023	4482	4002	3570	3176	2816	2483	2173	1885	33
34	1.6269	1.1852	0.9708	8279	7206	6346	5629	5013	4474	3994	3563	3170	2810	2477	2168	1880	34
35	1.6143	1.1806	0.9680	8259	7190	6333	5618	5003	4466	3987	3556	3164	2804	2472	2164	1875	35
36	1.6021	1.1761	0.9652	8239	7174	6320	5607	4994	4457	3979	3549	3157	2798	2467	2159	1871	36
37	1.5902	1.1716	0.9625	8219	7159	6307	5596	4984	4449	3972	3542	3151	2793	2461	2154	1866	37
38	1.5786	1.1671	0.9597	8199	7143	6294	5585	4975	4440	3964	3535	3145	2787	2456	2149	1862	38
39	1.5673	1.1627	0.9570	8179	7128	6282	5574	4965	4432	3957	3529	3139	2781	2451	2144	1857	39
40	1.5563	1.1584	0.9542	8159	7112	6269	5563	4956	4424	3949	3522	3133	2775	2445	2139	1852	40
41	1.5456	1.1540	0.9515	8140	7097	6256	5552	4947	4415	3942	3515	3126	2770	2440	2134	1848	41
42	1.5351	1.1498	0.9488	8120	7081	6243	5541	4937	4407	3934	3508	3120	2764	2435	2129	1843	42
43	1.5249	1.1455	0.9462	8101	7066	6231	5531	4928	4399	3927	3501	3114	2758	2430	2124	1838	43
44	1.5149	1.1413	0.9435	8081	7050	6218	5520	4918	4390	3919	3495	3108	2753	2424	2119	1834	44
45	1.5051	1.1372	0.9409	8062	7035	6205	5509	4909	4382	3912	3488	3102	2747	2419	2114	1829	45
46	1.4956	1.1331	0.9383	8043	7020	6193	5498	4900	4374	3905	3481	3096	2741	2414	2109	1825	46
47	1.4863	1.1290	0.9356	8023	7005	6180	5488	4890	4365	3897	3475	3089	2736	2409	2104	1820	47
48	1.4771	1.1249	0.9330	8004	6990	6168	5477	4881	4357	3890	3468	3083	2730	2403	2099	1816	48
49	1.4682	1.1209	0.9305	7985	6875	6155	5466	4872	4349	3882	3461	3077	2724	2398	2095	1811	49
50	1.4594	1.1170	0.9279	7966	6960	6143	5456	4863	4341	3875	3454	3071	2719	2393	2090	1806	50
51	1.4508	1.1130	0.9254	7947	6945	6131	5445	4853	4333	3868	3448	3065	2713	2388	2085	1802	51
52	1.4424	1.1091	0.9228	7929	6930	6118	5435	4844	4325	3860	3441	3059	2707	2382	2080	1797	52
53	1.4341	1.1053	0.9203	7910	6915	6106	5424	4835	4316	3853	3434	3053	2702	2377	2075	1793	53
54	1.4260	1.1015	0.9178	7891	6900	6094	5414	4826	4308	3846	3428	3047	2696	2372	2070	1788	54
55	1.4180	1.0977	0.9153	7873	6885	6081	5403	4817	4300	3838	3421	3041	2691	2367	2065	1784	55
56	1.4102	1.0939	0.9128	7854	6871	6069	5393	4808	4292	3831	3415	3034	2685	2362	2061	1779	56
57	1.4025	1.0902	0.9104	7836	6856	6057	5382	4798	4284	3824	3408	3028	2679	2356	2056	1774	57
58	1.3949	1.0865	0.9079	7818	6841	6045	5372	4789	4276	3817	3401	3022	2674	2351	2051	1770	58
59	1.3875	1.0828	0.9055	7800	6827	6033	5361	4780	4268	3809	3395	3016	2668	2346	2046	1765	59
	0	1	2	3	4	5	6	7	8	9	10	11	12	13	14	15	

RULE:—*Add proportional log. of planet's daily motion to log. of time from noon, and the sum will be the log. of the motion required. Add this to planet's place at noon, if time be p.m., but subtract if a.m. and the sum will be planet's true place. If Retrograde, subtract for p.m., but add for a.m.*

What is the Long. of ☽ Feb. 28th, 1986 at 2.15 p.m.?
☽'s daily motion—14° 12′

Prop. Log. of 14° 12′	.2279
Prop. Log. of 2h. 15m.	1.0280
☽'s motion in 2h. 15m. = 1° 20′ or Log.	1.2559

☽'s Long. on Feb. 28th = 29° ≃ 57′ + 1° 20′ =
1° ♏ 17′

The Daily Motions of the Sun, Moon, Mercury Venus and Mars will be found on pages 26 to 28.

The Origin & History Of The Original Old Moore

THE WORTHY DOCTOR was born and lived in the Parish of Southwark, London, where he practised Medicine and Medical Astrology. He was attached to the Court of King Charles the Second as a Physician and was indeed a popular figure in Court circles. His original *Almanack* was published as a black and white Broad Sheet, printed in old English type, and included instruction for the making of herbal remedies by country folk, based on his knowledge of Medicine and Astrology in relation to the months of the year and diseases in those days which attacked the populace from time to time.

The background of the *Almanack*, so called, is extremely interesting. From evidence to be found at the British Museum, it would appear that the first almanack saw the light of day some three thousand years ago, in the reign of Rameses the Great. It was produced by its originator in the form of a parchment document and was inscribed with many curious hieroglyphics. Much space was devoted to religious ceremonies, and reference was made to certain charms. Birthday information similar in character to the birthday delinations found in more modern almanacks was included.

There is no trace of any other almanack having been published until the year 173 A.D.; but it is hardly likely that this was so, and doubtless there is evidence in existence which would tend to prove that the almanack was carried on by other astrologers, both before and after the advent of the Christian era.

From the latter end of the second century to the beginning of the eighth, almanacks had become comparatively numerous, and the almanack makers of those days devoted much space to religious festivals and Saints days. It is said that the priests were responsible for the Biblical phraseology.

The Norman period saw the almanack produced in very highly-coloured and finished state, and some exquisite copies may still be seen in the libraries of the famous European cities. The effect of the many varied colours used is extremely beautiful. These rare and expensive almanacks contained lists of lucky and unlucky days and notes on such subjects as astrology, medicine, and occult research.

The first English almanack was published about the year 1495, and a copy is now to be found in the Bodleian Library, Oxford.

The year 1697 is an interesting date in the history of almanacks, for it was not until Dr. Francis Moore published his Broad Sheet in this year that the question of prophecies was seriously dealt with by the compiler. At that time, the great universities in England were also responsible for the production of almanacks. But shortly after his death in 1715, in London, the original *Almanack* as produced by Dr. Francis Moore was taken over and published by the City of London Liveried Stationers Company until the nineteenth century, when the House of Foulsham acquired the copyright and issued a popular edition of Dr. Francis Moore's *Almanack*, which is now known in its popular format as *Foulsham's Original Old Moore's Almanack*.

The Almanack *is always published some months in advance of the year for which it is dated, since the essence of the* Almanack *lies in its prognostications for the year ahead.*